The Racial
Glass Ceiling

The Racial Glass Ceiling

*Subordination
in American
Law and Culture*

ROY L. BROOKS

Yale UNIVERSITY PRESS/NEW HAVEN & LONDON

Published with assistance from the
Mary Cady Tew Memorial Fund.

Yale University Press books may be purchased in quantity for
educational, business, or promotional use. For information,
please e-mail sales.press@yale.edu (U.S. office) or sales@yaleup.
co.uk (U.K. office).

Set in Minion type by IDS Infotech, Ltd.
Printed in the United States of America.

Library of Congress Control Number: 2016954830
ISBN 978-0-300-22330-9 (cloth : alk. paper)

A catalogue record for this book is available from the British
Library.

This paper meets the requirements of ANSI/NISO Z39.48-1992
(Permanence of Paper).

10 9 8 7 6 5 4 3 2 1

For James A. Thomas

Contents

Preface

Since the end of the civil rights period, the problem of racial inequality in the United States has largely been defined as a socioeconomic problem. Racial disparity in education, jobs, and income is seen as the primary indicator of racial inequality faced by African Americans, or blacks, in particular. While there is little disagreement in naming the race problem today, there is major disagreement in understanding what sustains the problem long after the end of the Jim Crow era. This disagreement breaks along political lines, with progressives arguing that the race problem, so defined, is sustained by racism, and with conservatives just as adamantly insisting that it is maintained by bad behaviors and values among blacks. But when I study the problem of black inequality post–Jim Crow, I see a more complex problem.

More than a socioeconomic problem, more than a problem that largely affects poor blacks, more than racism, more than a supposedly dysfunctional class of blacks, I see a three-headed hydra when I look at the problem of black inequality. I see a socioeconomic, socio-legal, and sociocultural race problem, with the latter two manifested largely as racial subordination.

By "racial subordination," I mean the act of impeding racial progress in pursuit of legitimate, nonracist interests. The race problem in law, as I see it, is due less to a racist Supreme Court than to a racially subordinating Court, and the problem in the American culture writ large is racial subordination as well as racism. In moving the discussion from discrimination discourse to subordination discourse, and in focusing on law and culture, I hope to further our understanding of a problem—black inequality in post–Jim Crow America—that has preoccupied the hearts and minds of scholars, pundits, policy-makers, and other concerned Americans. Interest in this problem has intensified with the election and reelection of a black president of the United States, and with a new round of racial discord over police encounters with African Americans.

Subordination discourse also affords us an opportunity to arrive at solutions to these unexplored aspects of the race problem—socio-legal and sociocultural—based on good social policy harvested on common ground. In the end, the success of any prescription for the race problem will depend, in my view, on our ability to engage each other with concern rather than fear—concern for what is right for others right in front of us.

Acknowledgments

I am deeply indebted to Perla Bleisch, my secretary for more than twenty years, and to several teams of research assistants who worked on the book at various times. Special thanks to Kevin Alexander, Mohammed Aly, Muna Amadi, Christra Buckley, Matthew Burgess, Claude Durden, Shannon Finley, Susan Gathman, Jarvis Lagman, Xiaowan Mao, Ariane Lisa Pan, Amalea Romero, Mellania Safarian, Kelly Smith, Benjamin White, and Heather Zak. My distinguished colleagues Judith Liu (sociology), Carlton Floyd (English), and Karen Teel (theology) read some of the chapters and offered priceless suggestions, as did my former student Jon Bialecki, who has become an extraordinarily gifted scholar. Wayne Shannon has been an irreplaceable source of wisdom and support for my entire professional life. Jaya Aninda Chatterjee, my editor at Yale University Press, was simply superb and a great pleasure to work with. Thanks also to Kate Davis, who did a first-rate job on the manuscript.

The Racial
Glass Ceiling

A New Understanding of
Racial Subordination

T wo billionaire owners of NBA teams. One, Donald Sterling, eighty-one-year-old owner of the L.A. Clippers, is recorded in a private conversation reproaching his thirty-one-year-old Latina assistant/girlfriend, V. Stiviano, for associating in public with African Americans, or blacks. He scolds her most severely for taking a picture with basketball Hall-of-Famer Earvin "Magic" Johnson and posting it to her Instagram account. In addition, he repeatedly depicts African Americans as racially inferior and implores Stiviano "not to bring them to my games." After an audiotape of these racist remarks was leaked to the press, several corporate sponsors withdrew from the Clippers, and players throughout the league threatened to boycott the games if Sterling remained an owner or associated with the team in any fashion. In response to these events, the NBA commissioner, Adam Silver, barred Sterling from associating with any NBA team in any capacity and fined him $2.5 million, the maximum allowed under the NBA rules. In addition, the commissioner asked the other NBA owners to force Sterling to sell his team.

Although the team was eventually sold by Sterling's wife (for $2 billion, yielding a very handsome profit), before the owners could vote on the matter, Mark Cuban, the billionaire owner of the Dallas Mavericks franchise, publicly announced that while he found Donald Sterling's racism to be abhorrent, he did not support the idea of forcing him to sell his team. That would create a "slippery slope," Cuban reasoned, one that would set a precedent for the league to oust owners based on their personal views. "Again, there's no excuse for his positions. There's no excuse for what he said. There's no excuse for anybody to support racism. There's no place for it in our league, but there's a very, very, very slippery slope." Ignoring or discounting a matter of keen importance for racial advancement—to wit, punishing unabashed, habitual racist conduct as severely as possible—Cuban argued that forcing Sterling to sell would be un-American: "But regardless of your background, regardless of the history they have, if we're taking something somebody said in their home and we're trying to turn it into something that leads to you being forced to divest property in any way, shape or form, that's not the United States of America. I don't want to be part of that."[1]

This was a revelatory moment for me. Not Donald Sterling's racism—as an African American I take that as a given in our society—but Mark Cuban's candor in expressing a racial mind-set that I had long known existed but up to then had misunderstood, as had so many other civil rights scholars, as "racism." Cuban's mind-set and concomitant actions add a dimension to the problem of race in post–civil rights America (the period since the end of the civil rights movement and the Jim Crow era, circa 1972) that has not been fully studied, if studied at all, in academic circles or discussed in the public arena. His position helps us understand why racial equality continues to elude even socioeconomically successful African Americans, including a black president of the United States.

In this book, I use the Cubanian mind-set as a springboard for making three principal points. First, although Sterling is a racist, as conventionally defined, Cuban is not; he is a *racial subordinator,* as defined in this book. Second, racial subordination hurts African Americans and society as a whole because it stands in the path of racial justice, thereby creating a racial glass ceiling. Doing nothing about racial subordination is bad social policy. Third, the American race problem in post–civil rights America is more than a socioeconomic problem, more than a problem that largely affects poor blacks. When I look at the race problem today and going forward, I see a three-headed hydra consisting of a socioeconomic race problem, a socio-legal race problem, and a sociocultural race problem, the latter two reaching all blacks, including the wealthy. The problem in law is manifested less by racism than by racial subordination—what can be called *juridical subordination*—and the problem in the American mainstream culture is indicated by both racial subordination—what can be called *cultural subordination*—and racism. Juridical subordination, which I define as Supreme Court decision-making in civil rights cases that freezes or impedes racial progress, and cultural subordination, defined here as the suppression of important black values or folkways in the American mainstream culture, are animated by norms that perform important rhetorical and regulatory functions in civil rights discourse. Each has the potential to promote or menace. I argue that deploying these norms in deference to the spirit of *Brown v. Board of Education* (1954) can eradicate racial subordination in law, and using them to resolutely enhance our racial democracy can reduce (but not entirely eliminate) racial subordination in the mainstream culture. This book is mostly devoted to developing that argument.

But I do not see myself as writing a book strictly about law or culture. Instead, my ambition is to use observations regarding law and culture to make a larger point about racial inequality in contemporary American society: namely, that beyond racism and class lies a realm of racial inequality that reaches even rich or famous African Americans. Moving reflection and discussion about civil rights or racial inequality beyond the usual coordinates of racism and socioeconomic deficiencies, one can find new answers to many thorny questions about racial fairness with which we struggle each day. Isn't making it to the middle class the race problem's silver bullet? How can it be said that blacks like President Obama, Oprah Winfrey, and Cornel West experience racial inequality? Is this a problem on which Americans should spend their limited time, energy, and emotional capital trying to fix? Why aren't the opportunities accorded to poor white immigrants transferable to poor blacks? Fresh answers to these and similar questions can be found by thinking outside of the box, that is, moving past questions of racism and socioeconomic class. In short, my goal is to provide a useful context from which discursive arguments on contested issues of racial equality can proceed. I begin with a brief elaboration of the three main points tendered in this book.

Point One. Racism is not the only structural, or external, source of racial inequality. Racial subordination also contributes to racial inequality. I define racism conventionally as racial animus or racial stereotyping. "Racial subordination" is a term that has been put in service by other scholars, none more prominent than critical race theorists (more about this to follow). Unlike these excellent scholars, I define racial subordination as any act that ignores or discounts matters of keen importance for racial advancement for the sake of pursuing an important (nonracist) matter. Hence, *racial subordination, as used in this book, occurs when an individual or institution consciously forgoes an opportunity to advance racial progress and does so for the sake of pursuing an important competing interest.* As a means of protecting private property or the right to privacy, Mark Cuban is willing to forgo severe public punishment of a person whom Cuban himself admits is a racist, and who is widely known to be a serial racist. A professional sports league that is overwhelmingly black and that associates itself with a known racist sets back the cause of racial progress to the days of Jim Crow, a time in which unabashed racists controlled the livelihood of African Americans. Blacks back then had to swallow their pride and take this degradation. Yet Cuban seems to believe that racial progress will just have to yield to important, nonracist competing interests. Cuban is a subordinator; Sterling is a racist.

Critical race theorists and progressive social scientists, whom I consider to be fellow travelers, would disagree with my use of the term "racial subordination." They would argue that racial subordination should be condemned as an expression of racism—for example, "color-blind racism." In their view, there is little difference between racial subordination and structural barriers created during Jim Crow. When the perpetrator has his foot on the victim's neck, the victim cares little about the perpetrator's state of mind. The victim just wants the perpetrator to remove his foot. Hence, from the victim's perspective, racism is coextensive with racial inequality.[2]

I do not argue that racial subordinators should be taken off the hook; I simply argue that they are on a different hook. Racial subordination and racism have racial implications (they are, to borrow from Joe Feagin, "racialized"), but they are not coterminous concepts. There is a clear distinction with a real difference between Donald Sterling and

Mark Cuban. Unlike Sterling, there is no racial animus or racial stereotyping motivating Cuban's actions. Hence, challenging the mind-set of Cuban is far more difficult than confronting the motivation of Sterling. Because of his moral depravity, Sterling's racially harmful action is easily dismissed. Because he is motivated by what one must admit are legitimate or non-nefarious reasons, Cuban's racially harmful conduct cannot be so easily ignored.

We need to look at the process of racial inequality as well as its effects. Reducing all racial inequality to racism artificially simplifies the problem of race as well as its solution: just get rid of all the racists. But African Americans will still face racial inequality even after all the racists leave town. Thus, we unwittingly allow other forms of racial wrongdoing to fly under the radar when we treat racism as the reason for all racial wrongdoing. Furthermore, we give racial wrongdoers a convenient defense that shuts down discussion: "I'm not a racist, so I'm walking away from this insult." Injecting subordination discourse into discussions of racial inequality holds the racial wrongdoer personally accountable for impeding racial progress.

What makes it so tempting to merge racial subordination into racism is the fact that, unlike the days of Jim Crow, racism is often difficult to detect today. It is rare for white Americans to admit openly to being racist. Then there is what Ta-Nehisi Coates calls "elegant racism"—racism so cleverly coded that we don't even realize it's racism—to which I would include racism masquerading as racial subordination. But not all whites who act against the interests of blacks think in these terms. They are not all racists. Mark Cuban is Exhibit A, and the Supreme Court, as we shall see, is Exhibit B.[3]

Point Two. Racial subordination—consciously ignoring or discounting matters of keen importance for racial advancement in deference to important, nonracist interests—is not racially neutral or innocent. It is damaging to blacks and our society, and, for that reason, it is bad social policy. Subordinating racial progress is racially harmful not only because it returns us to Jim Crow conditions (see Point One above), but also, and more fundamentally, because *it makes it more difficult for blacks to climb out of the abyss of racial degradation wrought by slavery and Jim Crow.*

The racial abyss is often difficult for us to see because racial dynamics in our society have changed since the days of government-
sanctioned racial segregation and discrimination. Oversimplification is
tempting but dangerous. Yes, there has been unprecedented success for
blacks individually since the end of the civil rights movement, and, yes,
many if not most young blacks and whites do not have the same racial
issues as those who grew up in the civil rights era, which is to say that
racial mixing is more fluid among the young who seem more tolerant
than their parents or grandparents. But such undeniable racial progress
has taken place against a backdrop of continued racial inequality. Racial
despair still shadows the existence of the vast majority of blacks. I give
many speeches each year. Blacks in the audiences tell me over and over
that they are suffering racial depression *sub silentio.* Even blacks who
have "made it" (which is my crowd) have a sense that they are not equal
in social status in spite of their socioeconomic success and the election
and reelection of a black president—the world's most powerful man,
who was impotent when it came to raising racial issues in his own administration. Black intellectuals like Cornel West, Michael Eric Dyson,
and Tavis Smiley have criticized President Obama for being a "racial
wimp." I felt their anger and frustration, but I now understand that the
president had no choice. African Americans still remain, to quote James
Baldwin, "that shadow which lies athwart our national life, not as a
threat or a curse but as a constant reminder of the injustice and inequality that belie the American Dream and the promise of the nation's foundational ideals."[4] Even the recent immigrant knows, as Toni Morrison
reminds us (and as Mexico's former president Vicente Fox has said in so
many words), that "no matter his immigrant status, he stands above the
long-suffering Black American citizen."[5]

That many African Americans, including financially successful
ones, feel a sense of racial reductionism today is strong evidence that all
things racial are not equal. Blacks are not at equal risk with whites or
nonblack racial minorities in the quest for racial equality. It still *means
something* in this society to be a black person. An unarmed black male is
twenty times more likely to be killed by a police officer than an unarmed
white male is. Even a black U.S. senator from South Carolina, Republican Timothy Eugene "Tim" Scott, reports on the floor of the Senate that

he has been stopped and released by the police seven times in one year, explaining that "the vast majority of the time I was pulled over for driving a new car in the wrong neighborhood or something else just as trivial."[6] Social scientists such as Orlando Patterson, Jennifer Lee, and Frank Bean report that African Americans are the least assimilated racial or ethnic group, that although Asians and Latinos are disengaging their national origins from racial identity, similar to European immigrants of the past, African Americans (including multiracial blacks) are perceived as being "black," and choose to identify as "black." These identities are abetted by the fact that African Americans intermarry at a rate that is significantly lower than the rates for Asians and Latinos. African Americans came out of both slavery and Jim Crow with jobs, schools, housing, and social esteem worse than whites. Four decades into the post–civil rights period, blacks still have jobs, schools, housing, and social esteem that are worse than whites. In fact, the racial differentials are little changed from the end of Jim Crow and, in some instances (for example, the income gap between college-educated males) have gotten *worse*. Happiness and worldly success are not independent of race and color in post–civil rights America. This is not surprising given the fact that "the oppression visited upon African Americans by this country was more extensive than that faced by other racial groups"[7] Racial subordination is objectionable, in my view, because it ascribes a low social value to African Americans, which, because of the racial chasm in which blacks are stuck, only adds to the burden of being black. Yes, all lives matter; but black lives *really do* matter.[8]

Maintaining a state of inequality between blacks and whites— a racial glass ceiling—is not only morally wrong but also costs the American economy trillions of dollars each year, denies African Americans the opportunity to fully connect to the nation's resources and assets, and discourages young African Americans from feeling invested in the future of our country—a dream deferred yet again. After the shooting of Trayvon Martin and the subsequent police killings of unarmed blacks, young African Americans have let it be known that they are less patient with racial disadvantage than my generation is. They are less willing to tolerate a society that refuses to make the personal and institutional sacrifices necessary to make black lives matter.[9]

Point Three. Cuban's commentary on race is atypical racial discourse in that it is directed at blacks who are financially well-off (NBA players), although the implications for poor blacks are quite clear. The lesson to be drawn here is that even well-to-do African Americans are racially vulnerable. Their inequality is not in the area of income, housing, employment, education, or other capital disparities (socioeconomics), but in matters of culture and law. For example, unlike Oprah Winfrey, Donald Trump has not had to deal with racism in his life. Nor has he ever had to admonish his sons, "It's unlikely but possible that you could get killed today. Or any day. I'm sorry, but that's the truth. Black maleness is a potentially fatal condition."[10] The mainstream culture marginalized President Obama, the most elevated black in America, when he raised racial issues. The most vivid instance occurred when the president publicly said that a white police officer acted "stupidly" when he arrested Harvard professor Henry Louis Gates Jr. for prying open a door to get into his own house, which he was locked out of. A nasty public fight over racism ensued, the president's approval ratings went down, and the media accused the president of being racially divisive by "playing the race card." The race card, in fact, has become the trump card in silencing middle-class blacks who dare to raise racial issues in public. The quickest way for a black professional or executive to lose face within his or her organization, even among white friends, is to raise a racial issue. So it is that in his 2015 memoir, *Black Man in a White Coat: A Doctor's Reflection on Race and Medicine,* Dr. Damon Tweedy recounts how time after time he was discouraged from calling out discriminatory administrative practices or white doctors who mistreated black patients for fear of being labeled "too difficult" or "too sensitive" by his white peers.[11]

Within the mainstream culture, the white view on racial matters typically trumps the black view, such as the very legitimate black belief that "[t]he best way to combat racism . . . is to seek it out every minute of every day and expose every instance we find."[12] Some of this cultural pushback is, of course, racist; but not all of it is. Some of it is racial subordination, in that the perpetrators, not unlike Mark Cuban, honestly believe they are acting on the basis of legitimate interests. Take the matter of big government, for instance. The normative assumption or belief within the mainstream culture for less intrusive government expresses

cultural subordination (not racism) when it trumps the very legitimate
African American cultural preference for an active government in rooting out age-old racism. To me, racial subordination is a more realistic
and productive way to understand many cultural clashes, especially
among whites and blacks of probity and intelligence. But here is the rub:
*if we accept cultural subordination then we are saying to African Ameri-
cans that the price for socioeconomic success, which is what we want for all
Americans, is cultural displacement and racial degradation.* In this book,
that's not racial equality; it is a racial glass ceiling.[13]

The same is true with law. Legally, employers can no longer refuse
to hire blacks, but Supreme Court justices are free to exercise their inter-
pretative powers in ways that brazenly weaken employment protections
granted to blacks in civil rights legislation. Indeed, the Supreme Court
and Congress have been locked into an awkward dance during the entire
post–civil rights period in which the Court cuts back on the civil rights
protections Congress legislates and Congress passes new legislation
to restore those cuts. In case after case, one sees a growing insensitivity
and even hostility within the Court toward the black equality interest.
Representative John Lewis, a living legend of the civil rights movement,
speaks directly to the Court's juridical subordination:

> President Lyndon Johnson signed the Voting Rights Act into
> law in 1965, 100 years after the conclusion of the Civil War
> and following the marches from Selma to Montgomery,
> Alabama. These marches witnessed countless non-violent
> protesters attacked by state troopers. I was among those beat-
> en for trying to secure our most fundamental and precious
> right: the right to vote free from discrimination. [Rep. Lewis
> was beaten to within an inch of his life during the march to
> Montgomery.]
> . . . [T]he Supreme Court invalidated one of the Voting
> Rights Act's key provisions this past year in *Shelby County v.
> Holder,* a case that could compound the issue of voting rights
> for years to come. At issue was whether Section 4 of the act,
> which requires all or parts of 16 "covered" states with long his-
> tories and contemporary records of voting discrimination,

mostly in the south, to seek approval for changes in voting procedures from the federal government, was still appropriate.

The court ruled that Section 4 was unconstitutional, despite the massive record we compiled during the 2006 reauthorization showing its continued need and ongoing discrimination in those jurisdictions. . . .

In a democracy such as ours, the right to vote is precious. It is almost sacred. It is the most powerful nonviolent tool the people have in a democratic society. . . . It is not a partisan issue—it is an American issue.

We have come a long way as a nation, and we don't want to go back. We want to move forward. But without Section 4, voting rights—a fundamental tenet of our democracy—may be legally denied, and these unjust laws will be enforced unless a lawsuit provides some eventual relief. The act contained a preapproval process that pre-empted disenfranchisement because waiting for litigation to conclude permits discrimination to prevail, if only temporarily. As Martin Luther King Jr. said, "Justice delayed is justice denied."

The court's premise that the success of the law was the reason it needed to be eliminated is unreasonable, especially in light of the thousands of pages of evidence Congress entered into the record. It demonstrates, and the court even admitted, that there was continued, blatant discrimination in the south and in jurisdictions across America. I feel hopeful that in conjunction with my colleagues . . . that Congress will come together to develop a fix for the act.[14]

The Court's decision in the case, in my view, was not juridical racism but juridical subordination. I just don't think that Justice Clarence Thomas or the other justices are acting with racial antipathy or stereotyping. It is more likely that they are making decisions in what they calculate to be the best civil rights interest of blacks considering the competing interests. But these calculations must be brought into public view for all to see and evaluate, as I attempt to do in this book. Juridical subordination makes the Supreme Court itself the subject of civil rights scrutiny, as well it should be given its racial history (discussed in chapter 1 of this book).

My argument, then, is that African Americans today face not one but three related race problems. I see, in addition to the much-discussed socioeconomic race problem, a socio-legal and sociocultural race problem. The cultural race problem feeds into the legal race problem, which feeds into the socioeconomic race problem. Justice Oliver Wendell Holmes spoke to the symbiotic relationship between culture and law when he observed, on more than one occasion, that "The life of the law has not been logic, it has been experience."[15] And Justice Thurgood Marshall, *Brown v. Board of Education*'s principal lawyer, addressed the law and socioeconomic connection when he wrote, "What is striking is the role legal principles have played throughout American history in determining the condition of Negroes."[16] Thus, it is not surprising that one year after the Court's decision in *Shelby County v. Holder*, several states "advanced a variety of tactics—from voter ID laws to cuts to early voting—that restricted access to the ballot for minorities. . . . And those tracking the fallout from the decision say it greased the skids for voting restrictions not just in the covered areas, but also in places that weren't directly affected."[17] Researchers at the University of California San Diego have reported that these restrictions, for the most part politically motivated, have reduced the turnout of black voters. Those who showed up at the polls, such as ninety-three-year-old Willie Mims, who had voted in every election in Escambia County, Alabama, since 2000, were not allowed to cast a ballot. The issue is not whether SCOTUS is racist; it is whether SCOTUS can say to the American people that it is effectuating good social policy—that it is being faithful to the spirit of *Brown*—when it interprets a long-standing civil rights statute in a way that allows a political party to gain political advantage at the expense of racial advancement.[18]

UCSD Research

I focus on racial subordination in law in chapters 1 and 2 and in culture in chapters 3 and 4. The arguments presented therein are complex and nuanced, as any serious discussion of the race problem requires. I do not address the socioeconomic race problem, as there is no dearth of excellent scholarship on that subject.[19]

The Spirit of *Brown*

Juridical subordination, as used here, is judicial decision-making that inhibits racial advancement by suppressing the black equality interest in civil rights cases. That interest was relatively easy to define during the civil rights period. *Brown v. Board of Education* (1954) defined it as "formal equal opportunity," meaning racial omission (color blindness) or racial integration (racial mixing). Vindicating these norms in civil rights cases was thought to be the best strategy for achieving racial equality through the law. Indeed, the Supreme Court in the decade following *Brown* rendered decision after decision striking down racial segregation not only in the field of education but also in transportation, employment, housing, and other segments of American life, all of which profoundly improved black lives socio-legally and socioeconomically. As the Jim Crow era came to a close, however, blacks began to lose important civil rights cases. Faced with legitimate, nonracist interests that directly competed with the black equality interest, the Court began to rule against the latter in many cases, including school cases like *Milliken v. Bradley* (1974) and affirmative action cases like *Regents of the University of California v. Bakke* (1978). Formal equal opportunity had become more foe than friend to African Americans. With diminished socio-legal power, blacks began to lose the socioeconomic gains they had recently achieved, especially in earnings and college participation. Yet, most Supreme Court justices, both then and now, remain faithful to racial omission or racial integration, finding them to be conceptually solid normative stances. So too do many civil rights scholars and pundits. I call those who subscribe to the racial omission norm *traditionalists,* and I call those who adhere to the racial integration norm *reformists.* Others, mostly young civil rights scholars, offer alternative theories or strategies for achieving racial equality. *Limited separatists* and *critical race theorists* advance very different post–civil rights theories, from which we get very different articulations of the black equality interest and, consequently, very different ways of unearthing or conceptualizing juridical subordination. These norms— racial solidarity (limited separatists) and social transformation (critical race theorists)—cannot be reconciled with racial omission or racial integration for the most part. The all-important question is: Which of these post–civil rights norms should the Supreme Court assert in its civil rights cases? My answer is that the Court should be guided not by any one of these norms per se, but by what can be called the "spirit of *Brown,*" by which I mean the *Brown* Court's attempt to reverse the Supreme Court's inglorious racial history. This principle, in my view, trumps all post– civil rights theories and concomitant norms, all expressions of the black equality interest, all argumentations as to what constitutes juridical subordination. If the Supreme Court follows the path charted by its most important civil rights precedent, it will, in my view, eliminate juridical subordination.[1]

That argument unfolds in this and the next chapter. Chapter 1 marshals detailed evidence to support my reading of *Brown.* Chapter 2 shows how each post–civil rights theory and its attendant norm maps out racial equality in civil rights cases, applies these calculations to several Supreme Court cases to test for juridical subordination, and determines which of these applications furthers the spirit of *Brown.* I maintain that if the Supreme Court decides civil rights cases in this manner, it will promote good social policy.

The Supreme Court's Inglorious Racial History

The post–Civil War amendments to the Constitution—the Thirteenth Amendment, Fourteenth Amendment, and Fifteenth Amendment— give evidence of a degree of commitment to the ideal of racial equality by the American people during the postbellum period. So difficult and burdensome is the passage of a constitutional admentment, requiring a two-thirds majority in both the House and Senate plus ratification by three-quarters of the state legislatures, that, more than the enactment of a statute, it reflects the most serious attention and consideration the American people can give to lawmaking. Congress further indicated its fealty to the ideal of racial equality by passing a series of postamendment statutes designed to enforce the Reconstruction Amendments. These criminal and civil statutes empowered the federal courts to hold individuals and institutions accountable to the amended Constitution. Like the Reconstruction Amendments, these early civil rights statutes have informed the civil rights statutes enacted during the 1960s civil rights movement.[2]

Rather than treating the Reconstruction civil rights laws as a mandate for promoting racial advancement, the Supreme Court used these laws to shackle the recently emancipated enslaved to second-class citizenship. Indeed, the Court's civil rights jurisprudence had changed little from the antebellum period, and would remained essentially the same until liberated by *Brown v. Board of Education* in 1954. Throughout the South and to a lesser extent in other regions of the country as well, blacks could not attend the best public schools, use the cleanest public restrooms or drinking fountains, occupy the best seats on streetcars or in theaters, vote in elections, or sit on juries. Blacks were accorded neither due process nor equal protection of the laws. Segregation and racial discrimination were so widespread across the nation that they can hardly be called aberrations of the South. They were part of our national legal narrative largely written by the Supreme Court. As Lawrence Goldstone observes, "The descent of the United States into enforced segregation, into a nation where human beings could be tortured and horribly murdered without trial, is a story profoundly tragic and profoundly American. And the Supreme Court was a central player in the tale."[3]

Was the Court's complicity in the subversion of racial equality the work of a few rogue justices, a judicial irregularity, or was it an ongoing pattern and practice of judicial decision-making at the highest reaches of our judiciary? There were simply too many cases both predating and postdating the Reconstruction civil rights laws to call the Court's sabotage of racial equality a judical hiccup. The historical record leads to no other conclusion.

In recounting this history, I would be remiss if I did not begin with *Dred Scott v. Sanford* (1856). This case, which predates the post–Civil War laws, is without a doubt the most infamous of the Court's decisions. To understand *Dred Scott,* as well as the jurisprudence of racial justice that the Supreme Court could have imbibed, one must first understand a famous English precedent, *Somerset v. Stewart* (1772), written by the distinguished English jurist Lord Mansfield.

James Somerset was an enslaved American brought to England by his master, Charles Stewart. The slave escaped and was recaptured, setting off a long period of litigation regarding his status. Lord Mansfield ruled that slavery was "so high an act of dominion, . . . so odious, that nothing can be suffered to support it, but positive law."[4] Finding no positive law (no statutory law) in England authorizing slavery, the court set Somerset, the slave, free. But the significance of the ruling extends beyond the facts of the case. The court established the precedent in Anglo-American law that a slave became free upon coming into a nonslave-holding jurisdiction because of the absence of positive law authorizing slavery therein.[5]

Fast forward to the *Dred Scott* case. In this 1856 case, a runaway slave took up residency in the "free" state of Illinois. Once there, he invoked the *Somerset* precedent. But rather than deciding the substantive issue, Chief Justice Taney, writing for the Supreme Court, decided the case on procedural grounds, ruling that Dred Scott, even though he resided in Illinois for four years, was not a citizen of the state and, hence, could not invoke the federal court's diversity jurisdiction. In other words, the federal courts lacked authority to decide the case. To cut off the prospect of Dred Scott suing in state court, the Supreme Court went on to rule *sua sponte* that blacks were "regarded as beings of an inferior order . . . unfit to associate with the white race" and, as such, "they had no rights which the white man was bound to respect." The Court concluded that "the negro might justly and lawfully be reduced to slavery for his benefit."[6] These words come from the highest Court in the land. The Court's ruling not only precluded an action from being filed in state court, but it also overturned the Missouri Compromise of 1820, which had divided new states between slave and free states, on the ground that it violated Fifth Amendment substantive due-process rights by allowing a slave to shed his status as property upon stepping into a free state. Taken together, *Somerset* and *Dred Scott* underscore an essential teaching about Anglo-American law: to wit, law is less a body of rules than a state of mind.[7]

Although the Civil War amendments changed the Constitution from a slaveholder's document to one that resonated with the Declaration of Independence, the Supreme Court issued decision after decision that effectively kept the new citizens in a state of semislavery. These decisions by the highest court in the land crippled rights African Americans had just acquired under the Thirteenth, Fourteenth, and Fifteenth Amendments. With few exceptions, the civil rights decisions issued prior to *Brown v. Board of Education* established and exposed the Supreme Court's inglorious racial history. To illustrate the Court's overall racial history prior to *Brown*, I shall begin with *United States v. Cruikshank* (1875), *United States v. Reese* (1875), *Civil Rights Cases* (1883), *United States v. Plessy* (1896), *Williams v. Mississippi* (1898), and *Giles v. Harris* (1903).[8]

In *United States v. Cruikshank,* the Supreme Court severely undermined the ability of African Americans to protect themselves against racial violence perpetrated by private citizens. The Court was called upon to review the criminal convictions of three white defendants who had been found guilty of violating the Enforcement Act of 1870, also known as the First Ku Klux Klan Act. The defendants had participated in a brutal attack on African Americans in what became known as the "Colfax Massacre." This massacre took place in Louisiana, only three years after ratification of the last of the Reconstruction Amendments— the Fifteenth Amendment—and was instigated by the events following Louisiana's widely contested 1872 gubernatorial election. Both the Republican and Democratic candidates claimed to have won the election. To the chagrin of white Democrats and the delight of African Americans, a Republican federal judge determined the Republican candidate William P. Kellogg was the victor. In rebellion, a group of white Democrats, including many white supremacists, seized the Colfax courthouse in an attempt to set up their own government but were forced out by

African Americans. On April 13, 1873, a mob of whites armed themselves and marched on the Colfax courthouse, then occupied by black Republicans. Outgunned, the African Americans surrendered to the white mob and turned over their weapons. Nevertheless, the white mob set the courthouse on fire and began slaughtering African Americans. Hours after the attack had begun, as many as one hundred African Americans lay dead—burned alive in the courthouse, attacked outside its doors, and hunted down in the surrounding woods.[9]

Responding to the Colfax Massacre, the state indicted nearly one hundred of the white attackers for violating section 6 of the Enforcement Act. Of these, only three were convicted. On appeal, the Supreme Court reversed the convictions, holding, in part, that the Fourteenth Amendment applied to states and not to private actors.[10]

The Court began by explaining that in order for a defendant to be found guilty of violating the Enforcement Act, he must have banded together or conspired to violate a right "granted or secured by the constitution or laws of the United States." But this prohibition did not apply to everyone. Since the Enforcement Act was predicated on the Fourteenth Amendment, it could not protect against a private citizen's interference with statutory rights. It only protected against state intrusions. The Court thus articulated the "state action doctrine," now a fundamental principle of constitutional law. Based on that doctrine, the Enforcement Act was inapplicable to the facts of this case.[11]

Similarly, the Court dismissed other charges in the indictment on the basis that the charges failed to allege that the defendants had violated rights secured by the Constitution or federal laws. For example, the justices ruled the Fifteenth Amendment was inapplicable because it protected against racial discrimination in exercising the right to vote. Because the indictment did not specifically state that the defendants had intended to interfere with voting rights *based on their race*, it did not properly allege a violation of a federal right and, by extension, the Enforcement Act.[12]

The Court was very wrong on both counts. As to the Fourteenth Amendment issue, the Court should have seen that state action was implicated in the case because the massacre was all about state political power and it could not have happened without the assistance of local authorities. The KKK always acts with local authority working behind the scene. At the very least the Court should have remanded the case to determine the extent to which local authorities had participated in or sanctioned the massacre. That would have easily brought the case within the state action doctrine. Failing to do so, the *Cruikshank* Court failed to secure justice for African Americans who were so brutally slaughtered by racist thugs. The Court's decision certainly helped to open the door to forms of racial violence, such as lynching, that were characteristic of the Jim Crow era. The state action doctrine itself, one should note, is quite problematic. It artificially restricts the scope of the Bill of Rights incorporated in the Fourteenth Amendment, in this case leaving the former slaves to the mercy of their former slaveholders and white supremacists. Withdrawing federal protection made it open season on blacks in the southern states at the hands of private racists who usually acted under the closet authority of public officials. How could the Supreme Court have turned a blind eye to that and call it justice? As to the Fifteenth Amendment issue, the massacre was clearly about political power and the exercise of the franchise by blacks. It was about the integrity of the recently passed Fifteenth Amendment. Had there not been a gubernatorial election in which blacks voted for the first time, there would not have been a massacre of blacks. Federal rights were certainly implicated in *Cruikshank,* but the Court was too blind to see them.[13]

In *United States v. Reese,* the Supreme Court further undercut African American progress by invalidating sections of the Enforcement Act that criminalized unlawful interference with voting. In *Reese,* the Supreme Court questioned whether two southern election officials could be punished under the Enforcement Act for refusing to allow William Garner, a qualified African American voter, to vote in a municipal election in Kentucky. The election officials claimed they did not allow Garner to vote because he had failed to pay the required $1.50 poll tax. Garner countered that he had attempted to pay the poll tax but his payment had been refused. The officials were indicted for violating the Enforcement Act, which provided federal punishment for interfering with a citizen's Fifteenth Amendment voting rights.[14]

On review, the Supreme Court examined whether the election officials could be indicted under the third and fourth sections of the

Enforcement Act. Section 3 prohibited an election official from wrongfully refusing to receive or count the vote of an eligible voter who presented an affidavit stating that a different state official had unreasonably
failed to register that voter. Essentially, section 3 protected the voting
rights of eligible voters who had followed voting registration instruc-
tions but nonetheless had been wrongfully turned away. Section 4
promised punishment to any person who used "force, bribery, threats,
intimidation, or other unlawful means . . . to hinder, delay, prevent, or
obstruct, any citizen from doing any act required to be done to qualify
him to vote, or from voting."[15]

The Court began by noting that Congress's power to create legislation governing state elections came from the Fifteenth Amendment.
Next, it explained that the Fifteenth Amendment prohibited interfering
with an eligible citizen's voting rights based on race, color, or previous
condition of servitude. Finding that the third and fourth sections of the
Enforcement Act reached beyond these parameters by criminalizing not
just racial but *any* unlawful interference with voting rights, the Court
declared those sections unconstitutional. The Court found no federal
law under which the election officials could be charged. For that reason,
it sustained the defendants' demurrers.[16]

With the stroke of the pen, the *Reese* Court wiped away federal
voting protection for African Americans. More than forty lower-court
cases were waiting to see how the Court would rule. The Court could
have construed sections 3 and 4 in ways that brought them within the
scope of the Fifteenth Amendment, such as by ruling that as applied to
the facts of *Reese*, these sections were limited to race. The election officials were clearly motivated by race in denying the right to vote in this
case. Moreover, when the act is read in its entirety, there is little doubt
that Congress intended to limit sections 3 and 4 to race-based voting
violations. As Justices Clifford and Hunt pointed out in dissent:

> 1. That the intention of Congress on this subject is too plain
> to be discussed. The Fifteenth Amendment had just been ad-
> opted, the object of which was to secure to a lately enslaved
> population protection against violations of their right to
> vote on account of their color or previous condition. The act

is entitled "An Act to enforce the right of citizens of the United States to vote in the several states of the Union, and for other purposes." The first section contains a general announcement that such right is not to be embarrassed by the fact of race, color, or previous condition. The second section requires that equal opportunity shall be given to the races in providing every prerequisite for voting, and that any officer who violates this provision shall be subject to civil damages to the extent of $500, and to fine and imprisonment. To suppose that Congress, in making these provisions, intended to impose no duty upon, and subject to no penalty, the very officers who were to perfect the exercise of the right to vote— to wit, the inspectors who receive or reject the votes—would be quite absurd.[17]

By invalidating sections 3 and 4 of the Enforcement Act in their entirety, the Court eliminated the only legislation reinforcing and supporting the black Americans' newfound voting rights. Again, the Court signaled it was open season for white supremacists to intimidate, threaten, and thwart racial advancement in this country.[18]

In the *Civil Rights Cases,* the Supreme Court declared that sections of the Civil Rights Act of 1875 securing equal treatment for African Americans in public accommodations were unconstitutional. Five similar lawsuits were consolidated in this case. Essentially, five African American plaintiffs had all filed separate lawsuits alleging that certain hotels, theaters, and public transit companies had violated the Civil Rights Act of 1875 by denying them services or banning them from areas reserved for whites. Section 1 of the Civil Rights Act of 1875 stated that "all persons within the jurisdiction of the United States shall be entitled to the full and equal enjoyment of accommodations, advantages, facilities, and privileges of inns, public conveyances on land or water, theaters, and other places of public amusement; subject only to the conditions and limitations established by law, and applicable alike to citizens of every race and color, regardless of any previous condition of servitude."[19] Section 2 of the act imposed a punishment on any person who violated section 1. Under section 2, a person who violated section 1 of the Civil Rights Act would have to pay five hundred dollars in damages to the person he had wronged, receive a misdemeanor conviction, and have to pay an additional fine or be given a minimum of thirty days of imprisonment.[20]

The Court had to determine whether sections 1 and 2 were constitutional under the Thirteenth or Fourteenth Amendment. As to the latter, the Court, as it had done in *Cruikshank*, limited the reach of the Fourteenth Amendment to state action and ruled the Civil Rights Act unconstitutional thereunder as a regulation of private conduct. As to the Thirteenth Amendment, the Court came to the same conclusion. While "Congress has a right to enact all necessary and proper laws for the obliteration and prevention of slavery, with all its badges and incidents," refusing service to a person based on their skin color "ha[d] nothing to do with slavery or involuntary servitude."[21] Thus, the ability to redress private citizens' refusal of service to African Americans was outside Congress's power and instead lay with the state.[22]

Justice Harlan filed a strong dissenting opinion. He criticized the majority's opinion as "narrow" and "artificial," and, like Justices Clifford and Hunt dissenting in *Reese*, asserted that the majority had thwarted congressional intent. Justice Harlan read the Thirteenth Amendment as prohibiting more than just slavery: "the Thirteenth Amendment may be exerted by legislation . . . for the eradication, not simply of the institution [of slavery], but of its badges and incidents. . . ." Public transportation, hotels, and places of public amusement were public or quasi-public, Justice Harlan continued, and "such discrimination practiced by corporations and individuals in the exercise of their public or quasi-public functions is a badge of servitude." The Civil Rights Act of 1875, in short, is proper exercise of the power granted to Congress in section 2 of the Thirteenth Amendment to protect "freedom and the rights necessarily inhering in a state of freedom."[23]

Moving to the Fourteenth Amendment, Justice Harlan argued that Congress has authority thereunder to limit the actions of private citizens as well as states. Congress has the power to protect all that is necessary for the enjoyment of rights and privileges granted to African Americans as citizens under the Fourteenth Amendment. Moreover, railroad corporations, innkeepers, and managers of places of public amusement are public agents because they provide services to the public. Hence, "a denial, by these instrumentalities of the State to the citizen, because of his race . . . is a denial by the State within the meaning of the Fourteenth Amendment," Justice Harlan insisted.[24]

The African American press decried the Court's decision in the *Civil Rights Cases,* calling it "a farce." In his dissent, Justice Harlan made special note of the fact that the Court's twisted construction of yet another civil rights statute impeded racial progress: "It is, I submit, scarcely just to say that the colored race has been the special favorite of the laws. . . . The one underlying purpose of the congressional legislation has been to enable the black race to take the rank of mere citizens. The difficulty has been to compel recognition of the legal right of the black race to take that rank of citizens, and to secure the enjoyment of privileges belonging, under the law, to them as a component part of the people for whose welfare and happiness government is ordained."[25] As bad as the decision in the *Civil Right Cases* was, *Plessy v. Ferguson* was worse.

Second only to *Dred Scott* in its infamy, *Plessy v. Ferguson* provided constitutional cover for relegating blacks to second-class citizenship in virtually every walk of life for generations to come. The Court in *Plessy* upheld the constitutionality of segregation in public transportation under the doctrine of "separate but equal." Plaintiff Homer Plessy was charged with violating Louisiana's statute that prohibited whites and African Americans from riding in the same railway car. To the naked eye, Plessy looked like a white man. Although he likely could have ridden in the white railway car without issue, Plessy announced to the conductor that he was one-eighth black, which, under the "one-drop rule," meant he was "colored" in the eyes of the law. Not unlike Rosa Parks a half century later, Plessy intended to test the validity of southern segregation policies on public transportation. After refusing to sit in the colored car, Plessy was removed by the police, taken to a local jail, and criminally charged. He filed a lawsuit challenging the statute on the ground that it violated the Thirteenth and Fourteenth Amendments.[26]

In an 8–1 decision, the Supreme Court upheld Louisiana's statute, finding that it violated neither the Thirteenth nor the Fourteenth Amendment. In finding no Thirteenth Amendment violation, the Court reasoned that the statute did not "re-establish a state of involuntary servitude" by simply making a legal separation between whites and blacks.

Second, the Court held that the statute did not violate the Fourteenth Amendment because the purpose of that amendment was to treat the races equally before the law, *not* to abolish racial distinctions or create social equality. To support its segregationist stance, the Court pointed to school segregation policies, "which have been held to be a valid exercise of the legislative power even by courts of states where the political rights of the colored race have been longest and most earnestly enforced."[27] The Court dismissed Plessy's argument that the statute was unreasonable because it stamped blacks with "a badge of inferiority." Blacks, the Court insisted, were responsible for their own feelings of racial inferiority.[28]

In a powerful dissent, Justice Harlan famously declared that "Our constitution is colorblind, and neither knows nor tolerates classes among citizens."[29] The true purpose behind the Thirteenth, Fourteenth, and Fifteenth Amendments, Justice Harlan wrote, was to "remove the race line from our government" and secure equal civil rights for all Americans regardless of race. Louisiana's statute interfered with the right of African Americans to travel about freely. Justice Harlan rejected the argument that the statute was nondiscriminatory because it equally limited both whites and blacks in their seating options. He pointed out the obvious: the statute was meant to keep African Americans out of the white railway cars, not the other way around. Summing up his position, Justice Harlan maintained that Louisiana's segregation law was invalid because it was facially inconsistent with our color-blind Constitution. A harbinger of contemporary civil rights sentiment, Harlan predicted that the majority's opinion would come to be seen as equally shameful as *Dred Scott*.[30]

In *Williams v. Mississippi*, the Supreme Court upheld southern voting laws that blatantly operated to prevent African Americans from voting. The plaintiff, Henry Williams, was indicted on a murder charge by an all-white grand jury in Mississippi. Williams moved to quash the indictment alleging that Mississippi's voter registration laws violated the Fourteenth Amendment.[31]

Mississippi's voter registration laws required eligible voters to pay a poll tax and pass a literacy test. The laws also gave election officials complete discretion in administering the literacy test and determining whether an eligible voter had passed. Moreover, citizens of Mississippi were only eligible to serve on juries if they were registered voters. Thus, the purpose of Mississippi's voting requirements was two-fold: prevent African Americans from voting and serving on juries. The Mississippi circuit court denied Williams's motion to quash as well as his subsequent motion to remove the case to federal court from state court. An all-white jury convicted Williams and sentenced him to be hanged.[32]

Williams appealed, arguing that Mississippi's voter registration laws violated the Fourteenth Amendment because, despite their facial neutrality, they gave election officials absolute discretion to determine voting eligibility, which in turn determined ability to sit on a jury.[33] The Supreme Court recognized that Mississippi's law afforded the election administrative officials enormous discretion: "This officer can reject whomsoever he chooses, and register whomsoever he chooses, for he is vested by the [Mississippi] constitution with that power. . . . The officer is the sole judge of the [literacy] examination of the applicant, and, even though the applicant be qualified, it is left with the officer to so determine; and the said officer can refuse him registration."[34] However, the Court determined there was insufficient evidence to prove that the voter registration laws had *actually* been administered in a discriminatory fashion. To bolster this contention, the Court pointed out that the plaintiff had brought suit against the law, not against any election officials. Ultimately, the Supreme Court upheld Mississippi's voter registration laws because they were facially neutral and evidence had shown only the likelihood—not certainty—that the laws had been administered in a racially discriminatory manner.[35]

The *Williams* decision effectively eviscerated African Americans' right to vote. It nullified the Fifteen Amendment as far as black Americans were concerned. By placing a heavy evidentiary burden on African Americans seeking to challenge the administration of state voting laws, the Court intentionally sought to impede racial progress. There is no other way in which to understand the case.

Giles v. Harris is another important voting-rights case. The Supreme Court declined to strike down Alabama's voter registration laws even though they were clearly intended to prevent African Americans from voting. In *Giles,* the African American plaintiff brought suit against the Board of Registrars of Montgomery, Alabama, on behalf of himself and five thousand other African Americans. The plaintiff alleged that the Board of Registrars had unfairly refused to register him and other eligible African Americans to vote before August 1, 1902, and that portions of Alabama's state constitution dealing with voter eligibility violated the Fourteenth and Fifteenth Amendments. Alabama's voting registration laws were split into two categories depending on whether a person had registered to vote before or after January 1, 1903. For those who registered to vote before January 1, 1903, the eligibility criteria were more relaxed. They also received lifetime voting rights. Alabama residents who registered to vote on or after January 1, 1903, faced stricter voting eligibility criteria, including literacy or wealth requirements.[36]

The federal district court dismissed the suit for lack of jurisdiction. On appeal, the Supreme Court affirmed the district court's dismissal on different grounds. The Court found it "impossible to grant the equitable relief which is asked." because the plaintiff was asking that his name and the names of eligible African American voters be placed on the pre-1903 voter registration list while at the same time asserting that Alabama's voting registration scheme was unconstitutional. The Court refused to register the plaintiff under a potentially fraudulent voting registration scheme, while "express[ing] no opinion as to the alleged fact of the [laws'] unconstitutionality. . . ."[37] Moreover, the plaintiff could not sue the state of Alabama in federal court. If the state of Alabama had violated the plaintiff's political rights, only that state, Congress, or the executive branch could grant relief. Three justices dissented. Justice Harlan was one of them. Although he made several impressive legal arguments, as usual, one observation he made stands out: "Although the case involves questions of considerable importance, it was submitted here without oral argument."[38] What an inglorious racial history.

Institutional Redemption

Responding to pressure exerted by a relentless litigation campaign waged by the NAACP, the Supreme Court began to chip away at the regime of second-class citizenship it had helped erect since the Court's inception. There were many NAACP victories. Three are especially important: *Missouri ex rel. Gaines v. Canada* (1938); *McLaurin v. Oklahoma*

State Regents for Higher Education (1950); and *Sweatt v. Painter* (1950).[39] Each of these cases laid the foundation for the Court's decision in *Brown v. Board of Education* (1954).

In *Missouri ex rel. Gaines v. Canada*, petitioner Lloyd Gaines, an African American, was refused admission to the state's all-white law school at the University of Missouri. There were no Missouri law schools for blacks. The respondent admitted at trial that the petitioner's "work and credits at the Lincoln University [his undergraduate school] would qualify him for admission to the School of Law of the University of Missouri if he were found otherwise eligible." The petitioner was refused admission based solely on the fact that it was "contrary to the constitution, laws and public policy of the State to admit a negro as a student in the University of Missouri."[40] The respondent advised the petitioner to apply for aid under a state statute that allowed the state superintendent of schools to arrange for the admittance of blacks to law schools in other states, including adjacent states, where nonresident blacks are admitted. The statute also allowed the superintendent to pay the tuition of these law schools.[41]

Siding with the petitioner, the Supreme Court held that the state violated constitutional equal protection when it failed to provide an in-state law school for blacks. The Court pushed aside the respondent's arguments that there is "a legislative declaration of a purpose to establish a law school for negroes at Lincoln University whenever necessary or practical," and that "pending the establishment of such a school, adequate provision has been made for the legal education of negro students in recognized schools outside of this State."[42] The Court rejected the promise of a black law school as nothing more than words—"a mere declaration of purpose, still unfulfilled"—certainly not a "mandatory duty." Similarly, the Court found the state's "generous" offer to arrange for and pay the tuition of petitioner to attend an out-of-state law school to be constitutionally insufficient:

> Manifestly, the obligation of the State to give the protection
> of equal laws can be performed only where its laws operate,
> that is, within its own jurisdiction. It is there that the equal-
> ity of legal right must be maintained. That obligation is

imposed by the Constitution upon the States severally as governmental entities—each responsible for its own laws establishing the rights and duties of persons within its borders. It is an obligation the burden of which cannot be cast by one State upon another, and no State can be excused from performance by what another State may do or fail to do.[43]

Under this rationale, there would be a constitutional violation if Missouri "arranged for the attendance" and paid the "reasonable tuition fees" of blacks to attend Harvard Law School.

The fact that the petitioner was the first person to demand a law school at Lincoln University was no excuse for not providing one beforehand. As the Court ruled, the constitutional right at issue was a "personal" one. The petitioner was therefore entitled to equal protection of the laws as an individual, regardless of whether other members of his putative class sought the same opportunity. Of course, a personal right in the discrimination context is only comprehensible by reference to characteristics that form the basis for the animus, which, in turn, are common to other members who might suffer the same discrimination. Group rights and personal rights are not mutually exclusive in civil rights cases. Perhaps the Court invoked the idea of "personal rights" because it thought that admitting Mr. Gaines to the law school as a matter of personal right might seem less threatening to the status quo than declaring the rights of African Americans as a group.

Indeed, although *Gaines* was a major victory for all African Americans because it was the first Supreme Court case that expressly held that separate education must actually be equal, the case still very much maintained the status quo. It did not require desegregation or integration. Blacks remained separate but equal, which is to say they continued to be regarded as second-class citizens under the Court's civil rights jurisprudence. The Court, in short, was not prepared to overrule *Plessy*.[44]

Yet, the Court's attitude toward black advancement was clearly changing, and *Gaines* was an unmistakable manifestation of that change, not only in the Court's holding and reasoning on the substantive issues but also on the procedural ones. Whereas in earlier cases the Court's anti-black rulings often had turned on minor procedural errors by the petitioners,[45] the Court was quite willing to push aside arguably more serious pleading errors, for example, the failure to exhaust all remedies, in *Gaines*. Eschewing legalisms, the Court ignored or downplayed pleading problems in support of racial equality.

In two cases handed down on the same day in 1950, the Supreme Court continued to move toward rectifying its shameful past. The first case was *McLaurin v. Oklahoma State Regents for Higher Education*. As a condition for enrolling in a graduate program at an all-white university under the *Gaines* precedent, appellant G. W. McLaurin, an African American Ph.D. candidate, had to comply with a state statute that required him "to sit apart at a designated desk in an anteroom adjoining the classroom; to sit at a designated desk on the mezzanine floor of the library, but not to use the desks in the regular reading room; and to sit at a designated table and to eat at a different time from the other students in the school cafeteria."[46] Not unlike it did in *Gaines*, the Court pushed aside the state's main argument (that the conditions it imposed were "merely nominal") to rule in favor of black advancement on equal protection grounds. The educational conditions imposed on the appellant are so humiliating and segregative that he "is handicapped in his pursuit of effective graduate instruction. Such restrictions impair and inhibit his ability to study, to engage in discussions and exchange with views with other students, and, in general, to learn his profession."[47] The Court not only found that the appellant had an equality interest— integrated education—which interest, as the interest in *Gaines*, was "personal and present," not dependent upon similar requests made by other blacks and ripened with the establishment of similar educational opportunities for whites, but for the very first time linked the black equality interest to good social policy, *black role models*:

> Our society grows increasingly complex, and our need for trained leaders increases correspondingly. Appellant's case represents, perhaps, the epitome of that need, for he is attempting to obtain an advanced degree in education, to become, by definition, a leader and trainer of others. Those who will come under his guidance and influence must be directly affected by the education he receives. Their own

education and development will necessarily suffer to the extent that his training is unequal to that of his classmates. State imposed restrictions which produce such inequalities cannot be sustained.[48]

In the next case, *Sweatt v. Painter*, the Court continued the process of historical reversal. The Court, in fact, came very close to overturning *Plessy v. Ferguson*. The issue was whether a new law school built for African Americans in Texas offered the petitioner, Heman Marion Sweatt, "privileges, advantages, and opportunities for the study of law substantially equivalent to those offered by the State to white students at the University of Texas" from which Sweatt had been denied admission because of the color of his skin. The Court answered this question in the affirmative. It held that the petitioner must be admitted to the state's white law school because the state's black law school was unequal in physical facilities and "reputation of the faculty, experience of the administration, position and influence of the alumni, standing in the community, traditions and prestige. It is difficult to believe that one who had a free choice between these law schools would consider the question close."[49] While reiterating that the equality interest the petitioner sought to assert—an integrated or quality education (same difference in this case)—was "personal and present," the Court did not link the vindication of this interest to good social policy. The Court kept the interest "personal."[50]

McLaurin and *Sweatt* have important differences that make the former the more important case. *McLaurin* explicitly links black advancement to good social policy; *Sweatt* does not. Perhaps the Court thought that the black interest asserted in *Sweatt* has no significance beyond the individual who asserts it. Neither case, however, changed the legal status of blacks, who remained second-class citizens. Separate but equal was still the law of the land. In fact, *Sweatt* explicitly refused to "reach petitioner's contention that *Plessy v. Ferguson* should be reexamined in the light of contemporary knowledge respecting the purposes of the Fourteenth Amendment and the effects of racial segregation."[51] That task was left to *Brown*.

With the momentum of cases that chipped away at the separate-but-equal doctrine, *Gaines, McLaurin,* and *Sweatt* in particular, a unanimous Supreme Court in *Brown v. Board of Education* raised and answered the dispositive issue: "Does segregation of children in public schools solely on the basis of race, even though the physical facilities and other 'tangible' factors may be equal, deprive the children of the minority group of equal educational opportunities? We believe that it does."[52]

The Court then went on to sign the execution warrant for Jim Crow. It ruled that "in the field of public education the doctrine of 'separate but equal' has no place. . . . [S]uch segregation is a denial of the equal protection of the laws."[53] *Brown* changed the sociopolitical environment for racial relations in our country. From that point forward, the law would regard blacks as people whose lives mattered. Equal opportunity before the law—formal equal opportunity—was now the law of the land, first in the field of education, then spreading to other segments of society.

Looking back at the decision a decade later, Judge Robert Carter, one of the NAACP lawyers who argued the case before the Supreme Court, wrote that *Brown*'s decision engendered "a social upheaval the extent and consequences of which cannot even now be measured with certainty," and changed the legal status of black Americans from mere supplicants "seeking, pleading, begging to be treated as full-fledged members of the human race" to persons entitled to equal treatment under the law.[54] Effectively ending racial segregation, a relic of slavery, the decision was, in the view of Judge Louis Pollak, who had for most of his professional life been an advisor to the NAACP lawyers, "probably the most important American government act of any kind since the Emancipation Proclamation."[55] Hence, Judge Pollak, who had served as the dean of Yale Law School and of the University of Pennsylvania Law School prior to becoming a judge, saw the decision in the same light as did Judge Carter. In a 2004 interview on NPR, he observed that "even though it was a decision about schools, [*Brown*] became a precedent for, in the next half-dozen years, a series of Supreme Court decisions where they didn't even have to write opinions, where they knocked out segregation in buses, in parks, in swimming pools and the whole array of public institutions that had been blanketed with Jim Crow for half a century."[56]

What was the motivation behind *Brown*? What does the opinion stand for? Many contemporary legal scholars view *Brown* in materialistic terms. They argue that the Supreme Court's decision to overturn well-established law was motivated less by a racial awakening or fulfillment of the American Creed—the Court's response to the American Dilemma made plain by Gunnar Myrdal—than by material considerations. Not only had we just fought a war to save democracy for the world, but black soldiers returned home with a new militancy. They were unwilling to accept second-class citizenship.[57]

There were also geopolitical considerations. At the time of *Brown*, the United States was in the throes of the Cold War in which a major objective was to win the hearts and minds of the black, brown, and yellow people of the Third World. Foreign press reports, letters from United States ambassadors abroad, and other communiqués clearly and persistently indicated that the United States could not win the Cold War if the world news organizations continued to carry stories of lynchings, murders of young blacks like that of fourteen-year-old Emmett Till (whose murder for allegedly whistling at a white woman was so monstrous that it helped to inspired Rosa Parks's civil rights defiance), racial discrimination against African delegates to the United Nations in places of public accommodation, and other domestic incidents of racial oppression. So serious were these concerns that the United States Department of State filed an amicus curiae brief in *Brown* that sided with the NAACP. This was the first time in American history that the government sided with the NAACP in a segregation case. The government's amicus curiae brief referred to Secretary of State Dean Acheson's report stating that "racial discrimination in the United States remains a source of constant embarrassment to this Government in the day-to-day conduct of its foreign relations; and it jeopardizes the effective maintenance of our moral leadership of the free and democratic nations of the world."[58] American racism made it difficult for the United States to market democracy as a protector of personal freedoms.[59]

I see another motivation for the Court's decision in *Brown*. The Supreme Court's decision is a reaction to its own history in racial relations, its inglorious racial past. When viewed within that context, *Brown* stands for something quite different, and what it stands for is not inconsistent with the materialistic take on the case.[60]

Well aware of its sordid precedents, the *Brown* Court arguably sought to end the harm that prior Supreme Courts had visited upon generations of blacks. At its most basic level, *Brown* should be understood as a case of juridical redemption, a case in which the Court seeks to atone for its inglorious racial history enshrined in cases like *Dred Scott* and *Plessy*. The *Brown* decision sought to reverse course, to support racial advancement rather than to continue to impede it. And it sought to do so less because it felt sorry for blacks or wanted to accord them special treatment than because it saw racial advancement as good social policy. The Court, in fact, explicitly noted "the importance of education to our democratic society."[61] School segregation was fundamentally inconsistent with quality education. It also weakened democracy's internal morality—human dignity. To find the social good in racial advancement, the Court had to reject *Plessy*'s "finding" that the segregation statutes did not stamp blacks with a "badge of inferiority," that any suggestion of black inferiority arising from racial segregation came from a twisted black perspective. Heeding the voices of black children spoken through the "doll test" (the work of black psychologists Kenneth and Mamie Clark), *Brown* went in the opposite direction of *Plessy*, finding that "Segregation of white and colored children has a detrimental effect upon the colored children. . . . Any language in *Plessy v. Ferguson* contrary to this finding is rejected."[62] *Brown thus embraced racial advancement as a matter of good social policy.*

In similar fashion, the Supreme Court today ought to push hard for racial progress. In the spirit of *Brown*, the Court should maximize racial progress unless there is an exceedingly important societal reason not to do so. Though, necessarily, this determination must be made on a case-by-case basis, it generally means that socio-legal victory for blacks should not unnecessarily trammel the civil rights interests of others. With this judicial mindset, the Supreme Court should be able to avoid juridical subordination.

Juridical Subordination

J uridical subordination describes judicial decision-making in civil rights cases, especially at the Supreme Court level, that inhibits racial advancement for nonracist reasons. Unearthing juridical subordination necessarily requires a deeper understanding of the black equality interest in civil rights law. That interest was first articulated in *Brown*. In overturning the separate-but-equal doctrine, the *Brown* Court embraced a rather ambiguous concept of the black equality interest—formal equal opportunity. In the decades following *Brown*, Congress and the Supreme Court fashioned two potentially conflicting norms that gave meaning to formal equal opportunity—racial omission and racial integration. These norms not only defined the black equality interest ordained in *Brown* but have also guided the Supreme Court and Congress in the creation and application of civil rights law both during and after the civil rights era.[1]

As we shall see, *Brown*'s twin norms and the implementing law crafted during the civil rights era are not the only ways to pursue racial advancement in today's post–civil rights society. Indeed, they may not be the best or even sound positions to take in every civil rights case that comes before the Supreme Court today. One of the questions staring us in the face is whether the civil-rights-era equality norms—racial omission and racial integration—continue to have currency in post–civil rights America. Have they become instruments of juridical subordination? To answer these questions, I begin with the civil rights era.

Civil Rights Period

Taken together, the racial-omission and racial-integration norms define the black equality interest under a regime of equal rights. Racial omission defines the black equality interest as racial neutrality. The government's stance on matters of race should be neutral, or color-blind. Race must be omitted from governmental rules and policies regarding education, employment, housing, and other areas of American life. Racial groups are entitled to equal treatment (or racial neutrality) from the government in all aspects of life. White Americans should not be given any government-sanctioned freedoms or privileges not also available to African Americans, and vice versa. As racial omission's sibling tenet, racial integration defines formal equal opportunity as racial mixing. All aspects of the government and government-supported segments of American society—whether educational, economic, or social—should be racially mixed. Racially integrated settings create opportunities for blacks and, at the same time, remove from the public arena all vestiges of prior systems of racial oppression. However beneficial racial integration might be for blacks and the nation as a whole, the racial-integration tenet, unlike the racial-omission tenet, is permissive rather than mandatory, at least in the Supreme Court's deployment of the tenet. Governmental entities need not take affirmative steps to promote racial mixing, and, in fact, can only do so under very limited circumstances. They must, however, take affirmative measures to ensure that their policies and practices are race neutral. These rules apply to private institutions for the most part.[2]

Clearly, the racial-omission and racial-integration norms presuppose racial desegregation. No government could logically or successfully operate a public policy that mandates the omission of race from legal considerations or calls for racial mixing without first (or at least simultaneously) removing legal designations that exclude and stigmatize a racial group. The failure to do so would be disingenuous and certainly would create institutional dysfunction, if not cognitive dissonance among Americans, on racial matters.

The racial-integration and racial-omission norms sometimes collide with each other. This happens most famously in the case of affirmative action, which typically promotes racial integration in a race-conscious manner. Yet, the norms need not collide necessarily. Color-blind decision-making can support the racial-integration norm on the theory that it allows racial mixing to unfold naturally, that is, by the removal of the artificial barrier of racial segregation rather than by affirmative measures taken by an institution. When the norms collide, one of them must yield. Usually civil rights law requires the racial-integration norm to give ground.[3]

There are myriad federal statutes that both proscribe racial discrimination and permit racial preferences. The Civil Rights Act of 1964, the Voting Rights Act of 1965, the Fair Housing Act of 1968, and the 1972 amendments to Title VII of the 1964 Civil Rights Act are the most significant federal antidiscrimination and racial-preference laws implementing the racial-omission and racial-integration norms. Vindicating the racial-omission norm, the 1964 Civil Rights Act has eleven titles, each of which prohibits discrimination "on the basis of race or color" in a major sector of American life, such as voting (Title I), public accommodations (Title II), public education (Title IV), and employment (Title VII), to mention just a few. Similarly, the 1965 Voting Rights Act, which vastly improves the voting protections provided in Title I of the 1964 Civil Rights Act (which mainly establishes standards applicable to voter registration), bans all forms of discrimination in voting (from literacy tests to complex schemes of vote dilution) "on account of race or color." The 1968 Fair Housing Act makes it illegal for certain property owners, real estate agencies, and lenders to discriminate "because of race, [or] color" in the sale or rental of housing. Finally, the 1972 amendments to Title VII of the 1964 Civil Rights Act, inter alia, strengthened the Equal Employment Opportunities Commission, the government agency charged with enforcing Title VII, by giving it the power to investigate and prosecute charges of employment discrimination (making Title VII more than just a toothless tiger) and by extending the prohibition against employment discrimination to states and local governmental entities. The 1972 amendments brought an official end to the Jim Crow era and began the post–civil rights era.[4]

Vindicating the racial-integration norm, many federal statutes also permit the use of racial preferences as a remedy for a proven violation of statutory law or as a voluntary remedy under certain conditions. Title VII, for example, permits employers to establish race-conscious affirmative action voluntarily to eliminate manifest racial imbalance in traditionally segregated job categories so long as it does not unnecessarily trammel the interests of white males. The 1965 Voting Rights Act authorizes the creation of "majority-minority voting districts," a form of affirmative action, to remedy historic patterns of voting discrimination. The 1968 Fair Housing Act has in the past permitted affirmative-action housing policy on a limited basis.[5]

Statutory antidiscrimination and racial-preference laws are triggered by the "intent test" and, sometimes, the "effects test." The former test requires the plaintiff to show that the defendant, whether it be a private party or governmental entity, purposefully made a race-conscious decision that disadvantages the plaintiff. The effects test requires the plaintiff to show that the defendant used a racially neutral policy or practice that falls more harshly on the plaintiff's civil rights class than on one or more of the other civil rights classes. Because whites constitute a civil rights class (a "protected class"), these laws also protect them.[6]

Like statutory law, constitutional law enforces formal equal opportunity through the creation of antidiscrimination and racial-preference laws. In constitutional law, the "strict scrutiny test" has become the Supreme Court's chief means of enforcing the racial-omission and racial-integration tenets. A two-prong equal-protection test, the strict scrutiny test prohibits a governmental entity from intentionally (the intent test) using a racial classification unless the classification is narrowly tailored (commonly called the "means prong" or "means test") to serve a compelling state or governmental purpose (commonly called the "ends prong" or "ends test"). Imbued with the constitutional authority of the Equal Protection Clause, the strict scrutiny test is intended to severely limit the use of race in the formulation of public law or policy. To that extent, the strict scrutiny test promotes the racial-omission tenet.[7]

Implicit in the strict scrutiny test is the constitutional authorization for the use of racial preferences by governmental entities. These institutions have constitutional permission to intentionally use a racial classification, which would otherwise be illegal, if the classification meets the strict scrutiny's means and ends tests; that is, it must be narrowly tailored to serve a compelling governmental purpose. Few racial classifications pass the strict scrutiny test. Basically, the Supreme Court recognizes only two compelling state interests regarding race-conscious programs designed to assist blacks: the desire to remedy an institution's own past discrimination, and the desire to maintain a diverse student body. In sanctioning affirmative action, the strict scrutiny test promotes the racial-integration norm *pro tanto*. Mediating the tension between the racial-omission norm and the racial-integration norm, the strict scrutiny test typically favors the former. Basically, the racial-omission tenet trumps the racial-integration tenet in constitutional as well as most statutory civil rights law.[8]

This legal regime has governed the Supreme Court's decision-making during both the civil rights and post–civil rights periods. The problem is this: racial dynamics have changed since the civil rights era, not a little but a lot. New strategies for achieving racial advancement have emerged to challenge the old norms. Judicial decision-making has to keep up with changing attitudes about racial justice if it is to avoid juridical subordination.

Changing Racial Dynamics

Racial conditions in contemporary American society are quite different from what they were at the time of *Brown* and during the Reverend Martin Luther King era. The Supreme Court in 1954 was dealing with a system of American apartheid. The South had Jim Crow laws, and the North, for the most part, had Jim Crow practices. For example, blacks in the South were prohibited not only from going to the same schools as whites, but also from eating in the same restaurants, drinking at the same public water fountains, using the same restrooms, or sitting in the same seats at movie theaters. Common signage at the time warned: WHITES ONLY; RESTROOMS FOR COLORED; NO DOGS OR NIGGERS; COLORED WAITING ROOM; and STAFF AND NEGROES USE BACK ENTRANCE. Blacks could be lynched for such infractions as attempting to register to vote, filing a lawsuit against a white person, or, in the case of black men, making eye contact with a white woman ("eyeball rape"). Lynching was more than a hanging. It typically had a prelude and finale, the former consisting of torture, burning, maiming, and dismemberment, and the latter consisting of harvesting from the corpse such "souvenirs" as ears, nose, lips, and genitals.[9]

In 1972, the racial dynamics of American society changed significantly and for the better. Jim Crow died with the passage of the Equal Employment Opportunity Act of 1972. The civil rights movement as well as the civil rights period ended, and what scholars call the post–civil rights period began. Some four decades into the post–civil rights period, blacks have experienced unprecedented success individually, including the election and reelection of a black president of the United States. Yet capital deficiencies—financial, human, and social—continue to overwhelm the vast majority of African Americans, and the Supreme Court has significantly slowed the pace of racial progress. While formal equal opportunity was seen as an effective and fair response to Jim Crow, many civil rights scholars today question its soundness in our current racial environment.[10]

Indeed, at least four distinct norms, including the old ones, now speak to the question of formal equal opportunity's utility in civil rights cases: racial omission, racial integration, racial identity or solidarity, and social transformation. Each norm is a calculation as to the best strategy for racial advancement in contemporary American society. The racial-omission norm is primarily espoused by traditionalists. These largely conservative scholars believe that race no longer matters in our post–civil rights society; ergo, formal equal opportunity (FEO) is conceptually sound provided that the racial-omission norm trumps the racial-integration norm in civil rights cases, as it usually does. The racial-integration norm is favored by reformists. Loosely tied to the liberal side of the political spectrum, reformists, unlike traditionalists, believe race still matters in post–civil rights America; ergo FEO is conceptually sound but operationally flawed precisely because the racial-integration tenet is typically subordinated to the racial-omission tenet. Limited separatists proceed from the normative position that racial identity or solidarity matters most these days. FEO leaves no room for racial identity; for that reason it is conceptually unsound. The critical race theorists' core post–civil rights stance is that white hegemony matters most. FEO protects and perpetuates white privilege—it offers no social transformation—and for that reason it is conceptually unsound. What follows is a more detailed explanation of these normative stances.

Post–Civil Rights Norms
TRADITIONALISM

Traditionalism's basic orientation toward the American race problem, its core belief about racial relations and black progress, is quite simple: race no longer matters. Adherents of this post–civil rights theory are clearly not saying that racism does not exist; they are saying that the racism that does exist does not prevent African Americans or any other racial group from achieving worldly success and personal happiness in our post–civil rights society. Similarly, they are clearly not saying that African Americans face no problems today; they are saying that the problems African Americans face in today's society are self-inflicted. These problems are internal, not external; they are cultural, not racial.[11]

Given this core belief about black equality in post–civil rights America, one can easily see that traditionalists are largely in sync with the civil rights era's dominant view about racial progress. Racial omission was a sound strategy during the days of Martin Luther King Jr. and remains sound after the election and reelection of a black president. Now as then, formal equal opportunity is both conceptually and operationally sound. The only caveat is that its constituent norms must be strictly applied; in other words, the racial-integration norm must always be enforced in a racially neutral fashion; it must never cross paths with the racial-omission norm in application. If, however, their paths do cross through an ill-advised attempt to bring about racial integration in a race-conscious manner, then the racial-omission tenet must trump. Blacks and society as a whole are better off when we do not pollute the social environment by making too much fuss about race when, in fact, race no longer matters. Race-conscious policies are racially divisive, pure and simple.

This thinking certainly provides the subtext for most of the Supreme Court's decision-making in civil rights cases since the end of the civil rights period. The Court simply does not want to make too much about the problem of race in our society. Chief Justice Roberts, a steadfast traditionalist, spoke to this point in one of his opinions, writing, "Simply because the school districts may seek a worthy objective does not mean they are free to discriminate on the basis of race to achieve it. . . . The way to stop discrimination on the basis of race is to stop discriminating on the basis of race."[12] George Will, another traditionalist, strongly believes not only that race no longer matters but also that race only matters when the government uses it in policy-making. Whether invidious or benign, "negative" or "positive," race-conscious governmental policies are discriminatory and, hence, ipso facto, "racist."[13]

Giving blacks special treatment is not only racially divisive but is also counterproductive for blacks. It signals to society that blacks are hapless victims in need of special treatment. This message undercuts the black equality interest by depicting blacks as a people less than equal to whites. Blacks are akin to wards of the state. Justice Clarence Thomas has made this point quite often and with no dearth of passion:

> [T]here can be no doubt that racial paternalism and its unintended consequences can be as poisonous and pernicious as any other form of discrimination. So-called "benign" discrimination teaches many that because of chronic and apparently immutable handicaps, minorities cannot compete with them without their patronizing indulgence. Inevitably, such programs engender attitudes of superiority or, alternatively, provoke resentment among those who believe that they have been wronged by the government's use of race. These programs stamp minorities with a badge of inferiority and may cause them to develop dependencies or to adopt an attitude that they are "entitled" to preferences. . . . In my mind, government-sponsored racial discrimination based on benign prejudice is just as noxious as discrimination inspired by malicious prejudice. In each instance, it is racial discrimination, plain and simple.[14]

Racial charity, in short, undermines racial equality.

REFORMISM

Reformists proceed from a different normative stance. Glenn Loury, a onetime traditionalist, has become a most effective advocate of reform- ism. He argues that the traditionalist belief that "it's time to move on" is "simplistic social ethics and sophomoric social psychology."[15] When re- formists look at the American race problem, they see a problem of race rather than a narrower problem that inheres in the culture of the lowest socioeconomic class in black America.

For reformists, race still matters, just the opposite of what tradi- tionalists believe. For example, they argue that even though we have a black president, the most powerful person in the world lacks the power to raise racial issues with a strong voice in his own administration. General Mills reports a strong racist response to its 2013 commercial showing an interracial family eating its iconic cereal, Cheerios. Back- stage racism (for example, revealed by former NBA owner Donald Ster- ling in a private conservation) seems more prevalent than front-stage racism (racism expressed in public places). Reformists also point to the Department of Justice (DOJ) report on Ferguson, and to FBI director James Comey's acknowledgment of the "hard truth" that racial bias is a fact of life among police officers policing black communities. Yes, there is black-on-black crime, as traditionalists point out, but, reformists ar- gue, the traditionalists fail to point out that FBI statistics also show that the rate of white-on-white crime is virtually identical to the rate of black-on-black crime. Reformists want the Supreme Court to be more sensitive to the racially disadvantaging effects of these and other racial- ized conditions.[16]

But reformists are not revolutionaries. "With due humility," Glenn Loury insists, "I am a reformer, not an 'abolitionist.' "[17] Hence, reform- ists, like traditionalists, would seem to embrace formal equal opportu- nity in concept. Racial-omission and racial-integration norms are fine in concept in our post–civil rights, post–Jim Crow society. The differ- ence lies in the way the Supreme Court typically applies these tenets. Reformists believe formal equal opportunity, though conceptually sound, is operationally flawed because the Court does not place enough emphasis on the racial-integration norm in its administration of both racial-preference and antidiscrimination law. Reformists want more rather than less racial integration, even if that means more race-conscious, less color-blind decision-making. Black equality is most enhanced through racial integration, as the mainstream is where the best of everything is—the best schools, jobs, and so on. The difference between reformists and traditionalists, in short, lies in the relative emphasis given to the racial-omission and racial-integration norms. For traditionalists, the racial-omission norm trumps the racial-integration norm. For reformists, the racial-integration norm trumps the racial-omission norm.[18]

Rivaled only by Justice Ginsburg, whose opinion in a Title VII case will be discussed in due course, Justice Sotomayor begins one of her dissenting opinions by borrowing from the title of reformist Cornel West's book *Race Matters*. It is for that reason that she, like all reformists, believe in race-conscious affirmative action. Racial preferences are the strongest implementation of the racial integration norm. Justice Sotomayor's defense of affirmative action is just as passionate as Justice Thomas's renunciation of it, discussed a moment ago. She writes in her memoir:

> I had no need to apologize that the look-wider, search-more affirmative action that Princeton and Yale practiced had opened doors for me. That was its purpose: to create the conditions whereby students from disadvantaged backgrounds could be brought to the starting line of a race many were unaware was even being run. I had been admitted to the Ivy League through a special door, and I had more ground than most to make up before I was competing with my classmates on an equal footing. But I worked relentlessly to reach that point, and distinctions such as the Pyne Prize, Phi Beta Kappa, summa cum laude, and a spot on *The Yale Law Journal* were not given out like so many pats on the back to encourage mediocre students. These were achievements as real as those of anyone around me.[19]

Reformists see affirmative action as the gateway to integrating American institutions, which in turn is the best strategy for racial advancement.

LIMITED SEPARATION

Limited separatists have a clear post–civil rights orientation, a clear understanding of what matters most in the quest for black equality in today's society—racial identity or solidarity. Racial self-sufficiency is the sine qua non of racial advancement for African Americans. Yet blacks, limited separatists believe, suffer from a dearth of racial unity, a paucity of racial pride. Blacks are too preoccupied with gaining acceptance from whites or making their fame and fortune in white institutions. Hence, there is not enough black pride, black heritage, black solidarity, self-reliance.[20]

Given this posture, one can safely surmise that limited separatists have an unfavorable opinion of formal equal opportunity. Both the racial-omission and racial-integration norms are conceptually incompatible with limited separatists' core message of racial solidarity, a message that is both race conscious and out of sync with racial integration. Thus, unlike traditionalists and reformists, limited separatists reject formal equal opportunity at the conceptual level. Formal equal opportunity, in the view of limited separatists, is at best an inchoate norm and at worst a dangerous norm in the context of today's post–civil rights society.

Even during the civil rights era, many African Americans viewed the racial-omission and racial-integration norms with suspicion. While African Americans in general initially greeted the Supreme Court's decision in *Brown* with exuberance, a fair amount of apprehension set in among many blacks, especially in the South, upon sober reflection. The fear was that formal equal opportunity might mean the closure of black institutions or the end to public funding of such institutions. The NAACP lawyers who argued *Brown* were aware of these concerns—for example, Judge Robert Carter and Judge Constance Baker Motely mention these concerns in their memoirs—but dismissed them as unfounded. These fears have, by and large, proven to be true.[21]

Indeed, the Supreme Court simply does not place much value in maintaining or creating black institutions. For most of the post–civil rights period, it has waged a sustained war against publicly funded black institutions on the ground that they make a mockery of *Brown*.

For example, the Court placed Historically Black Colleges and Universities (HBCUs), which are quintessentially black institutions, under a constitutional duty to dismantle their racial identity in deference to the racial-omission norm. In *United States v. Fordice,* the Supreme Court held that current policies traceable to de jure segregation that have a discriminatory effect "must be reformed to the extent practicable and consistent with sound educational practices."[22] Understanding the threat that this standard—"racial identifiability" attributable to de jure segregation—poses to the existence of HBCUs, Justice Clarence Thomas, the lone black justice on the Court who, if nothing else, is proudly black, attempted to spin the majority's opinion in such a way as to save HBCUs. The Court, he opined in a concurring opinion, "do[es] not foreclose the possibility that there exists 'sound educational justification' for maintaining historically black colleges as such."[23] And, in another case, he wrote, "*It never ceases to amaze me that the courts are so willing to assume that anything that is predominantly black must be inferior*" (emphasis added).[24] Although a core traditionalist, Justice Thomas has a clear understanding of and appreciation for the limited separatist norm of racial pride.

Despite Justice Thomas's attempt to spin the holding in *Fordice,* HBCUs remain under attack. Indeed, on remand in *Fordice,* the lower court mandated color-blind admission standards at HBCUs in the state of Mississippi. This ruling was made over the vehement objection of blacks who argued that the new standards would cut black enrollment in half at Mississippi's three HBCUs. The Supreme Court denied an appeal in the case and, hence, refused to block the lower court's ruling.[25]

To illustrate the inadequacy of the racial-omission norm, limited separatists often point to Justice Harlan's famous defense of the norm in his dissenting opinion in *Plessy v. Ferguson.* As he set about defending the ideal of a color-blind Constitution, Justice Harlan assured the nation that America's racial hierarchy would *not* change. The very same paragraph in which he embraced the color-blind Constitution opens with Justice Harlan avowing, "The white race deems itself to be the dominant race in this country. And so it is, in prestige, in achievements, in education, in wealth and in power. So, I doubt not, it will continue to be for *all time,* if it remains true to its great heritage and holds fast to the

principles of constitutional liberty" (emphasis added).[26] Limited separatists ask, rhetorically, how could anyone who truly believes in racial
progress embrace the racial omission norm to the exclusion of all else?

CRITICAL RACE THEORY

Critical race theory's central post–civil rights message is that white hegemony matters most in the struggle for racial advancement. The antidote for white privilege is social transformation. Not unlike the racial
identity norm, the social transformation norm amounts to a condemnation of formal equal opportunity. From the perspective of critical race
theory, formal equal opportunity is conceptually unsound, dead on ar-
rival, so never mind about its application. Unlike limited separatists,
however, critical race theorists do not believe formal equal opportunity's defects can be cured through artful repositioning of the racial-
omission and racial-integration norms with other norms. That is the
rhetoric, but the reality is a bit different.

Critical race theory's core message of white hegemony, planted in
the writings of the late Harvard law professor Derrick Bell, comes from
an analytical framework that goes to the very structure of our society. As
Richard Delgado and Jean Stefancic, two pioneering critical race theorists, assert, "critical race theory questions the very foundations of the
liberal order, including equality theory, legal reasoning, Enlightenment
rationalism, and neutral principles of constitutional law."[27] Critical race
theorists believe that appearances can be deceiving, reminiscent of *The
Wizard of Oz*, and, hence, seek to "understand what is going on behind
the curtain."[28] Looking behind the curtain, critical race theorists see a
post–civil rights social order that is racially corrupt, and has been from
the very beginning. Look around, and what does one see?—whites on
top, people of color on the bottom. Everything important in our society
slants in favor of insiders who are overwhelmingly straight white males.
This racialized social order means that our society is "racist." Our society is not organically neutral or objective when it comes to matters of
race. Instead, it is "non-neutral" or "anti-objective," all of which is socially constructive. When people think color-blind, they do not see
monochrome; they see white.[29]

Some whites, known as "critical white theorists," acknowledge the privilege they have in the social order: "[W]hen . . . I apply for a job or hunt for an apartment, I don't look threatening. Almost all of the people evaluating me for those things look like me—they are white. They see in me a reflection of themselves, and in a racist world that is an advantage. I smile. I am white. I am one of them. I am not dangerous. Even when I voice critical opinions, I am cut some slack. After all, I'm white."[30] Critical race theorists can be understood to pose the rhetorical question Whose values does the law tend to vindicate?

Because it is part of a racially corrupt society, formal equal opportunity is necessarily "racist," critical race theorists insist. More than just a cog or mantelpiece, formal equal opportunity is an integral part of the social order, as it protects and perpetuates it. That, indeed, is the purpose of law, that is, to maintain the existing social order. Consequently, the racial-omission and racial-integration norms do nothing to unstack the deck—to disassemble the constructed racial hierarchy that inheres in our society—but does everything to legitimize it. "Formal equal opportunity," Delgado writes, "is calculated to remedy at most the more extreme and shocking forms of racial treatment; it can do little about the business-as-usual types of [racialized conditions] that people of color confront every day and that account for much of our subordination, poverty, and despair."[31] The criticalist critique of formal equal opportunity, then, is part of a more general critique of our socio-legal order.[32]

Precisely how does formal equal opportunity do its job? How does it protect and perpetuate the socio-legal order? It does so, critical race theorists contend, primarily by privileging the perspective of the people on top: straight white males, the "insiders." Created by insiders, formal equal opportunity, and, hence, the Supreme Court's implementation of the norm, is largely informed by the insider's perspective rather than by the victim's perspective. The insider's ultimate aim is to remain on the inside, to stay in power. This goal is camouflaged by the use of lofty legal language like "justice," "equal protection," and "due process" in legal reasoning. Such language endows the socio-legal order with noble rhetoric, which in turn is used to mollify outsiders. Opium for the masses.

In reality, though, critical race theorists are integrationists. They want in, but on better terms than reformists have. They want to change the fundamental relationship between race and power in our society, starting with and through the judiciary. Critical race theorists are not reformists, but they are at bottom integrationists. This read of critical race theory comes through clearly when one applies the social-transformation norm to a few cases.

Juridical Subordination in the Supreme Court

Criticism of the Supreme Court's record on civil rights did not end with the Court's decision in *Brown*. In the 1960s, NAACP lawyers, including Robert Carter, the chief legal strategists behind the *Brown* victory and later a federal judge, criticized the Warren Court for having "struck down the symbols of racism while condoning or overlooking the in-grained practices that had meant the survival of white supremacy."[33] Derrick Bell took that criticism into the world of academia and developed critical race theory.[34] (The connection between Bell and Carter, or critical race theory and the NAACP, is little known. Bell, who was a close friend of Carter's, worked as a lawyer with the NAACP Legal Defense Fund, handling and supervising dozens of school desegregation cases, before embarking upon a fifteen-year career as a professor at Harvard Law School, where he became known as the "father of critical race theory." This theory is a major force in legal education today, having given birth to other "oppositional legal theories," such as critical feminist theory, critical race feminism, critical Asian theory, LatCrit theory, and queer crit theory.) More recently, Ari Berman demonstrates in *Give Us the Ballot: The Modern Struggle for Voting Rights in America* how the Supreme Court's voting rights decisions have persistently placed limitations and restrictions on voting rights enacted by a bipartisan Congress every time the Voting Rights Act of 1965 was renewed during the entire post–civil rights period, from 1969 to 2006. As another scholar, Jeffrey Rosen, writes, this "historical trend is clear." Simply put, the Supreme Court has not been a faithful friend of civil rights during the post–Jim Crow period. Appendix B provides the gory details.[35]

While the Court's civil rights record is a historical fact, the motivation behind that record is highly contested. Some civil rights scholars, such as the NAACP lawyers and critical race theorists, argue or have argued that the justices who rule against black claims are racists. Others, such as Berman, argue that these justices are political or "counterrevolutionaries" seeking to overturn the civil rights gains of the 1960s. I wish to offer a different hypothesis: these justices are neither anti-black, counterrevolutionaries, nor anti–civil rights. They are, instead, *pro–civil rights*. Some justices, traditionalists, believe that racial omission is the best strategy for blacks to achieve racial equality, that race consciousness undercuts the black claim for racial equality. Other justices, reformists, believe that racial integration is the best civil rights strategy. Importantly, it makes a difference which hypothesis is correct. A racist or politically motivated decision certainly lacks judicial and moral legitimacy. A traditionalist or reformist decision, in contrast, rests on defensible ground and, hence, invites a different kind of conversation, one that engages out-of-the-box normative stances that include matters of racial identity, social transformation, and, in the end, the spirit of *Brown*.

In the remainder of this chapter, I demonstrate a process of analysis that a pro–civil rights Supreme Court can use to avoid juridical subordination. The Court simply engages applicable post–civil rights norms and determines which norm or amalgamation of norms is within the spirit of *Brown*—maximizes racial progress unless there is an exceedingly important societal reason not to do so. Technical legal arguments are, of course, important; but they are used ex post facto to justify the Court's basic orientation regarding the best strategy for achieving racial equality. Supreme Court decisions in "hard cases"— cases that present polycentric issues—are rarely, if ever, deduced syllogistically from extant legal doctrine. "The life of the law," Justice Oliver Wendell Holmes wrote more than a few times, "has not been logic but experience." Perhaps more than in any other area of Anglo-American law (although intellectual-property lawyers claim ownership of this claim), civil rights law is less a body of rules than a justice's state of mind. Frustrated with this practice, in which he himself had engaged in other cases, Chief Justice Roberts protested in a hard civil rights case, "The majority's decision is an act of will, not legal judgment. The right it announces has no basis in the Constitution or this Court's precedent."[36] Such is the life of the law.

ANTIDISCRIMINATION LAW

I begin with a case in which all four post–civil rights norms are in agreement—a rarity—and that manifests no juridical subordination. To reach that result, the Supreme Court in *Robinson v. Shell Oil Co.* gave what legal scholars call a "veneer of reasoned inevitability to a tortuous logical path," thus once again proving Holmes's point. But it did so in the interest of racial advancement. In my book, that constitutes good social policy.[37]

Robinson was a case filed under Title VII of the Civil Rights Act of 1964, which prohibits employers from discriminating on the basis of such factors as race, color, or gender. A former employee who was discharged by the defendant employer filed a complaint with the Equal Employment Opportunity Commission (EEOC) alleging that his discharge was based on race. When the plaintiff applied for another job and received a negative job reference from his former employer, he claimed that his former employer was retaliating against him for filing the discrimination complaint with the EEOC. The issue before the federal courts was whether the alleged retaliation was actionable under Title VII. To give some context to the Supreme Court's unanimous decision, it is useful to begin with the lower court's opinion.

The United States Court of Appeals for the Fourth Circuit, with all the judges hearing the case, was divided on the issue. Seven judges denied the plaintiff relief; four dissented. Relying on a plain reading of Title VII, the majority reasoned that the statute unambiguously failed to protect the plaintiff because, at the time of the alleged retaliation, the plaintiff was not a current employee but rather was a former employee of the defendant. Title VII protects the "employee," defined in section 701(f) of the statute as "an individual employed by an employer." The majority reasoned that it was "simply prohibited from reading into the clear language of the definition of 'employee' that which Congress did not include." The court recognized that most of the courts of appeals had gone the other way on the ground that giving the statute a literal interpretation, as it had done, would produce results that undermined the underlying purposes of Title VII. But the Fourth Circuit majority believed, not unlike Chief Justice Roberts above, that such a reading of the statute lacked legal logic; it constituted an abandonment of "the established analytical framework for statutory construction" in deference to "broad considerations of policy." Interestingly, the majority stated that "these decisions fail to heed the Supreme Court's repeated mandate" to follow ordinary statutory textual meaning. The majority cited a Supreme Court opinion written by Justice Thomas, which itself was based on Justice Scalia's oft-stated belief that courts should follow "ordinary meaning" regardless of the consequences. The majority concluded that "although extending Title VII to cover former employees is tantalizing fruit, our judicial inquiry must cease when the language of a statute is plain and unambiguous. Such is the rule of law."[38]

On appeal, the Supreme Court, in an opinion written by Justice Thomas, no less, reversed unanimously. The Court held that the term "employee" or "employees" as used in Title VII included former employees. Justice Thomas reasoned that the word "employee" was used ambiguously in Title VII. On the one hand, it could mean former employees as well as current ones. After all, the definition of an employee is someone "employed by an employer," and that could mean someone who "is employed" or someone who "was employed," Justice Thomas wrote. Thus, absent a verb derived from the infinitive "to be" preceding the verb "employed," Title VII is ambiguous. In addition, Justice Thomas continued, some provisions of Title VII seem to suggest that the term refers to former employees, while others do not. Taking into account this broader statutory context along with the primary purpose of Title VII's antiretaliation provision—"maintaining unfettered access to statutory remedial mechanisms"—justified interpreting Title VII in such a way as to protect former employees as well as current employees from employment discrimination. Criticizing the Supreme Court's legal reasoning, one legal scholar has observed that "even if the majority of the Fourth Circuit was wrong to conclude that the definition of 'employee' was completely unambiguous, were they not right that the definition had an ordinary meaning excluding former employees? Justice Thomas worked hard to create enough doubt on the question of ambiguity to allow him to peek outside the provision at broader considerations. . . . *Robinson* suggests that, like beauty, ambiguity is in the eye of the beholder. In *Robinson* ambiguity becomes a magically liberating factor, a beautiful thing for judges–even if, or one might say, especially if, it is selectively employed."³⁹

Looking at *Robinson* from the post–civil rights norms, the outcome was never in doubt. Traditionalists (for example, Justices Thomas and Scalia) could support an expansive reading of the statute because such a nontextual reading promoted the racial-omission tenet. Employers could not take race into account even when dealing with former employees. Otherwise, employers could do an end run around the statute's general vindication of the racial-omission norm. For traditionalists, the integrity of the racial-omission tenet was very much at stake. Reformists (for example, Justices Ginsburg and Stevens) could support the Court's holding on the ground that it sustains racial integration. It does so by precluding employers from retaliating against former black employees who seek to integrate other predominantly white employment markets. While neutral regarding the racial-integration norm, as long as it does not undercut racial identity or solidarity, limited separatists have no taste for invidious discrimination. A nondiscrimination principle is, in fact, part of their normative stance. They would, accordingly, support the Court's holding. Finally, critical race theorists are integrationists, but, unlike reformists, they would want the Court's opinion to hit hard on the social-transformation norm. Giving Title VII protection to former employees strikes a judicial blow against a system of white privilege. None of these applied norms impedes racial progress. Each, in fact, furthers racial advancement by opening employment opportunities for African Americans without unnecessarily minimizing the employment interests of whites or other groups. The Court's opinion is squarely within the spirit of *Brown*. Not so the next case.⁴⁰

Another important Title VII case, *Ricci v. DeStefano,* involved an allegation that the city of New Haven, Connecticut, engaged in intentional racial discrimination when it decided to discard the results of written and oral examinations given to its firefighters. Although facially neutral, the examination results had a disparate impact on black firefighters. At the urging of the union, test scores were weighted 60 percent for the written scores and 40 percent for the oral scores. No practical, on-the-job examinations were given. The test results would determine not only which firefighters would be considered for promotions to the ranks of lieutenant and captain, but also in what order over a two-year period. When the results came back, it was discovered that the pass rate for blacks (and Hispanics) on both exams was about one-half the pass rate of whites. As a result, all ten persons promoted to the lieutenant position were white, and of the nine persons promoted to the rank of captain, seven were white and two were Hispanic. None were black. This established a prima facie case of disparate-impact discrimination under Title VII of the 1964 Civil Rights Act. Disparate impact refers to practices or policies that are not conscious of race but have a racial impact that (unlike racial subordination) was unknown to the defendant at the time the practice or policy was initiated. Indeed, had the city known that its tests would have had a disparate impact on blacks, it probably would not have given them.[41]

In an after-the-fact attempt to redress what even the Supreme Court admitted were "significant" racial disparities, the New Haven Civil Service Board (CSB) threw out the test results. This meant that everyone would have to retake the examinations. Most of the successful candidates (seven white and one Hispanic firefighter) filed a lawsuit claiming that the decision to throw out the test results constituted intentional race-based discrimination, given the fact that the successful candidates were mainly white and the unsuccessful candidates were mainly black. The city, in defense, argued that the sole reason it discarded the test results was to avoid disparate-impact liability under Title VII. The issue, as framed by the Court, in a 5–4 decision written by Justice Kennedy (in which Justices Roberts, Scalia, Thomas, and Alito joined), was "whether the purpose to avoid disparate-impact liability excuses what otherwise would be prohibited disparate-treatment discrimination."[42] The answer according to the Court: it depends.

The city can discard test results without violating Title VII's prohibition against discrimination on racial grounds (disparate treatment), the Court held, only if it can demonstrate by "a strong basis in evidence" that using the disparate exam results would cause it to lose a disparate-impact lawsuit brought, in this instance, by the black test takers. In other words, once the exam has been administered, the employer may discard the exam results on racial grounds only if it can show by "a strong basis in evidence" that had it not taken the action, it would have been

found liable by a court of law either on the basis that the disparate impact could not be justified as a necessity for doing business or on the
basis that the employer failed to pursue an equally valid but less discriminatory alternative test. The Court held that the city could not satisfy any of these conditions, that there was no evidence, let alone strong
evidence, of either a problem with the validity of the tests or of the avail-
ability of better testing alternatives.[43]

The traditionalist norm of racial omission is well represented in
the Court's opinion. Discarding the test results, as the city did, was a
race-conscious act and certainly the wrong way to pursue the black
equality interest in equal employment opportunity. Why? Race-
conscious action that seeks to benefit blacks is counterproductive. It
places African Americans in a negative light in that it portrays them as
losers, hapless victims in need of special governmental solicitude. As
Justice Clarence Thomas has offered, "Inevitably, such programs engen-
der attitudes of superiority or, alternatively, provoke resentment among
those who believe that they have been wronged by the government's use
of race."[44] The traditionalist norm is also behind the Court's subordination of disparate-impact discrimination (the effects test) to disparate-
treatment discrimination (the intent test). Traditionalists regard the
intent test to be less of a fishing expedition for racist motives than the
effects test. Playing down the effects test reinforces the core traditionalist belief that race no longer matters in post–civil rights society.[45]

Reformists would take issue with the Court's opinion for one specific reason: the Court's holding impedes the city's attempt to integrate the
command positions in its fire department. By not discarding the test results, qualified black firefighters are denied the opportunity to move up
and, thereby, integrate the command structure of the New Haven Fire Department for at least a two-year period. Without more racial integration,
the city's fire department will continue to look too much like it did during
"the days of undisguised discrimination."[46] This is the sum and substance
of the dissenting opinion written by Justice Ginsburg, a reformist.[47]

Clearly, then, requiring the city to retain the test results suppresses
racial integration. Allowing the city to discard them promotes it. The
Court opts for the former in deference to the racial-omission tenet.
There is a third option favored by limited separatists.

For limited separatists, the Court's opinion is defective because it misses an important opportunity to promote black self-sufficiency. There is nothing in the Court's holding or reasoning that supports black solidarity. Instead, the Court is trapped within the racial-omission / racial-integration vortex. Limited separatists reject the majority's obsession with the racial-omission norm and the dissent's obsession with the racial-integration norm, as if they were the only known or valid strategies for racial advancement. For limited separatists, both the majority and dissenting justices present flawed normative approaches to black equality. They both delegitimize black self-help. Neither approach allows the city to set up black fire stations in New Haven's black communities that would allow blacks to serve their own needs not currently met by the city. Black fire stations are race conscious and nonintegrationist. Yet, they are legitimate under a three-prong test that limited separatists use to test the legality of all racial classifications.

The test's three conditions are straightforward. First, the fire station must serve a "good end," meaning it must serve a racially compensatory or remedial purpose. Second, nonblacks must be allowed to apply for jobs at the fire station unless, third, the selection of one or more additional nonblacks would cause the fire station to lose its identity as a black fire station. Under that condition, race would be a bone fide selection qualification, or "BFSQ."

As to the good-end prong, New Haven's black community can certainly demonstrate a need for having their own fire stations. New Haven's white-dominated fire department has provided few opportunities for blacks over the years and, in a city that is about 60 percent minority, continues to deny opportunities today, especially at the supervisory ranks:

> Firefighting is a profession in which the legacy of racial discrimination casts an especially long shadow. In extending Title VII to state and local government employers in 1972, Congress took note of a U.S. Commission on Civil Rights (USCCR) report finding racial discrimination in municipal employment even "more pervasive than in the private sector." H. R. Rep. No. 92–238, p. 17 (1971). According to the

report, overt racism was partly to blame, but so too was a failure on the part of municipal employers to apply merit-based employment principles. In making hiring and promotion decisions, public employers often "rel[ied] on criteria unrelated to job performance," including nepotism or political patronage. 118 Cong. Rec. 1817 (1972). Such flawed selection methods served to entrench preexisting racial hierarchies. The USCCR report singled out police and fire departments for having "[b]arriers to equal employment . . . greater . . . than in any other area of State or local government," with African-Americans "hold[ing] almost no positions in the officer ranks." Ibid. See also National Commission on Fire Prevention and Control, America Burning 5 (1973). ("Racial minorities are under-represented in the fire departments in nearly every community in which they live.")

The city of New Haven (City) was no exception. In the early 1970's, African-Americans and Hispanics composed 30 percent of New Haven's population, but only 3.5 percent of the City's 502 firefighters. The racial disparity in the officer ranks was even more pronounced: "[O]f the 107 officers in the Department only one was black, and he held the lowest rank above private." *Firebird Soc. of New Haven, Inc. v. New Haven Bd. of Fire Comm'rs . . .* (Conn. 1975).

Following a lawsuit and settlement agreement, see ibid., the City initiated efforts to increase minority representation in the New Haven Fire Department (Department). Those litigation-induced efforts produced some positive change. New Haven's population includes a greater proportion of minorities today than it did in the 1970's: Nearly 40 percent of the City's residents are African-American and more than 20 percent are Hispanic. Among entry-level firefighters, minorities are still underrepresented, but not starkly so. As of 2003, African-Americans and Hispanics constituted 30 percent and 16 percent of the City's firefighters, respectively. In supervisory positions, however, significant disparities remain. Overall, the senior officer ranks (captain and higher) are nine percent African-American and nine percent Hispanic. Only one of the Department's 21 fire captains is African-American. ... It is against this backdrop of entrenched inequality that the promotion process at issue in this litigation should be assessed.[48]

New Haven's black community can also establish the second prong of the test, as the black fire station will certainly hire white and other nonblack firefighters. Limited separation does not permit black fire stations or other black institutions to bar whites or other nonblacks. Indeed, limited separatists welcome nonblacks to black institutions, not unlike historically black colleges and universities (HBCU) and most black churches, provided that there is no attempt to change the institution's mission, which is to serve the special needs of the black community. In the case of black fire stations, the mission is not only to put out fires but also to teach fire safety in a way that makes sense to the black community, to act as a community center (for example, hold Saturday-morning pancake breakfasts), and to provide positive role models, most especially for young African American males. Nonblacks cannot come to black institutions with the intent of changing the institution's mission.

The only time a nonblack could legally be denied employment at a black fire station is if his or her selection would constitute a BFSQ. This is the third condition under limit separations' legal regime. If the hiring of another nonblack would tip the fire station's racial balance from black to white, for example, no more nonblack applicants need be hired until the matter is corrected. Such a hiring freeze could only happen if there were too many nonblacks already working at the fire station, an unlikely situation.

The limited separatists' norm—black self-sufficiency—can be promoted in this case whether or not the test results are discarded. The Court's decision can stand or not stand while at the same time permitting the city to set up fire stations in black communities without fear of a constitutional challenge from traditionalists or reformists. Those who want to work in white fire stations can apply for jobs and promotions under the intent/effects test. Those who wish to work in black fire stations can apply under the three-prong-test regime. This gives blacks as well as whites options.

Critical race theorists would not like the *Ricci* Court's decision to keep the test results. The Court's decision merely perpetuates white hegemony, elevating the concerns of the white firefighters over that of the black firefighters and the black community as a whole. "The racial adverse impact here was significant." Those are the Court's own words. The racial disparities were "stark." That was the dissent's word. The outrageous disparity between white and black promotions was one of the few points on which all the justices, majority and dissenting, could agree.

Privileging the outsider's perspective, a critical race theorist is able to show most vividly how white hegemony is manifested in the Court's decision to uphold the test results. The dispositive question here is What does the decision to uphold the test results mean in New Haven's black community, the relevant outsiders? The testimony given by black city leaders during the five public hearings before the CSB leave no doubt about how blacks would view the Court's decision if they were asked. They would see it as a racial slap-down that traces back to slavery and Jim Crow. Remembering the days of Jim Crow, the black community would see an uncanny resemblance between the promotional examinations and the various voting tests, especially the literacy tests, discussed in the last chapter, used to reduce the number of eligible black voters. If we as a nation are serious about calling ourselves a racial democracy, critical race theorists would insist, then we simply cannot countenance these Jim Crow conditions.[49]

Continuing to privilege the outsider's perspective in this case, critical race theorists would see other examples of white hegemony in *Ricci*. By not acknowledging the efforts of the black firefighters in preparing for the examinations, while at the same time applauding Ricci's test preparation efforts, the Court not only stereotypes the black candidates as dumb or lazy or both but it also privileges the white candidates' perspective. The Court noted that "Ricci stated that he had 'several learning disabilities,' including dyslexia; that he had spent more than $1,000 to purchase the materials and pay his neighbor to read them on tape so he could 'give it [his] best shot'; and that he had studied '8 to 13 hours a day to prepare' for the test."[50] The Court, in turn, said nothing about the absence of equal access to the study materials or about how the black firefighters had no family connections with the fire department's testing practices on which to draw. One can doubt whether Justice Kennedy meant his tribute to Ricci's test-preparation efforts to be taken in these ways, but it is the outsider's perspective that defines the normative stance taken in critical race theory.

Critical race theorists would push for social transformation. They would want the Supreme Court to weaken the white power structure in the city's fire department by first and foremost jettisoning the exam. Conventional tests and other standards of merit, such as the one at issue in this case, are created in the image of insiders and merely perpetuate white hegemony. In place of the exam, critical race theorist would institute a quota system for promoting firefighters to the fire department's command structure. A strong affirmative-action program is the most efficient way to transform the power structure in the New Haven Fire Department.

Which perspective reflects the spirit of *Brown* the most? In my view, it is the reformist perspective. Discarding the racially discriminatory tests would promote *reasonable* racial advancement—racial advancement without unnecessarily trammeling the equality interests of whites—by opening employment opportunities for blacks through racial integration without a hard quota system. This in turn would help to change the command structure of the New Haven Fire Department and, as such, represent good social policy. So too would the creation of black fire stations in black communities. Not unlike the black church and HBCUs, racially identified fire stations would meet the legitimate needs of African Americans, including role models for black children, leadership training, places to organize for the purpose of planning effective solutions to community problems, and, to boot, men and women who could put out fires.[51]

RACIAL-PREFERENCE LAW

Abigail Fisher, a Texas resident, applied for admission to the 2008 freshman class at the University of Texas, Austin (UT), the state's highly selective flagship university and the premier university in the state, in its

Business Administration and Liberal Arts Schools. UT's admissions process was sui generis. It employed two tracks, one race neutral and the other holistic with race used as one of several subfactors. The former, called the Top Ten Percent Plan, automatically accepted individuals who graduated within the top 10 percent of their class in a state high school. This admissions plan was designed by the Texas legislature to comply with a federal appellate court ruling in *Hopwood v. Texas* (1996). There, the court absolutely barred the voluntary use of race in college admissions (specifically holding that diversity was not a constitutionally sufficient reason to establish a race-conscious affirmative-action plan). Though facially neutral, the Top Ten Percent Plan was not entirely blind to color or race, because it was responsive to the state's de facto segregated neighborhoods and schools. In any event, *Hopwood* was effectively overturned by the Supreme Court's 2003 holding in *Grutter v. Bollinger,* wherein the Court recognized student-body diversity as a compelling state interest and upheld an affirmative-action admissions program that used race as one of several factors in the admissions decision. UT's second admissions track was patterned after *Grutter*. The applicant's "Academic Index" (AI, which consists of the SAT score and high school academic record) is combined with his or her "Personal Achievement Index" (PAI). The latter is a holistic review containing numerous factors. In addition to the applicant's race, the PAI considers the applicant's leadership experience, extracurricular activities, awards/honors, community service, family responsibilities, socioeconomic status of the applicant's family or school, the language spoken at the applicant's home, and the extent to which the applicant lives in a single-parent home. Because the petitioner did not graduate in the top 10 percent of her high school class, she was eligible for admission only under the second track. Based on her grade-point average (3.59) and SAT score (1180 out of 1600), petitioner's AI score was 3.1 (out of 4.1). No holistic applicant for the fall 2008 Business Administration or Liberal Arts School freshman class was admitted unless his or her AI score exceeded 3.5. Thus, even if the petitioner had earned a perfect PAI score of 6, she would not have been admitted to the fall 2008 freshman class. The petitioner was denied admissions to UT. With the assistance of a conservative organization, the petitioner sued UT, alleging that the holistic plan, on its face, violated her equal protection rights under the Fourteenth Amendment.[52]

The Supreme Court decided the case twice. *Fisher I* (2013) was the first time. In that case, the Court ruled 7–1 against the constitutionality of UT's race-conscious admissions plan on the ground that the lower court, which had upheld the plan, was too deferential to UT in applying the constitutional means test, that is, in determining whether the affirmative-action plan was the most narrowly tailored means of achieving UT's diversity goals. Justice Ginsburg dissented and Justice Kagan recused herself. The case was sent back to the lower court. When it returned to the Court three years later, the justices upheld the affirmative-action plan 4–3. The Court agreed with the lower court that the plan satisfied strict scrutiny's means test. The majority opinion in this case, *Fisher II* (2016), was written by Justice Kennedy, who had concurred in *Fisher I*. What changed between *Fisher I* and *Fisher II*? The death of Justice Scalia, the most powerful traditionalist on the Court, was certainly an important factor in the Court's ruling, but it would not have changed the constitutionality of UT's holistic program. Joining the three dissenting justices (Chief Justice Roberts and Justices Thomas and Alito) to overturn the program, Justice Scalia's vote in *Fisher II* would have made the decision 4–4 (Justices Kennedy, Ginsburg, Breyer, and Sotomayor voting in favor of the plan, with Justice Kagan, again, recusing herself). Legally, this would make the court of appeal's decision the law of the case. The court of appeals ruled in favor of UT's plan, just as it had in *Fisher I*. Taken together, *Fisher I* and *Fisher II* illustrate rather dramatically how the justices deploy the post–civil rights norms. My discussion shall therefore combine both cases.

The Court's ruling in *Fisher II* is based on the interplay between UT's unique two-track admissions process. Seventy-five percent of the incoming freshman class was admitted through the Top Ten Percent Plan each year. The plan increased both the number and percentage of enrolled black and Hispanic students, from 2.7 percent and 3.0 percent, respectively, in 1997 (the first year of the program), to 4.5 percent and 16.9 percent, respectively, in 2004. Based on many months of study and supported by significant statistical and anecdotal evidence, UT determined that its race-neutral track was not achieving its diversity goals.

These goals, the Court found in *Fisher II*, mirrored the compelling interest in college diversity announced in *Grutter*, and were concretely and precisely articulated in a thirty-nine-page report. They included ending racial stereotypes, promoting "cross-racial understanding," preparing students for "an increasingly diverse workforce and society," and cultivating leaders with "legitimacy in the eyes of the citizenry." The report indicated that these goals could only be achieved by implementing a race-conscious admissions plan that could create a "critical mass" of minority students. A critical mass was needed because minority enrollment had stagnated under the Top Ten Percent Plan. For example, "only 21 percent of undergraduate classes with five or more students in them had more than one African-American student enrolled. Twelve percent of these classes had no Hispanic students, as compared to 10 percent in 1996." The dearth of diversity left many minority students feeling lonely and isolated. In addition, most of the minority students admitted under the *Hopwood* admissions plan came from lower-performing, minority schools. Though in the top 10 percent of their high school classes, these students tended to possess academic abilities, perspectives, and life goals quite different from minority students who graduated in, say, the top quarter of high-performing, predominantly white schools. Hence, UT wasn't getting a variety of perspectives among African Americans or Hispanic students. In agreeing with UT officials that "race-neutral policies and programs did not meet [UT's] goals," the Court in *Fisher II* characterized the Top Ten Percent Plan as a "blunt instrument" that may actually have been harmful to the university's diversity goals."[53]

Was the holistic plan the answer to UT's diversity problem? As to the effectiveness of the plan, the Supreme Court observed, "In 2003, 11 percent of the Texas residents enrolled through holistic review were Hispanic and 3.5 percent were African-American. In 2007, by contrast, 16.9 percent of the Texas holistic-review freshmen were Hispanic and 6.8 percent were African-American. Those increases—of 54 percent and 94 percent, respectively—show that consideration of race has had a meaningful, if still limited, effect on the diversity of the University's freshman class. In any event, it is not a failure of narrow tailoring for the impact of racial consideration to be minor. The fact that race consciousness played a role in only a small portion of admissions decisions should be a hallmark of narrow tailoring, not evidence of unconstitutionality."[54]

Fisher I and *Fisher II* are driven by post–civil rights norms. Dissenting in *Fisher II*, Justice Thomas succinctly states the traditionalist's position, which he also asserted in *Fisher I*: "I write separately to reaffirm that 'a State's use of race in higher education admissions decisions is categorically prohibited by the Equal Protection Clause. . . . The Constitution abhors classifications based on race because every time the government places citizens on racial registers and makes race relevant to the provision of burdens or benefits, it demeans us all.' "[55] Similarly, Chief Justice Roberts most emphatically expresses the traditionalists' norm when he asserts, "The way to stop discrimination on the basis of race is to stop discriminating on the basis of race."[56] Racial preferences are a form of reverse racial discrimination in the traditionalist way of thinking. They should not pass strict scrutiny, because the Equal Protection Clause "makes no exception for permitting governmental classifications of Americans based on race."[57] Race-based diversity can never be a compelling state interest. Demonstrating that traditionalists can be judicial activists, Justice Thomas would "overrule Grutter."[58]

Justice Alito makes clear in his very long dissenting opinion in *Fisher II*, in which both Chief Justice Roberts and Justice Thomas join, that the racial-omission norm offers the strongest statement of the black equality interest as it stands African Americans toe-to-toe with whites. Racial preferences, in contrast, give negative content to the black equality interest. Indeed, Justice Alito criticizes the majority for buying into the assumption that "the Top Ten Percent Plan admits *the wrong kind* of African-American and Hispanic students" (emphasis in original), "that the Top Ten Percent admittees are somehow more homogenous, less dynamic, and more undesirably stereotypical than those admitted under holistic review."[59] Thus, "instead of treating individuals as individuals, which the Equal Protection Clause requires, racial classifications demean, dehumanize, and stereotype individuals into meaningless skin-color-only groups."[60]

Reformists maintain that the best judicial expression of its central post–civil rights message—race still matters—occurs when the Court gives primacy to formal equal opportunity's racial-integration norm. Bringing blacks into mainstream institutions, wherein power and money reside, is the best way to concretize the black equality interest. As affirmative action has proven to be the most effective means of promoting racial integration, the Court ought to give maximum support to this measure.[61]

The reformist position very much animates the majority's opinion in *Fisher II*. Justice Kennedy, unlike the dissent, sees great value in UT's integrationist efforts. They mirror the efforts sanctioned in *Grutter*. Racial preferences, call it "reverse discrimination" if you like, was needed to counteract racial stereotypes and promote "cross-racial understanding" with the ultimate goal of preparing students for "an increasingly diverse workforce and society" and cultivating leaders with "legitimacy in the eyes of the citizenry." For reformists, racial integration *must* trump racial omission.

Though *Fisher II* is a reformist opinion, the Court does not go as far as reformism allows in service of racial integration. The Court could have articulated new compelling governmental interests beyond diversity or an institution's desire to remedy its past discrimination, and it could have extended these rationales beyond the educational context, even though these rulings would have only been *obiter dictum* (said in passing, not binding in the case). One compelling governmental interest the Court could have sanctioned is an institution's desire to prevent or remedy de facto resegregation. Race-based affirmative action satisfies the strict scrutiny test "where the program's abolishment would threaten a return to the *de facto* segregation that the plans originally sought to cure."[62] For reformists, just about any rationale that promotes racial integration would likely be an acceptable governmental interest in satisfying the constitutional ends test. Some might call this approach to racial-preference law "judicial slumming" because it is so indiscriminate in its selection of a compelling governmental interest. Reformists, however, might deny this claim or, alternatively, argue that it is better to get in rather than not to get in, that sometimes the ends do justify the means. In short, because racial-preference law is the reformist's counterpoison for racial disparity, they would not want to limit what counts as a compelling governmental interest.[53]

Fisher II as well as *Fisher I* completely ignore other post–civil rights norms that question whether the racial-integration or the racial-omission norm adequately promotes the black equality interest in racial-preference law. One such norm is the racial self-sufficiency, the norm of choice for limited separatists. This norm rejects any civil rights ruling that promotes formal equal opportunity at the expense of racial identity or solidarity. Thus, if an affirmative-action plan, such as the one critical race theorists prefer (more about this to come), does not undercut racial identity or solidarity, limited separatists would deem it to be acceptable. There is, however, a caveat: the Court must simultaneously direct some of its institutional imprimatur toward black identity or solidarity. Not unlike the legitimacy it bestowed upon formal equal opportunity during the civil rights era, the Court's recognition of racial identity or solidarity, even if *dicta,* gives "things black" important validation in the mainstream culture. Hence, the Court needs to, at the very least, balance the scale by acknowledging the importance of black identity, such as the importance of HBCUs, as it endeavors to support affirmative action, limited separatists would argue.

Limited separatists will *tolerate* racial integration under these conditions only because they support individual choice among blacks. They do not want to deny blacks the opportunity to choose between racial integration and racial solidarity on an individual, or personal, basis, as long as it does not undermine racial solidarity. Limited separatists do not want to place a stranglehold on healthy individualism; in fact, they want to support such individualism. But that is as far as they will go. Limited separatists will not *advocate* for racial integration or any means of achieving racial integration, especially when that challenges black identity.

On the other hand, affirmative action that undercuts black identity clashes with the racial-pride norm, and is therefore unacceptable to limited separatists. It is for this reason that limited separatists would probably reject UT's holistic affirmative-action plan. Predicated on diversity, the plan suggests that a black student needs to capture a white student to get a quality education and that the true value of a black student on a white college campus is to provide white students with a diverse experience. There is definitely a sense in UT's plan that black students in the state of Texas are better off at a predominantly white university like UT than at an HBCU like Texas Southern University. UT's low regard for black schools even goes down to the high school level. Justice Alito, in fact, noted in his dissenting opinion in *Fisher II* that the majority bought into the assumption that "the Top Ten Percentage admittees are somehow *the wrong kind* of African-American and Hispanic students" (emphasis in original).[64] Both the Court and UT made it clear that a major attraction of the holistic plan was to bring more minority students on campus to enrich the diversity experience of white students, especially in small classes. This kind of thinking is racially offensive, limited separatists would maintain.

A racially nonoffensive affirmative-action plan would certainly pass muster under the limited separatist's three-prong test, discussed earlier in this chapter in connection with the *Ricci* case. This test is used in lieu of the strict scrutiny test to gauge the legality of all racial classifications. Let us assume, *arguendo,* that UT's holistic affirmative-action plan is nonoffensive to black and Latino students. The first prong of the three-prong test is easily satisfied, as the absence of a critical mass of black and Latino students on the UT campus establishes a need for an educationally supportive environment at the school. The affirmative-action plan consists of racial preferences rather than racial quotas; hence, it does not deny admissions to other racial minorities or whites as a group. But even if it did involve a racial quota, the affirmative-action plan would still pass the second prong of the three-prong test, because it is not so broad as to govern all or even a substantial percentage of the admissions decisions made at UT. Seventy-five percent of UT's admissions are made through the Top Ten Percent Plan, and the great majority of the admissions under the holistic plan are given to nonminority students. As the Court observed, the plan "played a role in only a small portion of admissions decisions."[65] Given these considerations, there is no need to even consider the third prong of the test.

The social-transformation norm derives from critical race theory's core post–civil rights belief that American society and its major institutions, including the courts, are slanted in favor of straight white males. Judicial opinions that implement formal equal opportunity necessarily protect or preserve white hegemony, as that is their role in the culture and social order. The Court protects or preserves white privilege by issuing rulings that do not chip away at the fundamental relationship between race and power in our society, rulings that, in other words, eschew social transformation. *Fisher* is a prime example.

Although enthusiastic supporters of affirmative action, critical race theorists would find fault with the Court's use of the diversity rationale to support affirmative action. Derrick Bell, in an article titled "Diversity's Distractions," summarizes the critical race theorist's critique of the diversity rationale:

> For at least four reasons, the concept of diversity, far from a viable means of ensuring affirmative action in the admissions policies of colleges and graduate schools, is a serious distraction in the ongoing efforts to achieve racial justice: 1) Diversity enables courts and policymakers to avoid addressing directly the barriers of race and class that adversely affect so many applicants; 2) Diversity invites further litigation by offering a distinction without a real difference between those uses of race approved in college admissions programs, and those in other far more important affirmative action policies that the Court has rejected; 3) Diversity serves to give undeserved legitimacy to the heavy reliance on grades and test scores that privilege well-to-do, mainly white applicants; and 4) The tremendous attention directed at diversity programs diverts concern and resources from the serious barriers of poverty that exclude far more students from entering college than are likely to gain admission under an affirmative action program.[66]

Critical race theorists, then, believe that the diversity rationale upholds affirmative action on grounds acceptable to white elites rather than on grounds beneficial to outsiders, in other words, on grounds that explicitly acknowledge the relationship between race and power in our society. The diversity rationale prevents us from dealing with the real problem outsiders face—white hegemony. It does nothing to redress white control over the social order. Justifying affirmative action as a response to white hegemony, critical race theorists believe, offers not only a nonsubordinating rationale for an otherwise useful tool but also provides the most *truthful* way to justify the deployment of that tool. We would not even be talking about affirmative action were it not for the history of racial oppression in this country. Yet insiders who support affirmative action favor the diversity rationale because it assuages their uneasy feelings about supporting a race-conscious enterprise or perhaps even feelings of white guilt. The diversity rationale, in a word, expresses a white elite view of the value of affirmative action. It does not express historical truth or why affirmative action makes sense to outsiders. "While increasing diversity enriches the academic environment and enhances the curricular aims of education, the legal and rhetorical emphasis on diversity sidesteps the more challenging social issues of race and class inequality."[67]

The Court in *Fisher* failed to tell the truth about affirmative action—that its real value lies in the fact that it helps to counteract white privilege, to change the relationship between race and power in our society. The justices could "have accomplished a great deal more if they . . . acknowledged the poisonous consequences of near-exclusive reliance on objective admissions criteria and included a frank discussion of why those criteria produce racially skewed results."[68] The diversity rationale lacks the rhetorical heft needed to balance the racial scale in our culture. It can only maintain the existing racial differential. That chasm can only be traversed when the Court sets its sights on social transformation. And at that moment, the Court will come to understand the need for affirmative action not just in the form of racial preference but also in the form of racial quotas; in others words, as a means of sustaining an egalitarian response to white hegemony.[69]

Which view of *Fisher* does the best job of promoting the spirit of *Brown*? Which is good social policy? In my view, reformism, limited separation, and critical race theory contain features that, when joined together, promote racial progress within *Brown*'s spirit. Affirmative action is a powerful engine of racial advancement. African Americans made the most racial progress relative to whites during the heyday of affirmative action in the mid-1970s. I have no problem, therefore, with the reformist's attempt to expand the permissible grounds on which affirmative action could be sustained under the Constitution, but I do think that the critical-race-theory justification for affirmative action is the most racially progressive. Giving affirmative action a remedial purpose keeps our eyes on the prize—to wit, the abolition of racial injustice, including that caused by the Supreme Court's inglorious racial past.[70]

But I would not go so far as to accept racial quotas as critical race theorists would have us do. That would seem to unnecessarily trammel the white equality interest in higher education, although affirmative action is so limited in its use that it simply does not affect the vast majority of white students who apply to college. Of course, one of the main arguments against any form of race-based affirmative action is the traditionalist's belief that modern civil rights law should be individual focused rather than group focused. The best reasoning behind this conclusion is that in a society composed of diverse racial and ethnic groups, civil rights law can only work fairly and effectively on an individual level. The calculations become too complex at the group level. The problem with that argument, in my view, is that the horse is already out of the barn. As Judge Constance Baker Motely, who as a young NAACP lawyer worked on the *Brown* case, has remarked, *Brown* gave constitutional status to group rights: "Group rights, thus, became substantively as well as procedurally a distinct, new area in constitutional adjudication."[71] More importantly, racial inequality operates at the group-level in our society. When a black person experiences racial disadvantage, it is not because of who she is as an individual but because of her affiliation with a racial group. That is why it is called racial subordination (or racial discrimination) and not individual subordination (or individual discrimination). But still, I believe that affirmative action without racial quotas is reasonable racial advancement in a case like *Fisher.*[72]

So too is the limited separatist's strategy for racial equality. The *Fisher* Court should have sent a strong message of support for racial identity or solidarity for the very reasons limited separatists give. This could have easily been done by creating a place in its opinion for HB-CUs. Although it would have been purely advisory, the Court could have suggested that the state of Texas provide greater financial support for its

HBCUs or create more black liberal arts colleges. HBCUs are constitutional under limited separation's three-prong test.[73]

Fisher could have been decided in a way that furthered racial advancement. Combining reformism, limited separation, and critical race theory would have given greater deference to the spirit of Brown in a legally legitimate manner. Blacks, therefore, would have been closer to the goal of racial equality in higher education, and the Court would have given us all good social policy.[74]

Race and Culture

The cases discussed in the last chapter hint at the racial and cultural crosscurrents that inform our understanding of cultural diversity. Legal disagreements among the traditionalists and reformists on the Supreme Court pivot on that subtext. The conflicting values implicit in that discussion are brought under critical review as part of a larger argument regarding cultural diversity made in the final two chapters of this book. My contention is that beneath the surface of cultural diversity, commonly seen as a necessary condition for positive race relations, lies a source of racial inequality—cultural subordination.

My argument begins with a discussion of the values—questions and concerns—that shape the lives of black and white Americans. These values can be found in the racial and cultural crosscurrents of the middle and working classes. I make several assumptions about race and culture that should be noted before proceeding with my main discussion. They are as follows: culture can be expressed uniquely or held in common with other groups; some cultural expressions are "good" while others are "bad"; although self-identity is a personal right, identity is contingent, as it is largely externally imposed; and the American mainstream culture consists of elements of both "high" and "popular" culture.

Some values, or folkways, are unique to a specific group, others are held in common with other races or classes. For example, the attitudes toward race held by the black middle class are very different from those held by the white middle class, as we shall see. On the other hand, both groups, unlike the working class of both races, rank education, work, and family in the same order, as we shall also see. Similar intraclass racial comparisons can also be made for the working class, and they will be made in this chapter.

Cultural expressions can be "good" (life-affirming, moral, tolerant) or "bad" (life-negating, immoral, illiberal). Understand, I am not referring to simple matters of taste (for example, teenage boys wearing their trousers down) or classism (for example, placing higher worth on attending a Broadway play than a monster-truck rally). I am referring here to values and behaviors that allow the individual to reach her highest potential as a human being. Thus, racial antipathy, whether practiced by whites or blacks, is a bad folkway, as is the practice of *bacha bazi*, or "boy play," in Afghanistan. The essential point here is that no racial group has a monopoly on good or bad values.

In my view, individuals have a right to try to self-identify, or self-culture, in other words, to choose their own culture. I do not subscribe to the idea of cultural co-opting. Marshall Bruce Mathers III, better known by his stage name Eminem, the white working-class rapper, won a 1999 Grammy Award for Best Rap Album. I see nothing wrong with that. Yet, racial identity, particularly for blacks and other racial minorities, infrequently comes by way of one's own volition. An African American does not usually have control over how he or she is racially identified in our society. Racial identity is not normally a function of personal desire or effort. Indeed, Samuel R. Lucas and Marcel Paret argue that the racial-identity question is a moot question as a practical matter. Racial classifications in our society turn less on what a person feels about himself or herself than on what *others* will allow him or her to do or not do:

> While not denying the potential importance of one's stated racial identity for one's own experience, and without affirming or denying the putative biological basis of race, we draw on the history of socially defined racial exclusion. In that history, racial classification turned not on what one felt

but, instead, on what others allowed one to do. We believe that the exclusionary aspect of race may be as dominant now as it was in the past, and certainly remains important in the contemporary period. Thus, there is little need to address matters of personal identification or to resolve the biological facts of the phenomenon. Instead, one can attend to race with respect to its social role in determining how power will be wielded by significant social actors.[1]

Malcolm Gladwell's poignant account of his personal experiences supports Lucas and Paret's view that racial identity is largely imposed rather than chosen. A British-born Canadian of British and Jamaican heritage, Gladwell (author of such hugely popular books as *Blink* and *Outliers: The Story of Success*) once remarked in an interview with the *New York Times,* "I don't know what I consider myself. It's too complex. There are too many ways to define yourself, and [race is] not a way I have chosen to define myself anymore." But then something happened on the way to the forum: he grew an Afro, and began to be "stopped and frisked on the streets of America for no other reason than looking like a black American." Reflecting on his experience, Gladwell remarked, "That to the cop looking at you in that split second, or the employer sizing you up as you walk in the door—black is black is black."[2]

While Gladwell's dispatch supports the view that external factors largely shape identity, it also suggests that some blacks have the power to create (or re-create) their own identity to the extent that they can "fool" society. Blacks who look racially ambivalent, as Gladwell did before he grew an Afro, can make up their own identity. More typical is the black person whose skin is light enough to "pass" for white. For this person, as David Matthews describes in his memoir, *Ace of Spades,* racial identity and, hence, cultural identity are elective. Indeed, Matthews, who had a black father and Jewish mother, recounts how he "chose" to identify with the white kids in his elementary school by sitting with them at a lunch table on his first day at the school. He felt more comfortable with the kids who looked like him and acted like him, right down to their *Starsky & Hutch* lunch boxes. In what can only be disturbingly described as an extreme act of opting out of black culture, an older Matthews stepped into anti-black culture by joining a white friend in burning a cross (KKK style) in protest against their treatment by blacks. Clearly, some blacks have the power to choose their identity while others do not.[3]

Racial identity, then, is contingent. "[I]t depends," as Bliss Broyard writes, "on the neighborhood where you grow up, the schools you attend and the friends you hang out with; . . . it falls somewhere between how a person presents himself and how the world sees him." All this makes inquiry into racial or cultural identity quite delicate and complicated. But what contributes most to the "thorny nature" of the inquiry is our racial history. "The same American racial history that made the question of what one is matter in the first place now makes it difficult to answer, since necessary efforts to redress the past, like affirmative action and set-aside programs, and the polarizing debates about them, tend to reify black and white as separate and meaningful categories."[4]

My fourth and final premise is that there are two large currents (and, hence, potentially subordinating forces) that move through the American mainstream culture—"high" and "popular" culture. High culture (sometimes referred to as culture with a capital "C") purports to be esthetically elevating or institutionally functional, and, hence, worthy of preserving for the ages. It is timeless rather than timely. Without being judgmental, it is fair to say that high culture consists of the values and behaviors that come from society's elites, those who control our economic, social, legal, educational, and political institutions. Jazz may have begun as a "devious challenge[] to the conventions that had come to dominate popular music,"[5] but, as Peter Keepnews argues in his review of Harvey Cohen's book on the social and political significance of Duke Ellington, *Duke Ellington's America,* today the cultural elites regard "jazz as high art." Popular, or "pop," culture, in contrast to high culture, seeks to entertain (rather than educate) and/or titillate (rather than elevate). It seeks to distract, and aims for mass appeal. Pop culture makes no pretense of being anything more than a representation of the here and now. It is timely rather than timeless. "In music and the movies, even in TV, the designation of No. 1 is . . . besieged by the increasingly fast turnover in chart toppers and by the advent of new barometers of popularity. . . . [A]nd not everyone can even agree on what makes the measure of a No. 1."[6]

With these assumptions in mind, I turn to a discussion of the American middle class (white and black) and working class (white and black). Parsing through the cultural and racial crosscurrents of each socioeconomic class, my ambition is to identify some of the values that are unique to blacks regardless of class and, hence, to whites regardless of class. I shall end by arguing that middle-class whites exercise the most influence in shaping the American mainstream culture.

Middle-Class Culture

There is no definitive way to define the middle class in the United States. Scholars have yet to arrive at anything approaching a consensus definition. Bart Landry's decades-old description of the state of scholarship remains correct today: "There could be found no consensus in either scholarly or popular literature on the definition of middle class. Some writers defined the group by their *education* level, others by their *income,* and still others by their *occupations* or some combination of these characteristics" (emphasis added).[7] Karyn Lacy remarks, however, that the "key indicators of middle-class status . . . [are] wealth, housing, and income."[8] For present purposes, I shall use an income definition. As the median household income is $53,657 in 2014 dollars (2015 data will be released in September of 2016, after this book goes to press), it seems reasonable to set the household income range for the middle class from $50,000 to $150,000 per year. Above that range lies the upper middle class, and below it, as discussed later in this chapter, is the working class. That the middle class is an endangered class due to generations of wage stagnation is a different issue, superbly discussed by others.[9]

The middle class has many behaviors and values that distinguish it from the working class, regardless of race. Human capital is a major distinguishing feature. Besides financial capital, the middle class has more human capital than the working class. Barbara Ehrenreich goes so far as to assert that the former's "only capital is knowledge and skill."[10] Burton Bledstein agrees, asserting that the middle class owns "an acquired skill or cultivated talent" that is used to provide a service. This skill set is more than a commodity; it consists of "a human capacity . . . as unlimited in its potential expansion and its powers to enrich him financially and spiritually as the enlarging volume of his own intelligence, imagination, aspirations, and acquisitiveness."[11] What this means, then, is that scholastic achievement—education—occupies a central place within the mix of middle-class values.

Indeed, the middle class views education as the key to the American Dream, to prosperity and security, to worldly success and personal happiness, to a life well lived. Scholars have noted that the middle class highly values "credentials." Academic achievement gives one social status. One's identity is based on "the sum of accumulated grade acquisitions." The heads of most middle-class households have a college degree and take an active role in their children's education to the point of micromanaging it. Because of parental research and overall input, middle-class applicants typically go through a more efficient and successful college application process than working-class applicants do. Middle-class parents strongly believed that where one goes to college matters most. The more highly ranked and prestigious the school, the better. Yale, Harvard, and Princeton are the most elite and, hence, sought after colleges among the middle-class high school students who imbibe their parents' convictions about education. As a onetime visiting professor at Harvard has observed, "both they and I know that the main event in their lives has already taken place—that is, they were accepted at Harvard."[12]

The middle class's heavy involvement in the lives of their children extends far beyond the realm of education, revealing a deeper class schism. Malcolm Gladwell points to a fascinating study by Annette Lareau in her book *Unequal Childhoods: Class, Race, and Family Life* to illustrate this class division. Lareau studied a group of third graders, both black and white, from wealthy and poorer families. What she discovered was that the middle-class and lower-class families practiced two distinct parenting "philosophies." These parenting approaches divided almost perfectly along class lines rather than racial lines. As Gladwell describes:

> The wealthier parents were heavily involved in their children's free time, shuttling them from one activity to the next, quizzing them about their teachers and coaches and

teammates. . . . That kind of intensive scheduling was almost entirely absent from the lives of the poor children.

The middle-class parents talked things through with their children, reasoning with them. They didn't just issue commands. They expected their children to talk back to them, to negotiate, to question adults in positions of authority. If their children were doing poorly at school, the wealthier parents challenged their teachers. They intervened on behalf of their kids. The poor parents, by contrast, are intimidated by authority. They react passively and stay in the background. . . .

Lareau calls the middle-class parenting style *concerted cultivation.* It's an attempt to actively "foster and assess a child's talents, opinions and skills." Poor parents tend to follow, by contrast, a strategy of *accomplishment of natural growth.* They see it as their responsibility to care for their children but to let them grow and develop on their own. . . . [O]ne style isn't morally better than the other. The poorer children were often better behaved, less whiny, more creative in making use of their own time, and had a well-developed sense of independence. But in practical terms, concerted cultivation has enormous advantages. The heavily scheduled middle-class child is exposed to a constantly shifting set of experiences. She learns teamwork and how to cope in highly structured settings. She is taught how to interact comfortably with adults, and to speak up when she needs to. [T]he middle-class children learn a sense of *entitlement,* . . . [meaning (nonpejoratively) that the middle-class children] acted as though they had a right to pursue their own individual preferences and to actively manage interactions in institutional settings. . . . They knew the rules. Even in the fourth grade, middle-class children appeared to be *acting on their own behalf to gain advantages.* They made special requests of teachers and doctors to adjust procedures to accommodate their desires . . . .

By contrast, the working-class and poorer children were characterized by *an emerging sense of distance, distrust, and constraint.* They didn't know how to get their way, or how to "customize" whatever environment they were in, for their best purposes. . . . (emphases added).[13]

Is there a problem here? Elliot Currie argues in *The Road to Whatever* that the middle class's obsession with success, academic and otherwise, burdens middle-class youth culture. It creates an atmosphere of contingent worth and places enormous pressure on teens not just to succeed but to be number one. Gladwell disagrees. He argues that the sense of entitlement taught to middle-class children, and not to working-class and poor children, "is an attitude perfectly suited to succeeding in the modern world." As it turns out, being whiny has its cultural benefits. The whiny child learns to speak up and assert himself or herself. This is an important trait to have if one is to succeed in our highly competitive society.[14]

Occupational ambition and wealth accumulation, with a constant eye on the upper-middle class and super-rich, are important middle-class values. Whether white or black, the middle class is at once imitative and resentful of the upper class. As Christopher Lasch explained in his important book *The True and Only Heaven: Progress and Its Critics,* the middle class "resented social classes more highly placed but internalized their standards, lording it over the poor instead of joining them in a common struggle against oppression."[15] The middle class, in addition, believes that in America, people are often judged by what they do, not by who they are.[16]

Manual labor is historically the line of demarcation between working-class (or blue-collar) jobs and middle-class (or white-collar) jobs. Within the latter category are doctors, lawyers, engineers, teachers, government bureaucrats, scientists, advertising executives, interior designers, managers, journalists, and "quant jocks" (people who make their living working with numbers)—all requiring a degree of human capital. Some middle-class occupations rank higher than others. A doctor is ranked higher than a teacher, and a surgeon is ranked higher than a dentist. Such high-ranking jobs, including "jobs with a large payload of idealism" (such as in the green economy), are highly regarded by middle-class society.[17]

Homeownership is a nearly universal goal of the middle class. Although that attitude may have been affected by the burst of the housing bubble in 2007, historically, homeownership has been a defining goal of the middle class. "Ever since World War II, Americans have been taught that owning your own home is the ultimate investment, the ticket to long-term financial security, along with social acceptance and a nice tax deduction. . . . Homeownership is one of the most visible signs of participation in the middle class."[18]

The middle class also exhibits distinct attitudes toward religion. Surveys indicate that about 28 percent of people who identify themselves as middle class think it is somewhat important to live a religious life, and 53 percent think it is very important. This attitude should be distinguished from churchgoing. Although the middle class says it is religious, fewer people are going to church, as churchgoing in general has declined over the years. It is also important to note that even those who attend church may not subscribe to every aspect of religious doctrine. They may pick and choose from church teachings, as do the so-called "cafeteria Catholics," who dissent from church dogma on such matters as abortion, birth control, divorce, premarital sex, and homosexuality.[19]

An overwhelming majority of the middle class believes that having children is important. Yet, middle-class women exemplify the conventional feminist belief that women can work and be mothers at the same time. This attitude along with wage stagnation helped to fuel a nationwide, transclass trend toward greater female participation in the labor market. For example, in 2012, 71 percent of all mothers were in the labor force, compared to only 47 percent in 1975. Additionally, 62 percent of Americans surveyed "endorse[d] the modern marriage in which the husband and wife both work and both take care of the household and children."[20] The majority of American adults believe "that the trend of more women in the workforce has been a change for the better."[21] What is most significant here is that, historically, middle-class women see work less as a means of bringing in needed income than as a means of seeking intellectual fulfillment outside the home. Much of this work consists of volunteering. Home life is not enough.[22]

Finally, the middle class is a nervous class. Strange though it may seem, jitteriness is a character trait that helps define middle-class culture. It is not only that this comfortably situated class is continuously striving to reach the upper class, as mentioned earlier, it is also that, especially after the crash of the economy in 2008, the middle class lives in constant fear of slipping into the lower classes—the working class or, worse, the poverty class. But even in good times, the middle class is in constant pursuit of the upper class. The middle class is simply not satisfied or secure in what it has achieved.[23]

Middle-Class Racial Differences

My discussion of middle-class culture thus far has not indicated any significant racial distinctions. The folkways delineated so far are held in common by both the white and black middle class. For example, middle-class black parents tend to raise their children in the same way as their white counterparts. According to a study by Charles Willie and Richard Reddick, middle-class blacks, like their white counterparts, regard education to be the key to "making it." Black families also exhibit a pattern of shared power with their children. Like middle-class white parents, middle-class black parents strive to "promote a sense of accountability and obligation in their children." They want their children to "develop a sense of ownership and responsibility," especially toward education.[24]

Despite these cultural similarities, there are telling cultural differences between middle-class whites and blacks. Indeed, as Lacy notes, "Middle-class black and white families are assumed to be different, and an established body of evidence supports this perception."[25] Leland Ware and Theodore Davis concur, and, like others, have noted that some of these differences also differentiate middle-class blacks from working-class blacks, as we shall see.[26]

One difference between whites and blacks in the middle class is the contrasting attitudes each group has toward membership in the middle class. "Middle-class whites fit the public image of the middle class and may therefore take their middle-class status for granted, but blacks who have 'made it' must work harder, more deliberately, and more consistently to make their middle-class status known to others."[27] Members of the black middle class use what Lacy calls "public identities" in public settings "where they are likely to encounter white strangers who are not aware of their class position." The purpose of using public identities is to "demonstrate their middle-class status." One subject of a study explained that when he went shopping and wore a suit, he was signifying his middle-class status. He was actually doing more than that; for "[a] key strategy [of middle-class blacks] involves differentiating their group from lower-class blacks by amplifying similarities with the white middle class." Thus, not only do blacks struggle to join the middle class and to maintain their position therein, they also labor to put whites, especially the white middle class, on notice of their position. Let us call this *signaling*.[28]

Signaling actually entails both "exclusionary boundary work" and "inclusionary boundary work." It is the former when middle-class blacks consciously differentiate themselves from the culture of lower-class blacks. It is the latter when middle-class blacks intentionally associate themselves with the culture of middle-class whites. The black gentleman who wore a suit while shopping was both "exclusionary" and "inclusionary" because he sought to distinguish himself from lower-class black stereotypes and, at the same time, align himself with the American cultural norm, the white middle class. "Middle class blacks are aware of how society views poorer members of their race, and privately share some of those sentiments."[29]

Signaling could also be a way of preventing discrimination. Middle-class blacks spend more time in white spaces than working-class blacks do. Signaling could prevent "microaggressions," such as being seated at the table nearest the kitchen door in a restaurant or "macroaggressions," such as stop-and-frisk policies in policing black communities. Signaling may be an attempt on the part of middle-class blacks to provide a counternarrative to racial stereotypes.[30]

The upper-middle class (both whites and blacks) also engage in signaling, although it is not the same as for middle-class blacks. Upper-middle-class individuals or families will sometimes attempt to signal themselves as wealthy and rich, thus distinguishing themselves from the middle class and identifying with the upper class. The difference is that those who aspire to be in the upper-middle class are often signaling exactly what they are not, while the black middle class is signaling exactly what they are.

If taken too far, signaling can undermine deeply rooted black traditions that transcend class stratification. Houston Baker believes that many middle-class blacks have in fact committed just such a transgression. In his book *Betrayal: How Black Intellectuals Have Abandoned the Ideals of the Civil Rights Era,* Baker maintains that the lures of notoriety and economic status offered by mainstream American institutions have undercut a black ethos of racial kinship and identity ("racing") among middle-class blacks. Cornel West makes a similar point in *Black Prophetic Fire.* Both he and Baker believe there are fewer "race people" within the black middle class today than there were during the civil rights movement. Race people are men and women who, like Frederick Douglass, W. E. B. Du Bois, Martin Luther King Jr., Ella Baker, Malcolm X, Ida B. Wells, and Mary McLeod Bethume, dedicate their lives to advancing the interests of the black majority, often sacrificing personal wealth and white acceptance for "the cause." As Houston Baker explains, "In black American life and culture a race man or race woman is one who dedicates his or her life and work to countering the lies, ideological evasions, and pretensions to 'innocence' and 'equal justice for all' that prop up America's deeply embedded, systemic, and institutionalized racism."[31] Thus, race people are zealous advocates for the interests and well-being of the black Americans, especially the lower black classes. They are unwilling to compromise these ideals or withhold fervent and persistent criticism of societal forces that impede racial progress.

There is, however, a segment of the black middle class—mainly the young, urban, and successful within white mainstream institutions—that sees this new cultural phenomenon as a positive development. These blacks insist that the decline in the number of race people (aka "racing") moves the black middle class in the right cultural direction in post–civil rights America—from an antiquated black identity defined in Ralph Ellison's 1952 book *Invisible Man* (socially invisible to the American mainstream culture), to a modern black identity formed by Touré's "Visible Young Man." With economic prosperity comes not only the desire but also the ability to free oneself from the constraints of traditional roles and stereotypes externally or internally imposed on blacks. What is being expressed here is the very American ideal of individualism (a claim for which Ellison was ultimately arguing in his novel). The "post-black" African American refuses to be bound by race. As Touré explains:

> Now that we've got a post-black president, all the rest of the post-blacks can be unapologetic as we reshape the iconography of blackness. For so long, the definition of blackness was dominated by the '60s street-fighting militancy of the Jesses and the irreverent one-foot-out-the-ghetto angry brilliance of the Pryors and the nihilistic, unrepentantly ghetto, new-age thuggishness of the 50 Cents. A decade ago they called post-blacks Oreos because we didn't think blackness equaled ghetto, didn't mind having white influencers, didn't seem full of anger about the past. We were comfortable employing blackness as a grace note rather than as our primary sound. Post-blackness sees blackness not as a dogmatic code worshiping at the altar of the hood and the struggle but as an open-source document, a trope with infinite uses.
>
> The term began in the art world with a class of black artists who were adamant about not being labeled black artists even as their work redefined notions of blackness. Now the meme is slowly expanding into the wider consciousness. For so long we were stamped inauthentic and bullied into an inferiority complex by the harder brothers and sisters, but now it's our turn to take center stage. Now Kanyé, Questlove, Santigold, Zadie Smith and Colson Whitehead can do blackness their way without fear of being branded pseudo or incognegro.[32]

The internal struggle within the black middle class, then, is over what it means to be a middle-class black in the post–Jim Crow era. Is middle-class blackness in post–civil rights America to be defined by the civil-rights-era notion of racing? Does that identity continue to have any currency? Should the black privileged class approach life not with racial distance or restraint, but with easy familiarity and freedom? These are important questions to which the post–civil rights norms provide different answers in the next chapter.

Post-blackness may not be an accurate way to define the racial identity of most middle-class blacks in post–civil rights America. Alice Coner-Edwards and Jeanne Spurlock found in their study that despite the feeling expressed by some middle-class blacks that they can no longer be identified in relation to "the cause," most middle-class black families have a sense of racial solidarity; they have an appreciation for their blackness. This finding is consistent with a study conducted by the Pew Research Center and with Judge Harry Edwards's suggestion that although blacks exhibit growing class differences, they have "rejected the idea that they should 'blend in' with the majority, choosing instead to value their distinct racial identity."[33]

Beyond the question of racial identity, a cultural issue with which the white middle class never really has to deal, the black middle class has other distinctive cultural traits. These traits arise from the "unique race group patterns of historical experiences in the United States." For example, many middle-class blacks strongly believe that "[t]he life style of the new black middle class continue[s] to be constrained by racism still active in American society."[34] On the matter of racism, one finds significant convergence even between post-black blacks and other middle-class blacks. While the former do not believe racism is potent enough to prevent blacks from succeeding in life, they do acknowledge its existence and seek ways to outsmart it. In a *Time* magazine article titled "How to Talk to Young Black Boys About Trayvon Martin," written in the wake of the killing of an unarmed seventeen-year-old black male, Trayvon Martin, by an armed white man, George Zimmerman, patrolling his neighborhood, Touré admonishes young black men:

> It's unlikely but possible that you could get killed today. Or any day. I'm sorry, but that's the truth. Black maleness is a potentially fatal condition. I tell you that not to scare you but because knowing that could save your life. There are people who will look at you and see a villain or a criminal or something fearsome. It's possible they may act on their prejudice and insecurity. Being black could turn an ordinary situation into a life-or-death moment even if you're doing nothing wrong. . . . You will have to make allowances for other

people's racism. That's part of the burden of being black. We
can be defiant and dead or smart and alive.[35]

Touré's advice about dealing with "other people's racism," which seems
to undercut his bold assertion of post-blackness, expresses a conventional attitude held by the black middle class—to wit, *soyez méfiant* ("be
mistrustful"), discussed in greater details in a moment. His advice also
seems to reiterate Lucas and Paret's point, mentioned at the beginning
of this chapter, that society imposes racial alignments upon individuals,
that although one might select a particular racial identity on a governmental form or desire not to be limited by a specific racial identity, one's
racial identity is ultimately shaped by one's experience. Simply walking
down the street will decide the issue.

Racism may explain the high level of alienation among middle-
class blacks. Although feelings of alienation among blacks tend to
decrease as education or income increases, 70.3 percent of middle-class
blacks experience feelings of social alienation compared to only 37.8
percent of middle-class whites. Alienation is a racial characteristic that
"cuts across class lines in black America."[36]

A large percentage of blacks of all classes, unlike their white counterparts, rely on the black church as a "bulwark against racism" and "as
an ally in combating negative imagery" in the media's portrayal of black
men and black women. Thus, it is no surprise that the black middle class
is more religious than the white middle class. One study shows that 64.5
percent of middle-class blacks consider themselves to be religious,
compared to 55.1 percent of middle-class whites. Robert C. Smith and
Richard Seltzer boldly assert, "Faith in God . . . is perhaps the single
most distinctive attribute of Afro-American culture in the United
States." They trace this cultural trait "to the spirit of evangelical Protes-
tantism and the hope for deliverance that emerged in the slave culture."[37]

There is also racial difference within the middle class on the question of abortion. Substantially more middle-class whites are pro-
abortion than are middle-class blacks, 64.1 percent to 52.8 percent,
respectively. These attitudes toward abortion, call them the abortion
folkways, are not class bound; they do not apply only to the middle class.
They cut across classes, as shall be seen in due course. The abortion folk-

ways of black women help to explain the relatively high incidence of out-of-wedlock babies in the black community. Thus, far from being more promiscuous than white women, black women, some might argue, are very moral. Clearly, they have a different attitude about abortion.[38]

Other behaviors and values among middle-class blacks also transcend class. There is, for instance, a strong belief among the great majority of African Americans of all classes that because slavery and Jim Crow continue to significantly limit opportunities for blacks (again, a sentiment not necessarily held by black traditionalists), racism and racial discrimination should be vigorously resisted at every turn in one's personal or professional life. Accordingly, a top priority of government and private institutions alike should be to eradicate racial evils from the American landscape root and branch. The Pew Research Center reports that 62 percent of blacks and only 22 percent of whites believe that society should do everything possible to improve the conditions of blacks and other racial minorities, including giving blacks preferential treatment.[39]

Racial uplift, a visceral connection to "the cause" (or "the struggle") for racial justice, racial solidarity, a communal spirit (as opposed to possessive individualism), black is beautiful, reverence for the black mother, and *soyez méfiant* when around whites all define a quintessential black culture. So too does the black imperative for success—that a black person has to be "three times" better than a white person to succeed in this country—as well as the "African American Survival Maxim," which admonishes young blacks: "You have the right to be angry about centuries of racial exploitation as well as present-day racism and racial discrimination. But you do not have the right to dwell on that anger, to feel guilty about these matters, to suffer low self-esteem, or to react in other self-destructive ways."[40] Steven Barboza's wonderful book *The African American Book of Values* explains and illustrates dozens of black values, both shared by the white culture and unique to the black culture. Far from racial defeatism, the folkways delineated in this book speak of both personal and collective responsibility. For example, Langston Hughes's poem "The Negro Mother," considered by scores of blacks to be the most important poem ever written about the black experience, captures many unique black values of this quality. The poem begins:

Children, I come back today
To tell you a story of the long dark way
That I had to climb, that I had to know
In order that the race might live and grow.[41]

This poem was written in 1931, as the Harlem Renaissance was coming to an end, in honor of Mary McLeod Bethune, the leading black woman of her day. In the poem, the black mother is praised for overcoming racial burdens and injustices, but more so for nurturing her children and encouraging them "to look upward and keep on climbing 'up the great stairs' of life."[42] Similarly, Alice Walker provides a tribute to her great-great-grandmother, who as a slave walked from Virginia to Georgia "with two babies on her hips." Hence, the image of the black mother looms large in the black culture regardless of class. "Blood has been spilled and lives even lost in the African American community in defense of a mother's honor."[43]

More than whites, blacks of all classes have placed a great deal of value on the community. In an essay in *The African American Book of Values* titled "Voices of Respect," Maya Angelou explains why: "Neither the slaveowner nor the slave overseer was likely to speak to a servant in anything but the cruelest language. But in the slave society Mariah became Aunt Mariah and Joe became Uncle Joe. Young girls were called Sister, Sis, or Tutta. Boys became brother, Bubba, and Bro and Buddy."[44] The black community traditionally and in modern times is a place where blacks do not have to prove their humanity. There is no burden placed on blacks to painstakingly try to persuade others that racism has a lethal legacy and crippling presence in today's society. These perspectives are simply accepted as truth, because most blacks have experienced racism in their lived experiences.

Those few middle-class blacks who, having lived a life of high triumph, embrace a post-black culture, on the sly or openly, certainly strike at the heart of this heritage. Post-blackness envisions an anti-black African American community. Post-black African Americans would self-consciously unglue the bonds that bring together an eclectic group of individuals tied at the hip by an African heritage and a common history of racial oppression in this country.

Although there are many black behaviors and values that transcend class stratification within the black community, there are also cultural differences between the black middle and working classes. These differences are primarily associated with the general cultural divide between the middle and working classes.

Working-Class Culture

The working class can be defined as those who earn less than fifty thousand dollars a year and more than the poverty rate, which is about twenty-five thousand a year for a family of four. This class comprises a large segment of American swing voters. Here, again, I am less interested in their political strength or buying power than in their basic values and behaviors. As with the middle class, my focus will be on the working-class culture; that is, the folkways of the class, the questions and concerns that preoccupy the class writ large.

If there is one word that most defines the working class's collective identity it is "struggle." The working class harbors the rather grim attitude that life for them is a continuous struggle. Economic privation, physical danger, emotional turmoil, and, more broadly, the inability to control one's life are the conditions that define the world in which the working class lives. Struggle is the iconography of the working class. It unifies them. It pushes them to endure, to move forward in the challenging world in which they live. Struggle as a collective identity is reinforced by the mass media, which often represents the working class as a battle-weary cultural unit, constantly reaching for the American Dream, the middle class.[45]

One born into the working class will usually remain there for at least one generation. But one's ties to the working class, and the constant reminder of the working class's struggles, are not likely to be severed after "making it." Long after moving up to the middle class, alumni of the working class typically stay connected to one or more working-class networks. These networks operate variously through families communities, and work. Alumni are often immersed in tight social networks, in part because their extended family often resides within a few miles of their new, middle-class homes. Many retain strong roots in working-class communities through a variety of extracurricular activities, such as serving as a Little League coach, volunteering as a firefighter, or participating in some capacity in a neighborhood school, church, or American Legion post. Thus, the alumni are often reminded of the struggles from which they came.[46]

Several important working-class folkways have emerged in response to the life-is-a-struggle attitude. Among the most important are hard work, "providing," "protecting," personal integrity, straightforwardness, and respect for religion and other traditional expressions of morality. The word "work" in hard work is part of the working class's name. It is a word that has a distinct set of meanings in the working-class culture, to which the middle class would not necessarily subscribe. Working hard is a working-class cultural metaphor for masculinity. It is a way of expressing manliness—self-sufficiency and industriousness—especially when it involves physical labor. Hard work is also viewed as the individual's and community's main source of financial stability. There are few income-generating assets (stocks, bonds, real estate, trusts) among families within the community; hence, hard work is the only realistic way to build wealth within the family and community. Hard work even has meaning beyond the individual, family, and community. It is the basis for a particular view of democracy, one in which the demands of citizenship, economic contributions, and social utility converge. Under this view, democracy is recognized not as a license for self-expression but as a call for self-reliance, not as a basis for self-abasement but as a foundation for self-respect, and not as a path to self-abandonment but as a means to self-rule.[47]

Working-class men typically labor at jobs that are tedious in nature. This makes the work they do hard, both physically and psychologically. It takes "emotional energy and moral fortitude"—discipline—to persevere at these types of jobs. Consequently, those who show up for work on a consistent basis, year after year, often receive the admiration of their coworkers, families, and friends. Work, then, is a source of personal and family pride. It is the one stage on which a working-class man can show technical competence and moral fiber.[48]

Beyond longevity, competency and efficiency at one's job also carries cultural significance. The ability to do one's work well and with speed gives the unskilled worker "a sense of autonomy and control" over a job that offers little creativity. Work takes on even greater importance for most blue-collar workers because it is the primary, if not the only, way to advance in society. Not so for the middle class, for whom education is deemed to be the key to moving up socially.[49]

However important work is to the working class, it is not as important as family. Blue-collar males put family above work more so than white-collar males do. The former find greater personal satisfaction in family than in work, perhaps in part because of the nature of the work they do. Family is the realm of life in which the working-class male can be in charge ("king of his castle") and gain status from doing so. Family is also a realm of life that gives the working-class male intrinsic satisfaction. It is difficult to find such joy in a job that is not only mundane and dull but offers limited financial rewards.[50]

Given the importance of family in the working-class culture, it is not difficult to understand the value this culture places on providing for one's family. Working-class men in particular derive their self-worth from their ability to discipline themselves to take responsibility for providing for their families—providing not wealth but an orderly and safe life for their families. "Providing" functions as an alternative to an economic definition of success that is so prevalent in middle-class culture. It gives the working class dignity and moral standing in the face of financial burdens. "Providing" plays a very prominent role in the working-class male's sense of who he is, and, equally important, who he is *not*. "Providing" can, however, create problems for working-class families. A working-class family can suffer financially when the husband bent on "providing" passes up a better-paying job or promotion so as not to lose time with his family.[51]

"Providing" also means that the wife is encouraged to be a homemaker rather than work outside the home. Working-class men and women traditionally believe that "being able to keep the wife at home" is the hallmark of a "high-quality family life." This traditional value is, of course, merely aspirational rather than actual today, given the percentage of stay-at-home working-class wives. Only 16 percent of working-class wives interviewed stay at home as full-time homemakers. Most working-class wives are coproviders. Some even have the prime "providing" responsibility.[52]

The financial and psychological care and attention working-class males give to their families ("providing") is related to another working-class cultural trait—protecting oneself and one's family from a threatening environment. "Protecting" requires street smarts, which is defined as "the ability to survive in one's environment by knowing how to navigate around its perils and how to negotiate shady characters whose sole purpose in life is to exploit and defraud the innocent." Street smarts, in other words, is a form of intelligence made necessary by the nature of the neighborhoods in which the working class lives. It may be smart, for example, to place iron bars on one's windows or get a large attack dog.[53]

"Protecting" evokes certain cultural images within the working class—"willpower, honor, courage, discipline, and physical strength"—which carry geopolitical implications for this group of Americans. It means that the United States must be willing and able to protect and defend our sacred ideals, including our dominance on the international stage through the use of military force if needed. The idea that freedom, liberty, and all that the United States represents must be defended at all costs might reflect a working-class self-image of courage and strength. "[T]erms like honor, patriotism, cowardice, bravery, and duty are hard to distinguish as either nationalistic or masculine since they seem so thoroughly tied both to the nation and to manhood." The working class, then, sees itself as maintaining "moral order not only in the home and neighborhood, but also in the world at large." This, indeed, is one of the more meaningful cultural aspects of American life in which the working class has an opportunity to participate.[54]

Charles Murray asserts in his book *Coming Apart* that integrity as honesty has decreased in working-class America as evidenced by increases in crime, dishonest business practices, and bankruptcy therein. Elizabeth Warren challenges the view that personal bankruptcy, filed by millions of families each year during economic recessions, is an attempt to scam the system. She argues that predatory lending practices by credit-card companies and banks plus decades of wage stagnation have placed the average worker just one large medical bill, one layoff, one unexpected life event from bankruptcy. "The single best predictor that a family would go bankrupt was if they had a child." In the year after the 2000 recession, "More children lived through their parents' bankruptcy than their parents' divorce; more women would file for bankruptcy than would graduate from college; more people would file for bankruptcy than would be diagnosed with cancer."[55] Michele Lamont, like Warren, insists that America's working class does in fact value personal integrity. She maintains that integrity is an especially important class value because the working class is highly interdependent. The typical working-class male or female has limited financial resources, has little or no private space at work, and lives in a neighborhood where houses are set very close to one another. It is difficult for members of the class to buffer themselves from the actions of coworkers, neighbors, friends, and kin. Compared to his or her professional or managerial counterpart, a working-class white or black cannot readily escape crime, drugs, congestion, and undesirable people by moving to a pricier neighborhood. Hence, family, friends, and the community have to "show up." But showing up has its costs in terms of aggravation, disappointment, inconvenience, and the expenditure of time and emotional capital. There is a level of discomfort in having to depend on others.[56]

America's working class also values straightforwardness, which means "standing up for one's principles even in the face of adversity." This trait can, however, be problematic. Straight shooting can lead to conflict and inflexibility on the job, as when a headstrong worker has constant run-ins with a coworker or supervisor. This is not something that professionals or supervisors are likely to do, as the middle class values conflict avoidance and flexibility. Indeed, it is unlikely that one could become a supervisor without a healthy measure of flexibility.[57]

The overwhelming majority of working-class men do not consider themselves to be religious in any particular sense. But for those who do self-describe as religious, faith "plays an important role in clarifying rules and enforcing protection against the environment in which they live." Faith helps them cope with a challenging, struggling life. These men wear their religion as a badge of honor. Religion gives the faithful a feeling of moral superiority over the nonbeliever. Faith is "a source of status."[58]

Although it is not particularly religious, the working class holds to a fairly rigid moral code beyond "providing" and "protecting." Compared to the middle class, the working class is "less supportive of freedom of choice and self-expression (adult 'entitlement'), especially in the area of sexual morality, divorce, and abortion." This moralistic attitude has been described as "cultural fundamentalism," or "the cluster of values that . . . support adherence to traditional mores, respect of family and religious authority, asceticism, and control of impulse."[59] Based on this moral code, it is not surprising that working-class men, more than middle-class men, tend to "draw boundaries against" people and activities they consider to be morally corrupt. Morality functions as a shield that protects against temptation, including excessive gambling or use of alcohol, illicit drugs, and sexual promiscuity.[60]

The working class also constructs boundaries against the middle class. While middle-class men emphasize entitlement and conflict avoidance, working-class men accord little respect to these cultural traits. Placing more value on straightforwardness and personal integrity, the working class draws boundaries between itself and the white middle class built on the notion that the latter lacks personal integrity and sincerity. To this extent, the working class dissociates socioeconomic status from moral worth. It elevates itself above the middle class based on working-class standards—personal integrity and straightforwardness— to which they attach overarching importance.[61]

Working-Class Racial Differences

Not unlike middle-class whites, working-class whites draw racial and class boundaries between themselves and groups to whom they feel superior secularly—blacks and the poor. Working-class whites draw these boundaries on the basis of a particular moral code, one based on the "disciplined self." The working-class work ethic and commitment to family ("providing" and "protecting") are seen as bright lines that separate working-class whites from blacks and working-class whites from poor whites.[62]

Racism, a negative cultural tradition in white America, remains a visible part of white working-class culture. Nearly 20 percent of those who voted for Donald Trump in the 2016 South Carolina Republican primary, mostly working-class whites, believed ending slavery was a mistake. No wonder. Many working-class whites believe blacks are lazy, "welfare cheats" and responsible for an unspecified amount of the economic misfortunes of the white working class. Given these views, it is not surprising that the white working class tends to view affirmative action as an unfair practice that takes jobs away from deserving white men. Curiously, if a working-class white receives or has received some form of special assistance, whether private (for example, nepotism or union legacy) or public (for example, food stamps, assisted-living allowance, or disability), this is seen as deserving rather than freeloading. A study in 2014 revealed "rampant nepotism" in the Los Angeles County Fire Department despite its antinepotism policy. The working-class view of affirmative action is actually complex. Although many working-class whites complain about the unfairness of affirmative action, they do recognize situations in which it is acceptable. For example, "women should be privileged for *certain* jobs dealing with women and children, and blacks and Hispanics should be privileged in jobs dealing with crime" (emphasis in original).[63]

The black working class has a different set of racial experiences and perspectives. For them, race matters in most walks of life—from education to jobs to policing. This racial outlook is framed by a historical context of racial segregation and discrimination that working-class whites tend not to see as relevant or understand at all, and by a post–civil rights context of lingering racism, de facto segregation, and racial subordination, which, again, working-class whites tend not to see as relevant or understand at all. It is no wonder, then, that the working class, not unlike the rest of the country, is divided along racial lines when it comes to large racial events like the O. J. Simpson trial or the Trayvon Martin murder.[64]

More working-class African Americans than working-class whites describe themselves as very religious. Indeed, 47 percent of working-class whites say that they "never or rarely participate in religious activities," compared to only about one-third of working-class blacks. This is not surprising, because church participation—that is, the black church—has since the days of slavery been an important cultural marker of respectability within the black working class. One's religiosity is used as a proxy for moral character in the black working class much more so than in the white working class. This can be viewed as a form of "protecting," because "being able to use clear signals to distinguish between good and bad people is crucial in a dangerous world where one cannot know whom to trust." In addition, working-class blacks are more likely than working-class whites to verbalize their dependency on religion as a guide through life's minefields. The former "cite the Bible and refer to the presence of Satan around them, [even] at a time when references to sin are declining in American society." Hence, in addition to providing moral guidance in the affairs of everyday life, religion gives working-class blacks hope for a better tomorrow, a belief that God can accomplish what humans cannot.[65]

In response to the unwelcoming environment in which they live, working-class blacks appear to be tougher defenders of traditional morality than their white counterparts. Researchers have observed that the former "draw stronger boundaries" than the latter: boundaries against temptations and sins relating to "drugs, alcohol, promiscuity, and gambling," and boundaries that respect "family and religious authority, asceticism, and control of impulses." Based on this behavior, Lamont suggests, rather controversially, that "[b]y criticizing moral laxity . . . [blacks] may be attempting to counterbalance the racist association between blackness and oversexualized behavior," thereby "signaling their own moral character." Many working-class blacks "condemn black criminals for bringing down the entire race by reinforcing negative racial stereotypes" and by physically harming other blacks.[66]

The black working class also exhibits a pronounced sense of altruism. For example, many of these African Americans express a desire to "try to help a lot of people, create jobs for them, and keep them working," or to just "help people if I could." As one black worker explained, "I would like to be able to have enough in my house that if somebody else comes to my house and needs help, I can help them. . . . I don't have to take a trip every summer." This altruism seems to come from their strong religiosity. "If you don't share it you lose it . . . because God will not bless you if you don't put it to good use."[67]

Working-class blacks have a different cultural expectation than working-class whites regarding the desirability of having wives work. Unlike the latter, working-class blacks, both men and women, believe wives should work as well as husbands. This belief is consistent with the historical rate of participation of black women in the labor force. That rate is "twice the rate of white women." Quite simply, the stay-at-home wife is not a cultural norm to which working-class blacks subscribe.[68]

Racial solidarity is a far more noticeable cultural trait among working-class African Americans than working-class whites. "When asked to choose from a list of qualities that they value, more than a third of blacks, as compared to only a fifth of whites, chose 'shows solidarity.' " Fighting for "the cause" (civil rights) and cultivating racial kinship are deeply rooted traditions in the black community. "Racial solidarity is valued in and of itself as a source of self-worth by a people who might otherwise be [viewed in] a negative light by the larger society." Racial identity provides a social narrative that blacks can use to organize their efforts for racial progress and to otherwise make sense of their world.[69]

Because they have no history of collective oppression in this country, working-class whites do not articulate a desire to extend a helping hand to other whites or a need for self-support to counter group-based hostility to the same extent that their black counterparts do. For working-class whites, "a collectivist discourse" typically comes through labor unions, churches, and civic or fraternal organizations. But these institutions have had a dwindling influence in post–civil rights America and, as such, have "been unable to counteract the discourse of individualism that has become omnipresent in the media and political debates since the Reagan years. The Catholic Church in particular has been less effective in [promoting] a rhetoric of solidarity" within the white working class.[70]

The American Mainstream Culture

Each of the subcultures discussed in this chapter—the black and white middle- and working-class cultures—contributes to the American mainstream culture. But there is one subculture within the American culture that is the most dominant, the most influential, the most conventional. More than any other subculture, it establishes par value in the larger culture and, as such, drives society's most important institutions. Its narratives, language, heroes, traditions, holidays, "felt necessities," aspirations, questions, and concerns are the cultural canons of our society.

That subculture is white and middle class. To a large extent, it is the mainstream American culture.

Others have also noted that middle-class white folkways greatly shape our mainstream values and behaviors. Thom Hartmann argues that the middle class holds the key to our liberal, democratic society. "A true democracy," he notes, "both produces a middle class and requires a middle class for survival. Like the twin strands of DNA, democracy and the middle class are inextricably intertwined, and to break either is to destroy the viability of both." Hartmann concludes that "When there is no American Dream, when there is no middle class, there cannot be real democracy."[71] Similarly, W. A. V. Clark asserts that membership in the middle class is *the* American ideal: "The process of attaining the American Dream is in essence the process of becoming middle class, which encapsulates moving up the socioeconomic status ladder."[72] To borrow from the title of a book written by James Carville and Stan Greenberg, "It's the Middle Class, Stupid!" The white middle class also functions as the cultural gatekeeper, determining which values from other groups receive mainstream status. Jazz, racial equality, women's rights, and now gay marriage have been adopted to one degree or another by middle-class whites over the years. They are now commonly held, mainstream values.[73]

White and middle class, the American mainstream culture is sometimes in conflict with both the working-class culture and the black culture, regardless of class. Its notion of "success," defined in terms of wealth, and the belief that education is the key to obtaining such "success" (education trumps work and work trumps family) conflict with the working class's conviction about what constitutes "success" (family) and the best pathway to "success" (family trumps work and work trumps education). Mainstream American values can also clash with legitimate black values that transcend class stratification. These values, delineated in this chapter, coalesce around a sensibility about racial injustice shared by most blacks. The next chapter elaborates on this unique awareness and seeks to demonstrate the various ways in which its conflict with the mainstream culture can lead to cultural subordination, especially in a society committed to cultural diversity.[74]

Cultural Subordination Through Cultural Diversity

Not long ago, I attended a movie night at the Women's Museum of California. The movie was a documentary, *Pray the Devil Back to Hell,* about a large group of Liberian women who came together during the Liberian Civil War to challenge the country's corrupt regime, led by the infamous Charles Taylor, and the equally corrupt warlords who were fighting to oust him from power. Through the efforts of these women from all walks of life, peace was finally achieved in 2003. I was the only male in attendance at the film screening, but that did not prevent me from asking a few questions. I wanted to know what the bond was that brought these women from diverse backgrounds together to demonstrate for peace for such a long period of time. How is it that these women of such different backgrounds—Christians and Muslims, city dwellers and villagers, married and unmarried, mothers and childless, old and young—carried the same perspective? The initial responses were inconclusive. Seeking greater clarity, I asked the organizers of the event, "Do women have a unique way of looking at the world, which they hold in addition to other worldviews? Is there something like a woman's sensibility, a tagline for womanhood? How is it that members of your group also from diverse backgrounds—some mothers, others childless, some card-carrying members of the NRA, others card-carrying liberals, some rich, others middle class or working class, some businesswomen, others stay-at-home moms, some white, others black or Latina—could come together under the banner of this organization? What cultural markers does the word "women" in the Women's Museum of California indicate? The answer the group settled on was this: women in essence have a special receptivity for care and connection, especially toward children ("mothers always tell their toddlers that if they ever get lost, find a mommy and ask her for help"), and carry with them a sense of being at risk to male violence ("women carry Mace in their purses and whistles on their key chains"). Of course, not all women have these identities or even subscribe to the view that women have an identifiable set of attitudes or behaviors, in other words, values, or folkways. But, in the opinion of women in attendance, enough women do identify with these values, perhaps more descriptively than aspirationally, such that it makes sense to think of them as women's values. The question of black values is perhaps even more contentious.[1]

Black Values

There are those who think blacks are too fragmented ideologically and geographically to warrant any talk of black values. "The fact is that asking what something called 'black America' thinks, feels, or wants makes as much sense as commissioning a new Gallup poll of the Ottoman Empire," writes *Washington Post* columnist Eugene Robinson. He splits black America into four groups: the "Transcendent Elite"; the "Mainstream Middle Class," into which a majority of blacks fall; an "Emergent Community," consisting primarily of mixed-race families and black immigrants; and the "Abandoned," or large underclass of blacks living in the inner city or depressed areas in the rural South.[2] In contrast, linguist and political commentator John McWhorter discerns a black mind-set that he disapprovingly describes as a "double consciousness." This term was famously used in a different way by W. E. B. Du Bois in his most well-known book, *The Souls of Black Folk* (1903), to mean that every black American had "two souls, two thoughts, two unreconciled strivings," one being how we see ourselves, and the other being how we look at ourselves through the eyes of whites—in other words, being both black and an American. McWhorter uses the term to describe a mental outlook in which blacks privately preach hard work and self-help (black values to which I shall refer in moment) but embrace victimology in public. This double consciousness, he asserts, distorts what it means to be "authentically black."[3]

While I do recognize the many identities African Americans have, I do not think it can be denied that being black *means something,* even in today's society. And what it means is this: *a heightened sensibility or urgency about racial injustice—a black racial sensibility.* Similarly, Cornel West describes a black tradition of perpetual anger about the "state of black America," anger that "fuel[s] . . . boldness and defiance."[4] Black racial sensibility is a cultural condition, not a biological state. Tommie Shelby, a Harvard social scientist, explains in an interview the social conditions that give rise to this heightened sensibility about racial injustice: "I take it that the point of Black solidarity . . . is to try to bring about a more just society, a special society that satisfies the demand for racial justice. Black people obviously have a real stake in that because, being Black, they experience various forms of anti-Black prejudice and bias that limit our opportunities, limit our freedoms, make it difficult for us to flourish. . . . [B]eing subject to racial discrimination . . . [leads] us to think of ourselves as a unified political community."[5] Racial sensibility in blacks, then, comes from those parts of the black experience that are broadly similar, that represent the common trajectories in the lives of most blacks. Even Eugene Robinson cannot ignore a study by the Pew Research Center that shows that blacks earning more than one hundred thousand dollars a year "cling to the more traditional view that 'blacks can still be thought of as a single race because they have so much in common.' "[6]

Black racial sensibility is evidenced or expressed in myriad ways. Every time a racial event explodes on the American scene, such as those involving Trayvon Martin, Eric Gardner, and other police killings of un-armed black men, blacks of all walks of life—from President Obama to the unemployed protester, from the highly individualistic Touré to "race men" like Jesse Jackson and Al Sharpton—speak out pretty much with a single voice of racial condemnation and outrage. Black racial sensibility is at the bottom of Trayvon Martin's defiance when approached by George Zimmerman as a self-appointed neighborhood watchman. It is what motivates young black men to "mouth off" to police officers whom they deem to be racist or disrespectful. The truth is, blacks are more likely than whites to see racial injustice in a wide variety of social issues, such as the poor performance of public schools in black communities and the treatment of blacks by both the police and the courts in the criminal justice system. And they are likely to be right.[7]

Black racial sensibility is a foundational black value, or folkway. It fuels other black values. Among the latter are the beliefs that racism is omnipresent in our society, that special treatment is needed not as a handout but as a means of counteracting racial disadvantage, much of which lingers from slavery and Jim Crow, and that eliminating racism from society root and branch should be among the highest priorities of our government, thereby justifying big government. Self-respect, self-reliance, "black is beautiful," and respect for the black community are also important black values sustained by black racial sensibility. From the African American perspective, John Brown is a hero. W. E. B. Du Bois was right and Booker T. Washington was wrong. Both Martin Luther King Jr. and Malcolm X deserve holiday recognition. Jesse Jackson and Al Sharpton have done good things for blacks and therefore deserve our respect. African Americans have, in addition, developed strategies for survival in a society most blacks believe remains racist. Passed down to each new generation of blacks, one such strategy is *soyez méfiant* ("be mistrustful") of whites. Another survival strategy is imparted to young black men in particular: you have the right to be angry about past and current racial injustice, but you do not have the right to act in self-destructive ways. I received this talk from my father and later from my uncle when I was about twelve or thirteen years old. In my professional life, I have always referred to this talk as the "African American Survival Maxim." More commonly, blacks, including my African American students, refer to it simply as "The Talk."[8]

It is a fallacy to suppose that every black person has to be committed to a set of values before we can say that such a thing as "black identity" exists. As Shelby has noted, "but, of course, this has never been the case."[9] Conversely, although some whites do subscribe to some black values, an important benchmark of racial progress, such acceptance does not undercut the racial identity of these values any more than the participation of whites in the civil rights movement stripped that movement of its black identity. The fact that Joyce Carol Oates would write *The Sacrifice* to bear witness to the toxic cloud of racism and police violence that torment black lives is an important cultural event, but it does not belie the notion of black values.[10]

Black values not only exist, but they sometimes clash with mainstream values, creating the condition for cultural subordination. Black beauty is an example. While the mainstream American culture celebrates Beyoncé's light-skinned beauty, it regards dark-skinned women as unattractive. The issue was raised in the context of the "brown paper bag test" on an episode of *Black-ish*. This bold ABC sitcom shows an emergent blackness that is aware of the ways it is accommodating or acculturating nonblack forms within its blackness—hence "blackish"—such as the wife is mixed race, the son wants to be Jewish, and so on. Yet, the show, which first aired in the 2014–2015 season, stays close to black racial sensibility, such as the father's expressed anxiety concerning the children's seeming lack of racial awareness. Even more dramatically, Yale-educated Lupita Nyong'o, who won the 2014 Oscar for best actress in a supporting role in *12 Years a Slave*, left not a dry eye in the house when she confessed in a speech prior to receiving the award that as a young dark-skinned girl, she had wished her skin would become lighter: "I got teased and taunted about my night-shaded skin. My one prayer to God . . . was that I would wake up lighter-skinned."[11] Toni Morrison in *The Bluest Eye* writes about a black, poor, abused girl who wants blue eyes more than anything else. Referring, inter alia, to Serena Williams's reception in the white world of professional tennis, which she has dominated for more than a decade, Claudia Rankine notes poetically in *Citizen: An American Lyric* that black bodies still trouble whites.[12]

Other areas of conflict include discussions about the race problem itself. Whites in general think we talk too much about race, while blacks in general believe we do not talk enough about race. It is not surprising, then, that a black professional, black corporate executive, or even a black U.S. president has a difficult time raising the race issue on the job. Indeed, I have seen talented black executives or professionals lose credibility among their white peers by merely raising the issue of race on the job. Given the reluctance of most whites to even raise the issue of race, it is not surprising that they would feel less urgent about resolving the race issue than blacks do.[13]

When white and black values clash, something has to give way. When important black values give way in the mainstream culture, we have cultural subordination. Though it might seem counterintuitive, cultural subordination can occur even though our society is committed to cultural diversity. For the most part, this is so regardless of how one defines cultural diversity. To illustrate the point, I offer in this chapter four distinct definitions or models of cultural diversity. Each model is rooted in a specific theory, belief, or strategy regarding the best way for African Americans to achieve racial justice in today's post–civil rights society. As broached in the context of my discussion of juridical subordination, these post–civil rights theories are traditionalism, critical race theory, reformism, and limited separation. Extended to the cultural setting, each theory yields a specific vision of a diverse America, most of which can lead to cultural subordination. Racial subordination is manifested in the normal operation of these diversity models with the exception of one. Briefly, traditionalism, whose core belief is that race no longer matters in the quest for racial equality, suggests a form of cultural diversity—its own version of *cultural assimilation*—that peremptorily quashes black values held in conflict with mainstream American values. The latter are largely white middle-class values, the goal being to effectuate social cohesion. Critical race theory, whose basic civil rights orientation is that white hegemony matters most, suggests a cultural diversity model—*transculturalism*—that suppresses black values in conflict with mainstream values derived from a progressive blending of all American cultures (for example, "Happy Holidays" trumps "Happy Kwanzaa" in Macy's department stores). Reformism, whose core belief is that race still matters, implies a model of cultural diversity—what can be called *biculturalism*—that quashes black values in the mainstream through either cultural assimilation or transculturalism but that encourages ethnic expression at home and in other private places. Limited separation, whose core belief is that racial identity matters most in achieving racial equality, signifies a cultural diversity model—its version of *cultural pluralism*—that allows for more than one mainstream, each dominated by a single set of ethnic values, ergo, no cultural subordination. Although there are obvious similarities between these models of cultural diversity and their common namesakes, each model, or diversity norm, is self-consciously crafted in the image of its underlying post–civil rights theory. Each model uniquely informs racial justice discourse in today's post–Jim Crow society.

Before discussing these cultural diversity models, it is necessary to begin with a brief discussion of the legitimacy of cultural diversity in our society. This discussion will add important background information to my presentation of the cultural diversity models. More importantly, any solution to the problem of cultural subordination should, in my view, be faithful to the legitimacy of cultural diversity, that is, the reasons we as a society have a stated commitment to cultural diversity. We should want to vindicate the normative underpinnings of cultural diversity as we seek to resolve the problem of cultural subordination.

Legitimacy of Cultural Diversity

Cultural diversity's legitimacy in our society is based primarily on the fact that it enhances racial democracy—that is, human dignity (substantive democracy) and equal opportunity (Gunnar Myrdal's "American Creed"). The normative underpinnings of cultural diversity are very much in sync with the spirit of *Brown* discussed in chapter 1. That point will become clear as I unpack my argument.

When I think of the legitimacy of cultural diversity in our society (minimally defined as majority-minority mixing; more to come in due course), I think of a racial democracy. That term comprises two norms: democracy and the American Creed. Here, I am using the term "democracy" more in its substantive sense (its strong or broad sense) than in its procedural sense (its weak or narrow sense). Procedurally, democracy simply refers to a process of self-governance, directly or through representatives. Under self-rule, citizens find not only liberty, but also dignity and equality. This is the substantive side of democracy, a kind of "internal morality." As one distinguished jurist has put it, "Democracy has its own internal morality, based on the dignity and equality of all human beings." Substantively, the emphasis is on the qualities that make our society virtuous and stronger as a whole: "human dignity, equality, and tolerance. There is no [real] democracy without recognition of basic values and principles such as morality and justice."[14]

An equally important source of legitimacy for cultural diversity is what Gunnar Myrdal referred to as the American Creed. This rather uniquely American ideal refers to a society in which equal opportunity has "become the highest law of the land."[15] Some have argued that equal opportunity is the most important American value, that "[m]obility is the promise that lies at the heart of the American dream." America holds out the promise that persons born in poverty can die in wealth, noncitizens can become citizens and hold high office (not yet the highest office of the land), and citizens and noncitizens alike can obtain a free public education. True, we are constantly debating and refining our democratic ideals, such as the extent to which affordable health care should be included in the pantheon of our democratic ideals. But there is a widely stated belief in our society that a person's opportunities for success should not be fixed by arbitrary conditions such as birth or race.[16]

These, then, are the components of racial democracy—substantive democracy and the American Creed—which give legitimacy to America's embrace of cultural diversity. For a long time, however, there was very little commitment to cultural diversity in our society. This fact was reflected in the Supreme Court's civil rights decisions discussed in chapter 1. For example, the Supreme Court handed down the infamous case of *Plessy v. Ferguson* (1896). *Plessy,* as I discussed in chapter 1, constitutionalized a racial caste system. Even Justice Harlan's "great dissent," wherein he argued for a color-blind Constitution, saw America as a white society, as he wrote, "The white race deems itself to be the dominant race in this country. And so it is, in prestige, in achievements, in education, in wealth and in power. So, I doubt not, it will continue to be for all time, if it remains true to its great heritage and holds fast to the principles of constitutional liberty."[17] D. W. Griffith's hugely popular 1915 film *The Birth of a Nation* (originally titled *The Clansman*) affirmed this view of America. In that film, the Ku Klux Klan was portrayed as the defender of not just a white South but a white America.[18]

In contrast, most Americans today self-identify as a people committed to cultural diversity. Middle-class whites, in particular, seem far less inclined today to see the United States as a "white man's country" than they were during the days of Jim Crow. This cultural shift certainly informs what is arguably the Supreme Court's most important decision on cultural diversity—*Grutter v. Bollinger* (2003). Interestingly, other democratic societies, such as Canada, Germany, India, and countries fully committed to the European Union, have constitutional precommitments to diversity. The United States does not.[19]

A majority of the justices in *Grutter* ruled that student-body diversity constitutes a compelling governmental interest for purposes of satisfying the dictates of the Fourteenth Amendment's Equal Protection Clause. In constitutionalizing the diversity principle in *Grutter* as well as in its companion case, *Gratz v. Bollinger* (2003), the Court fully embraced the legitimacy of cultural diversity. Echoing both substantive democracy and the American Creed, the Court saw legitimacy in diversity's "potential to enrich everyone's education and thus make a law school class stronger than the sum of its parts."[20] This finding was based on hard evidence rather than mushy sentiment. As the Court wrote, "In addition to the expert studies and reports entered into evidence at trial, numerous studies show that student body diversity promotes learning outcomes, and 'better prepares students for an increasingly diverse workforce and society, and better prepares them as professionals.' "[21] This thinking clearly has legs; it applies beyond the facts of the case (higher education) as the Court subsequently indicated in *Parents Involved in Community Schools v. Seattle School District No. 1* (2007), a case involving K–12 schools. In that case, Justice Kennedy's concurrence read *Grutter* to mean that "racial composition . . . [is] one aspect" of "a diverse student body."[22]

The Court in *Grutter* made explicit reference to the fact that cultural diversity had become a high norm of the social order. Cultural elites and middle-class whites viewed cultural diversity as an essential component of a vibrant and changing America in the twenty-first century. They strongly believed that cultural diversity enriches society, that it makes society stronger than the sum of its parts, that it is a defining part of our democracy. This message was conveyed to the Supreme Court in no uncertain terms in amicus curiae (friends-of-the-Court) briefs filed in the case by cultural elites. The Court noted, for example, that:

> [M]ajor American businesses have made clear that the skills needed in today's increasingly global marketplace can only be developed through exposure to widely diverse people, cultures, ideas, and viewpoints. Brief for 3M et al. as *Amici Curiae* 5; Brief for General Motors Corp. as *Amicus Curiae* 3–4. What is more, high-ranking retired officers and civilian leaders of the United States military assert that, "based on [their] decades of experience," a "highly qualified, racially diverse officer corps . . . is essential to the military's ability to fulfill its principle mission to provide national security." Brief for Julius W. Becton, Jr. et al. as *Amici Curiae* 27 . . . To fulfill its mission, the military "must be selective in admissions for training and education for the officer corps, *and* it must train and educate a highly qualified, racially diverse officer corps in a racially diverse setting." Id., at 29 (emphasis in original). We agree that "it requires only a small step from this analysis to conclude that our country's other most selective institutions must remain both diverse and selective."[23]

Underscoring the power of cultural diversity in today's society, Walmart, the largest private employer in the United States, has instructed "its top 100 law firms that at least one person of color and one woman must be among the top five relationship attorneys that handle its business." What this means is that "law firms that pack their lower ranks with minorities and women while leaving white men in charge will lose business with the nation's largest retailer."[24]

Although *Grutter* spoke *ex cathedra* on the matter of cultural diversity, the opinion did not endeavor to define the term. Looking to the plain meaning of the term, the *Oxford English Dictionary* defines "cultural diversity" as "the existence of a variety of cultural or ethnic groups within a society," which is similar to at least one scholarly definition: "the representation, in one social system, of people with distinctly different group affiliations of cultural significance."[25] The representation could involve the simple mixing of different racial groups, the irreducible minimum definition, or, more ambitiously, the lateral transmission of folkways among racial groups in mainstream society. I find each of these definitions to be problematic because they beg an important question, a question that sets the stage for an inquiry into cultural subordination—to wit, *Which folkway of the various groups thrown into the mix should govern in the mainstream?* For me, this is (or should be) the all-important question in any discussion of cultural diversity. Four possible answers are suggested by traditionalism, critical race theory, reformism, and limited separation.

Traditionalism's Cultural Assimilation

Traditionalism's basic orientation toward the American race problem is quite simple: race no longer matters. Proponents of this post–civil rights theory believe that residual racism does not prevent African Americans from achieving worldly success and personal happiness in our post–civil rights society. They recognize that blacks face problems, but they see these problems as internal and, hence, self-inflicted.[26]

Given traditionalism's core belief, one might suppose that traditionalists have little or no desire for cultural diversity. Yet traditionalists understand that interracial marriage and immigration will continue to change the face of the American mainstream from "Beaver Cleaver pink" to "café-au-lait."[27] What they wish to preserve, however, are the values that control the mainstream. In other words, the faces in the crowd can be white, black, yellow, brown, or mixed, but the mind-sets and sensibilities that govern important questions must be of one unifying type— white middle class. This invokes the irreducible minimum definition of cultural diversity just discussed. It is a version of cultural assimilation— black face, white mind.

To be sure, minority values are represented in the American mainstream. But these values are consistent with or certainly do not threaten white middle-class values. Thus, some black esthetic folkways are thrown into the cultural mix ("co-opted" some would say)—such as Motown in pop culture and now jazz in high culture. But conflicting values are not. White racial sensibility (a preference for racial innocence) outweighs black racial sensibility (a steadfast resistance to racism), just as Mark Cuban would have it in the case of Donald Sterling's racism.[28]

Although majority-minority mixing under cultural assimilation may technically count as cultural diversity (distinct groups are represented in the mainstream), the exchange of values, if any, is quite low. For that reason, one can understand why some might not call this diversity at all. But diversity is measured in this case by individual inclusion rather than by a significant exchange of values. To Justice Thomas, this is "aesthetics" diversity; diversity is but a visual moment. Not only does this style of cultural assimilation offer the least amount of diversity possible, it is also a recipe for cultural subordination.[29]

The process of black adaptation to white middle-class values is almost certain to lead to cultural subordination. Culture flows mainly in one direction; white middle-class values trump important black values. Is this racism? Not necessarily. Most traditionalists merely wish to prevent the type of debilitating social conflicts that can erupt in heterogeneous societies. They desire social cohesion among diverse groups, and for that reason blacks are expected to "adopt[] the customs and attitudes of the prevailing culture."[30] People of different racial or ethnic backgrounds, thereby, become one. Assimilated blacks will come to see themselves as part of the dominant social group.[31]

My read of traditionalists is that they would not concede that their style of cultural diversity—the process of black adaptation to a white middle-class mainstream culture—constitutes cultural subordination. Instead, they would argue that it promotes racial advancement. "Ultimately, black social and economic progress largely depends on the sense that we are one nation."[32] African Americans can only be successful by blending in. They must not only speak and write standard English (with which I would agree), but they must also reject racial identity, spend less time thinking about race, especially slavery and Jim Crow, refrain from mouthing off to the police, make the best of the education given to them, and keep their families intact. Other cultural diversity models, as we shall see, take issue with this line of thought. I have my own concerns, which I shall present point by point shortly. Before turning to that discussion, it behooves us to dig deeper into the traditionalists' brand of cultural assimilation to gain a clearer understanding of its merits.[33]

The traditionalist idea of cultural assimilation is, in fact, a version of the "melting pot." It is a rather uncomplicated version that begins with the conviction that "Anyone could become an American" provided that he or she embraces our "common civic culture." Follow the path of the Irish, traditionalists would advise blacks. At one time, most Americans saw Irish immigrants "as drunks, ruffians and criminals." The vehicle used to transport arrestees, "paddy wagon," takes it name from a time when the Irish were frequent occupants. "America's elites . . . caustically scorned Irish cultural behavior . . . to the point that Irish leaders felt obliged to pretend at least to adhere to the standards of the larger society." With the help of private charities and the settlement-house movement, the "Irish rose to average levels of income and education by the 1950s, and in 1960 an Irish Catholic was elected president of the United States." Today, they have "conform[ed] to the standards of the larger society" and, hence, have "become interwoven into the fabric of American life."[34] Far from being a recipe for cultural subordination, traditionalists view this as a prescription for success in America, opened to all races and ethnicities.

One of the most prominent traditionalists is the black pundit Shelby Steele. He uses an example from his personal past to illustrate the process of assimilation he and other traditionalists envision. During his adolescence, a white woman helped him correct his grammar and eliminate his use of slang so that he might more easily and successfully move through the mainstream culture—high culture not pop culture. Initially reluctant and even hostile toward a white person's unsolicited attempt to change what he regarded as black identity, Steele soon appreciated the fact that the woman wished only to aid him in succeeding in the dominant culture. He came to understand that mainstream society would penalize him for his lack of standard verbal skills. Thus, for Steele, diversity means greater reliance on individual identity rather than black identity. Blacks should focus on being *successful individuals,* which will prepare them for successful assimilation into the mainstream culture. "[T]he next collective challenge for black America is simply to walk out and meet the words and ideas that make us tense."[35]

Other traditionalists sound a similar note. Thomas Sowell, a renowned scholar whom Justice Thomas has called his intellectual guru, suggests that African Americans are foolishly creating a system of social disadvantage when they celebrate cultural isolation. Racial identity,

Sowell insists, exacts a heavy racial toll on any group because "[f]ew, if any, of the great advances in human civilization have come from isolated peoples."[36] Thus, African Americans, Sowell continues, must endeavor to learn from those around them and pattern themselves after successful groups. Traditionalist Dinesh D'Souza agrees with Sowell and Steele. He counsels African Americans to follow the example of black immigrants, such as the West Indians, Haitians, and Nigerians, who have, in his view, successfully assimilated into mainstream American society. "Black immigrants from Africa average the highest educational attainment of any population in the country, including whites and Asians."[37] D'Souza believes the descendants of slaves can duplicate the success of black immigrants if they follow the latter's mind-set as expressed by a Jamaican immigrant: "I'm too busy working two jobs to worry about the white man's racism."[38] The best strategy for racial advancement, in D'Souza's opinion, is for African Americans to shut up about racism and realize that they are better off because of slavery. (This is like telling Jews that they should be grateful for the Holocaust because it helped create the state of Israel, and I doubt D'Souza wants to go there.) Is this a recipe for racial success or racial subordination?[39]

Arguably, cultural assimilation was on full display in one of the most successful shows in television history, *The Cosby Show*. Although the person for whom the show was named has subsequently dishonored himself with the revelation of alleged sexual misconduct spanning many years and many victims, this all-black sitcom was the most watched television show in the nation for four consecutive years in the 1980s. Indeed, "there were nights when more than half the homes watching television in the United States were in its audience."[40] *The Cosby Show* was not the first successful black sitcom on television. But unlike its predecessors, such as *Amos 'n' Andy* in the 1950s and *The Jeffersons, Sanford and Son,* and *Good Times* in the 1970s, *The Cosby Show*, as its adviser Dr. Alvin Poussaint, a black psychiatrist from Harvard, explains, avoided the "jivin,' jammin,' streetwise style stuff that is the worst kind of stereotyping."[41] *The Cosby Show* portrayed a black upper-middle-class family with dignity and humanity. Reformist Michael Eric Dyson agrees with Poussaint, noting "the most useful aspects of Cosby's dismantling of racial mythology and stereotyping is that it has permitted America to view black folk as *human beings*" (emphasis in original).[42] One TV critic argues that *The Cosby Show* brought to pop culture black personalities centered on universal family problems. The show's characters tackled these problems based on a positive approach to family life. Both parents taught the children such family-oriented values as personal responsibility, empathy, sharing, and respect for other people's possessions.[43]

Others, however, criticize the show for its unabashed cultural assimilation; and, in particular, for letting "racism off the hook."[44] Critics argue that *The Cosby Show* presented "a misleadingly cozy picture, a sugar candy world unfettered by racism, crime, and economic deprivation."[45] Reformist Henry Louis Gates Jr. suggests that the show's racial innocence, its avoidance of racism, made the Huxtable family, "in most respects, just like white people," and that this made the show seem unreal.[46] Jazz, black art, HBCUs, and track and field were frequently represented on the show, but not the thing that sits at the center of the black ethos—black racial sensibility. There was very little racism, racial discrimination, and other questions or concerns that preoccupy the hearts and minds of most African Americans regardless of socioeconomic class. This omission has impelled Dyson to conclude that the show's "lack of acknowledgment of the underside of the American Dream . . . was the most unfortunate feature of the Huxtable opulence."[47]

Responding to his critics, Bill Cosby, the show's co-creator, defended the show's cultural slant: "To say that they [the Huxtables] are not black enough is a denial of the American Dream and the American way of life. My point is that this is an American family—an *American* family—and if you want to live like they do, and you're willing to work, the opportunity is there" (emphasis in original).[48] Yet twenty-two years after *The Cosby Show* went off the air, another successful black sitcom, *Black-ish*, placed the black experience, in all its contemporary complexity, at center stage. Each week, the main male character, Dre Johnson, unlike Cliff Huxtable, expresses a heightened sense of racial justice at work and at home. Though as successful and wealthy as Cliff Huxtable, Dre Johnson worries constantly about whether the family's socioeconomic status has brought too much cultural assimilation into the family, especially the children who exhibit very little racial awareness openly. The name of the show says it all—*Black-ish*. Compared to this show or the sitcoms of the 1970s, *The Cosby Show* was indeed a celebration of cultural assimilation.

Another example of cultural subordination in pop culture is CBS's treatment of the hugely popular (and often vulgar) black comedian Dave Chappelle. In 2004, Chappelle signed a $50 million contract with Viacom, the parent company of CBS, to do a comedy show. Chappelle's salary was higher than the combined salaries of fellow employees Mike Wallace, Morley Safer, and Ed Bradley, all of whom were distinguished veterans of CBS's *60 Minutes,* TV's longest running news-magazine program. Chappelle was "asked" to include white characters in his racially charged comedy show to broaden his viewership. In response, Chappelle walked out on the deal, wondering aloud whether TV executives would have asked Jerry Seinfeld, the coproducer of *Seinfeld,* or the producers of *Friends* to add a black character, let alone several principal black characters, to their all-white shows. In 2014 *Saturday Night Live* added a black female to its cast in response to criticism that the show lacked diversity.[49]

Some traditionalists take a more flexible stance on the extent to which African Americans must embrace white middle-class values. Stephan and Abigail Thernstrom, for example, maintain that they are not asking "black Americans to turn their backs on all things 'black'—to deny all cultural differences associated with group membership." As they say, "Jews haven't; Armenians haven't; Ukrainians haven't. Many Americans arrange their private lives so as to spend much of their time with others of the same background. Purging all racial distinctions from our law and our public life would pose no threat to those who wish to live in a predominantly black neighborhood, attend an all-black church, and otherwise associate primarily or even exclusively with their fellow African Americans." Thus, the Thernstroms would confine cultural assimilation to the public sphere, allowing cultural identity to flourish in homes and private clubs. Steele, Sowell, and most other traditionalists do not believe it is possible or practical to turn off mainstream culture in private and turn it on in public. For them, public and private lives intertwine. Steele would point to his own life's journey as proof as well as to Jeff Hobbs's book *The Short and Tragic Life of Robert Peace: A Brilliant Young Man Who Left Newark for the Ivy League.* In this book, Hobbs recounts the life and death of a black Yale student who tried, unsuccessfully, to live in two cultures: a New Jersey ghetto and Yale University. More gifted than even the average Yale undergraduate, Peace, nonetheless, never felt "authentic" at Yale and consequently failed to take advantage of the opportunities Yale afforded to its undergraduates and graduates. Peace's life ended tragically in a drug-related murder in the home of one of his childhood friends from the hood.[50]

No traditionalist, however, would argue that black culture should trump white middle-class culture in the mainstream. Therein lies cultural subordination. It is all about the mainstream. The racial sensibility of white America trumps the racial sensibility of black America. Although African Americans appear within mainstream institutions, they have no distinctive, certainly no empowering, voice. Traditionalists see this as racial progress. They believe, for example, that when "ACME Corporation" hires an African American executive, it should do so not because the candidate is different, but because she is *not* different. The corporation should expect the African American executive's views to be interchangeable with the corporation's clientele, John Q. Public. It is in this way that the blue-chip executive brings value to the corporation. The value is purely in the form of intelligence and, hence, goes beyond race, gender, or ethnicity. It is the type of value that allows the minority employee to seamlessly assimilate into the corporation's mainstream culture rather than to stick out as a token. [51]

I reject cultural assimilation on several grounds. Most importantly, cultural assimilation, with its promotion of a one-way transmission of values, denies African Americans the opportunity to add their footprints in the American mainstream. Assimilation allows African Americans to be the entertainers of society—dancers, singers, athletes, and celebrities—but not the canon makers of the social order. Telling young blacks not to "mouth off" at police officers who hurl profanities at them denies them the opportunity to initiate a reshaping of the police culture, as well as their First Amendment rights. Cultural assimilation forces blacks to sacrifice their ethnic identity and emotional comfort. African Americans even have to waive the basic human right to name one's child, as studies have shown that résumés with distinctively black names (such as DeShawn, Shanice, or Ebony) tend to garner fewer job interviews than résumés with traditionally white names (such as Andrew, Katherine, or Hillary). Cultural assimilation also gives corporate executives license to tell the lone black female executive that she will not "perform" her job well wearing braids or an Afro hairstyle. Indeed, one of the most successful black graduates of my law school reports that she had to stop wearing an Afro when she was hired at a prestigious law firm. The partners made it clear to her that the Afro had to go if she wanted to stay and become a partner. She stayed and did become a partner, minus the Afro and minus her identity and pride. Cultural assimilation, in short, is cultural subordination in the worst way possible: it denies blacks the power to shape the racial conditions of the mainstream culture, leaving them stuck in the chasm of racial degradation.[52]

The major flaw in cultural assimilation is its assumption that African Americans (slave descendants) and other racial groups, including black immigrants, are similarly situated. African Americans have more difficulty assimilating into the American mainstream than do Asians, Latinos, or even black immigrants, the latter of whom, as we have seen, have the highest educational attainment in the country. No other group occupies a position of racial degradation comparable to blacks. Even the immigrant knows that "he stands above the long-suffering Black American citizen." My female law students from various African countries tell me that their parents have admonished them not to date or marry an African American. Every immigrant group has come to this country voluntarily looking for opportunities (they arrived here "on top of Plymouth Rock"). The ancestors of slave descendants were brought here against their will (they arrived here "under Plymouth Rock"). This makes a huge difference psychologically. "It has been a challenge for African Americans to look at their own history, and all too often, at their own personal experience, and not see our country in negative terms."[53] Even black immigrants, as columnist Clarence Page notes, "do not have a history of American slavery in their families." Slavery did not touch slave descendants lightly. They live amid the lost and the degradation of slavery and, therefore, find special meaning in First Lady Michelle Obama's remark, "I wake up every morning in a house that was built by slaves."[54]

Orlando Patterson, a Harvard social scientist, and other distinguished scholars raise the troubling issue of whether cultural assimilation is at all possible for blacks, even the black middle class. Patterson observes that "for nonblacks, assimilation is alive and well in America." He notes that "about 80 percent of the population define themselves as exclusively white," and that this sociological category is growing "thanks to the fact that almost half of all Hispanics now define themselves as 'white alone.' "[55] By contrast, Patterson writes:

> The great exception to this process of social incorporation is black Americans. . . . In private life blacks are almost as isolated from whites today as they were under Jim Crow. Whatever the reason—persisting covert racism, black racial preferences abetted by identity politics, or both—their isolation means that *the problem of ethno-racial relations in America remains, at heart, a black-white issue.* As the example of Henry Louis Gates Jr. demonstrates, even prominent upper-middle-class blacks risk being racially profiled and subjected to humiliating treatment by white policemen, as well as explicit racist abuse [emphasis added].[56]

Standing on its own, the traditionalists' justification for cultural assimilation (which in my view is cultural subordination) lacks merit. There is danger, traditionalists argue, in a society that celebrates or even recognizes racial differences over racial similarities in the mainstream. After 9/11, many Americans would probably agree with the late Arthur Schlesinger Jr. that "we ought to pay more attention to what holds the nation together," or that we are traveling down a dangerous road if we "decide that people belong irrevocably to one or another ethnic community."[57] The war on terror has created "new pressures on minority members to minimize any outward signs of difference."[58] But, as my colleague and literary scholar Carlton Floyd has remarked, Schlesinger's argument completely misses the point that the very issues he raises regarding holding this nation together are precisely what has subordinated African Americans, that good people like Schlesinger cannot or will not see that *it is the group, or "club," they want blacks to belong to that is the problem.* This club degrades black identity (things black), which is why so many blacks feel impelled to declare loudly that black lives matter.

I would add that the fear of difference does not justify the suppression of black values or racial progress. I would not equate the situation of blacks in America with that of, say, radical Muslims in the Netherlands. Although different, middle-class African American behaviors and values are not extreme and certainly pose no threat to the American way of life. One could even argue that African Americans have long demonstrated a deep belief in the core values of our liberal, democratic society more so than many whites, such as those who practice racism. Whether against slavery, Jim Crow, or present-day racial discrimination, the black struggle has always been a struggle for the American Dream. Far from subverting the culture of a free and open society, African American folkways—including the foundation value of a heightened sensibility about racial injustice—are supportive of that culture. African Americans have been on the right side of history when it comes to racial equality. Finally, unlike the Muslims in the Netherlands or other Western societies, African Americans are not new arrivals. African Americans have, in fact, been a part of this country from its inception. This gives African Americans a stake in American society and a concomitant status that allows them to have a certain say in shaping the mainstream culture.[59]

But can too much diversity in mainstream institutions be counterproductive? Sure it can. Studies show that cultural differences can be a hindrance in the corporate setting. Although a corporation desires executives who can think outside of the box ("informational diversity") and, hence, bring fresh ideas and information to the table, it cannot tolerate differences in the core value assumptions of its work groups ("value diversity"). If key employees do not share the same core values—hard work, dedication (meaning, inter alia, work trumps family), competitiveness, a common understanding of the corporate mission, and a common acceptance of their roles on the "team"—productivity will suffer. Diversity, then, can be a liability rather than an asset to businesses. This conclusion was reached in a seminal study of dozens of diversity reports: "From this study we can identify the types of diversity that are associated with various types of performance. For a team to be effective, [its] members should have high information diversity and low value diversity. For a team to be efficient, [its] members should have low value diversity. For a team to have high morale (higher satisfaction, intent to remain, and commitment) or to perceive itself as effective, it should be composed of participants with low value diversity."[60] Even entrepreneurs who operate illegal businesses understand the importance of low value diversity to the success of their enterprises. For example, in *Freakonomics*, Steven Levitt and Stephen Dubner describe a narcotics business run by a street gang called the Black Gangster Disciple Nation of Chicago (or Black Disciples). This business was run like McDonald's, complete with franchising arrangements and detailed account ledgers. The Black Disciples demanded low value diversity among its cohort of key employees: hard work, dedication, competitiveness, and commitment to the business's mission, which was to make money from the distribution of drugs buttressed by the use of violence to protect business interests. As a result, the business generated monthly revenue of thirty-two thousand dollars.[61]

Value diversity, in short, does not usually correlate with good performance either in the workplace or in society as a whole. Failure to assimilate to core values will likely foreshadow the failure of the society, institutions, and the individual, including African Americans. The success that comes from cultural assimilation will not only keep the country together, traditionalists believe, but will also improve the socioeconomic conditions of blacks as well as overcome much of the lingering racism that blacks continue to encounter.

None of this, in my view, justifies cultural subordination. I say, again, there is nothing in the middle-class African American ethos that demonstrates a disdain for core American or core corporate values. Chapter 3 clearly shows that value diversity between middle-class blacks and whites on core questions is quite low. Problems arise when racism, a *negative* American value, is brought into the mix. When middle-class blacks are repeatedly subjected to racial stereotyping and other forms of racism and racial discrimination, or when their employers' mission includes taking unfair advantage of the black community (such as by selling blacks worthless insurance policies or subprime mortgages or committing acts of environmental racism), or when racial subordination protects racism (as in the case of Mark Cuban) or is otherwise allowed to flourish, or when, in short, the mainstream culture does not see the urgency of pursuing racial advancement, value diversity is likely to be high, with a number of whites siding with African Americans.[62]

The traditionalist version of cultural assimilation raises no dearth of questions, none more important that these: Must blacks suffer the consequences of assimilation—the inevitable displacement and even degradation of black pride and heritage—for a piece of the pie? Must blacks suffer one form of inequality (cultural subordination) to alleviate another form of inequality (socioeconomic deficiency)? Is cultural assimilation even available for all blacks who seek it?

Critical Race Theory's Transculturalism

From the tenets of critical race theory comes a cultural diversity model—*transculturalism*—that is at the opposite end of the spectrum from traditionalism's cultural assimilation. If cultural assimilation offers too little cultural diversity, does transculturalism offer too much? Surprisingly, many of my minority students, who tend to be progressive, fall into the latter category. They see cultural subordination embedded in transculturalism. Black values are, indeed, subordinated to conflicting blended values.

Based on its core post–civil rights position—white hegemony matters—critical race theory's cultural goal is quite clear: a wholesale transformation of the American sociocultural order that gives all groups a seat at the table. This objective goes beyond mere reform, as reform is insufficiently transformative, incapable of generating the sociocultural revolution critical race theory envisions. As Derrick Bell urges, critical race theory seeks to create a "specific, more egalitarian, state of affairs. . . . [It seeks] to empower and include traditionally excluded views . . . [and to] see all-inclusiveness as the ideal."[63]

This ideal—"all-inclusiveness"—contemplates, at the very least, a merger of voices (or values)—outsider and insider. The resultant merger suggests a form of cultural diversity that is quite different from traditionalists' cultural assimilation, as it is more accepting of minority values. All cultures come together to form a new American melting pot, one marked not by one-way integration, as in the case of cultural assimilation, but by two-way (or multiway) integration—a true lateral exchange of values. The mainstream, therefore, is not white, nor is it black or brown or even gray (white and black mixed). Instead, it is mocha, a blending of all cultures. That's transculturalism.

Transculturalism, then, is not "a linear process of [racial] obliteration, but a dynamic one in which minority and majority cultures converge."[64] Each group contributes something of value to a new, blended mainstream culture. Although there is assimilation under transculturalism, "assimilation has less to do with one group adapting to another," as in the case of traditionalism's cultural assimilation or the hard form of biculturalism at its final stage (discussed in due course), "than with the blurring of boundaries among groups. . . . [M]ainstream culture is more malleable than monolithic."[65] My colleague, sociologist Judith Liu, refers to this as "assimilation-lite."

Critical race theory, thus, seems to envision a culture that is shaped by an increasingly multiracial population—a population mainly driven by marriage and immigration. In some respects, this cultural shift may already be taking place, primarily in pop culture. Beyoncé, Alicia Keys, Halle Berry, and other multiracial public figures feed the growing demand in the entertainment, advertising, and fashion industries for multiracial faces. Standards of beauty in pop culture seem to be changing from blond hair and blue eyes to something considerably more mixed. Men and women are increasingly found in nontraditional roles in the media and workplace. Gays and lesbians are certainly out of the closet.[66]

Critical race theorists are sophisticated enough to understand that although the mainstream in pop culture may be changing from white to mocha, we have a long way to go to reach what they would regard as cultural nirvana. Pop culture still "treats white as the default setting,"[67] and it is still tainted by racial stereotypes. High culture continues to be largely white. Mainstream political practices, business conventions, legal rules, educational policies, and other cultural standards are still set from the purview of middle-class-white-heterosexual males.[68]

Were transculturalism to come into full-blown existence, it would certainly create significant changes in our culture. It would require, for example, universities and colleges to incorporate courses on race and racism, gender and sexism into their core curricula rather than as special electives. Those in attendance at public events would be asked to observe a moment of silence for private reflection rather than be led into public prayer to a particular Supreme Being. A fundamental change in the concept of "merit" in higher education to reflect the sensibilities of outsiders would take place. Merit would include not only technical proficiency but also character traits. A racist physicist, for example, would be considerably less qualified for an opening in the physics department than a nonracist physicist, even if the latter had less technical proficiency yet was still solidly qualified. Although both are well educated, the former would be regarded as an educated fool (unable to function competently within a diverse culture) and, hence, unqualified for the position in a culturally diverse university setting.

In his book *La Nueva California*, David Hayes-Bautista gives us a partial glimpse (Latino/white) of what transculturalism might look like in California. He projects that by the year 2040, Latinos will become the largest racial or ethnic group in the state. Latino immigration to California, a high rate of Latino births, and the prevalence of interracial marriages to Latinos infuse the Golden State's mainstream culture with a heavy Latino influence. This new mainstream culture, which Hayes-Bautista calls "Californio," is presided over by a fictitious governor, "Governor Maria Isabel Rodriquez de Smith," whose very name suggests cultural fusion. Hayes-Bautista describes a "best-case" scenario for this mainstream culture. Soccer has become the sport of choice in the "Californio" culture. The soccer ball is jokingly referred to as a "globalized" version of the two-pointed football of bygone days. Medical schools have invested millions of dollars into researching culturally driven alternative medicine. The education system and its curriculum have been revamped in such a way as to tell the state's rich history in a culturally sensitive fashion, including a comprehensive account of the role of racial minorities in the development of the "Californio" identity. People in the state will speak with a pronounced "Californio" accent, eat distinctively fusion cuisine, and have a unique, brown-skinned, almond-eyed blond phenotype. By accepting its diverse population and harnessing its strengths, society has a brilliant future ahead.[69]

Transculturalism may be old wine in a new bottle. Arthur Schlesinger Jr. has reminded us that the original concept of the "melting

pot," broached in a 1908 play titled *The Melting Pot*, written by Israel
Zangwill, was "the idea that immigrants can be transformed into
Americans, producing a new, highly synthetic, or hybrid, culture." This
is an America in which everyone speaks English, although the language
becomes more colorful over the years with the addition of new ethnic
terms, or slang. It is an America in which everyone observes the work
ethic, but the way we work may change as businesses incorporate more
efficient means of production introduced by immigrants.[70]

Although in a technical sense it is perhaps true that critical race
theorists have embraced an old concept of diversity, it is also true that
transculturalism has never really taken shape in our society. More often
than not, Americans understood the term "melting pot" to mean one-
way integration, cultural assimilation. Indeed, this is how the "melting
pot" has largely played out in America. Perhaps the most famous example involves one of America's greatest industrialists, Henry Ford.

In 1914, Henry Ford increased wages at his automobile factory
from $2.34 for a nine-hour day to an unprecedented $5.00 for an eight-
hour day. This was less largess than a bribe. In exchange for the increased
pay, Ford's mostly immigrant workforce had to learn English, live the
"clean life," and become American citizens. These requirements were
enforced through the "Sociological Department," complete with 150 of
its own employees, which Ford created in his company. After taking the
oath of citizenship, each employee was required to go through a cere-
mony that symbolized the acquisition of a new identity—an American
identity. In dramatic fashion, each new citizen, wearing his or her ethnic
garb, marched onto the stage toward a large replica of a melting pot.
After switching into a business suit or a traditional American dress behind the melting pot, each new American emerged onstage to thunder-
ous applause. Critical race theorists seem to believe Ford's vision of the
melting pot remains transfixed in the minds of most Americans today,
certainly the traditionalists. And it is this image of the American mainstream that critical race theorists seek to change.[71]

Critical race theory's cultural diversity model is problematic. I see
in it a recipe for cultural subordination. Each group contributing to the
new melting pot will have to surrender some (perhaps most) of its own
identity as it assumes a new identity in the mainstream and in private.

Each member of the polity, including outsiders, must be willing to break through new boundaries. As there is but one mainstream under transculturalism, black values that clash with mainstream values are subject to suppression. For example, "Happy Holidays" could be the blended value that department stores, banks, the media, and other mainstream institutions use in lieu of the traditional greeting of "Merry Christmas." That value would trump all conflicting ethnic expressions, including "Happy Kwanzaa" and "Feliz Navidad," preferred by African Americans and Latinos, respectively. This is not racism; it is simply a choice made among competing legitimate values.

Transculturalism is difficult to effectuate. Julie Su and Eric Yamamoto demonstrate just how difficult it is to give up the characteristics that define one's cultural uniqueness. They discuss a lawsuit involving Thai and Latino garment-district workers. Each group had to surrender some of its identity if it hoped to forge a successful litigation. The coalition ultimately failed in part because the government and the media focused on the unique features of the groups, including the severe enslavement of the Thais. Common themes, such as sweatshop oppression, were underaddressed and underreported.[72]

What this clearly demonstrates is that critical race theory's cultural diversity model, transculturalism, can only work if the constituent groups are prepared to surrender some or much of their cultural identity; that is, to accept a degree of cultural subordination. Exactly what each group must surrender will presumably be determined in the marketplace of ideas, in other words, by what works best for society as a whole. But some racial minorities might be reluctant to surrender values they regard as precious and, hence, not subject to negotiation. Some Latinos, for example, regard bilingualism as a cultural necessity and may not be willing to give that up. Indeed, Latino educators in ten California school districts sued the state of California to end English-only testing of students who are learning English as a second language. Bilingualism does not work under transculturalism, which contemplates a more blended mainstream language, perhaps "Spanglish." But even that seems insufficiently blended. What happens if by consensus English only, mildly peppered with ethnic expressions, becomes the cultural norm? If that happens, I suppose critical race theorists could accept it on the ground that, unlike cultural assimilation, it is the product of a legitimate negotiation between outsiders and insiders and among outsiders.[73]

At first glance, transculturalism may appear to be the most progressive diversity model imaginable. But some might find it to be too progressive or perhaps progressive in the wrong way. Requiring a group to shed important features of its cultural identity undercuts the very notion of cultural diversity. Indeed, as I mentioned earlier, minority and female students in my civil rights seminars, who tend to be among the most progressive students in the law school, typically express frustration and even annoyance with what they regard as transculturalism's "self-satisfied imperialism." Maintaining one's cultural identity is very important to many young Americans of all colors. They do not wish to surrender their identity to a marginalizing mainstream culture. They will not suffer cultural subordination. Transculturalism, to say the least, will be a hard sell to the very people it is intended to help most.

Reformism's Biculturalism—Hard and Soft

The reformists' core post–civil rights belief—race still matters—suggests a unique way of reconciling conflicting majority and subaltern folkways—to wit, *biculturalism*. This model of cultural diversity envisions African Americans maintaining cultural ties in two civic places—public and private—in two different ways. In one model, what can be called "hard biculturalism," the public, or mainstream, culture is governed by white middle-class folkways; in the other, what can be called "soft biculturalism," the public culture is governed by blended values. The private domain (for example, home and private institutions) in both models is shaped by black values. Hence, the major difference between hard and soft biculturalism is that the former's mainstream consists of cultural assimilation, while the latter's mainstream entails transculturalism. "Like other groups in American society who retain their cultural identities, African Americans must master the dominant culture."[74]

Hard biculturalism has an unmistakable presence in the American culture. Matthew Jacobson argues that most Americans today view America not as a melting pot of any sort, but as a society in which ethnic groups maintain close connections to their roots. Most ethnic Americans, he argues, self-describe as hyphenated Americans, such as Italian-American, Mexican-American, and Jewish-American. Some have argued that the turning point in the evolution of biculturalism was the 1977 TV miniseries *Roots*. After that series, "not only blacks but all ethnic groups saw themselves whole, traceable across oceans and centuries to the remotest ancestral village. . . . Americans have become like those adoptees who demand the long-denied knowledge of heritage."[75] Jacobson disagrees with this view.

He submits that white ethnic groups' embrace of biculturalism actually began around the time of the Kennedy administration. The Kennedys are often described as the quintessential Irish-American clan. When President John F. Kennedy made a state visit to Ireland, his ancestral home, in 1963, he was greeted with an official welcome from Éamon de Valera, the Irish revolutionary, anticolonial leader, and statesman. President Kennedy was recognized as "the chief executive and first citizen of the great Republic of the West," as "the representative of that great country in which our people sought refuge when the misery of tyrant laws drove them from the mother land," and as the "distinguished scion of our race who has won first place amongst his fellow countrymen."[76] Responding to this warm welcome, President Kennedy referred to the United States as "a nation of immigrants," and then said to the crowd, "[T]his [Ireland] is not the land of my birth, but it is the land for which I hold the greatest affection."[77] Jacobson contrasts the president's sentiments with the preference for cultural assimilation expressed by the president's father, Joseph Kennedy. When he was referred to as an Irishman, the elder Kennedy blasted back, "I was born here. My children were born here. What the hell do I have to do to be called an American?"[78]

Whether hard or soft, biculturalism means that African Americans must function well in two different worlds. The African American Wall Street banker works in a white world, which includes socializing with her coworkers or blue-chip clients at the Wall Street Club during the weekdays, but "hanging out" with members from her own racial group on weekends. There is no mistake, however, as to where the mainstream culture lies: Wall Street. The Black Student Union (BSU) is the quintessential example of the hard form of biculturalism. This racially identifiable college institution is intended to help black students adjust to college life and, upon graduation, become comfortable with and successful in mainstream American institutions. BSU members are expected to be bicultural—black in private and white in the mainstream of college life. It is also expected that BSU members will become increasingly acculturated by graduation. As the acculturation process unfolds, ties to a former life may weaken and the black perspective may lose its relevancy. What one writer has said about acculturated Latinos applies with equal force to acculturated blacks: "[A]s Latinos prosper, they, like Asians, will develop attitudes and behaviors, including marital choices, that will make it difficult to distinguish their cultural traits from that of whites."[79]

Biculturalism, then, attempts to reconcile dominant and subaltern cultural interests by preserving the former folkways in the mainstream while protecting the latter in the private sphere. Whether soft or hard, biculturalism means that minority folkways that clash with mainstream folkways in the public sphere must be removed and replaced and used in private places. The two domains are not unconnected. Minority groups use their ethnic assets as stepping-stones to achieve a level of comfort and efficiency in the mainstream culture. Cultural identity provides a safe harbor as minority groups journey toward their public lives in the American mainstream. Thus, unlike cultural assimilation or transculturalism, biculturalism does not envision racial or ethnic groups bringing the mainstream culture home, at least not until one is prepared to do so. Public adaptation to mainstream values is expected to be gradual rather than happen cold turkey. Racial or ethnic groups are viewed as having "distinct points of entry into the American mainstream, assimilating at different rates."[80] Blacks may take longer than Asian Indians, for example, to assimilate, for a variety of reasons, including the fact that blacks have a unique set of historical references—slavery and Jim Crow. But, again, the ultimate objective of biculturalism is for blacks and other minority groups to become fully assimilated in America regardless of how long it takes.[81]

Whether hard or soft, both forms of biculturalism are rooted in reformism. The hard form of biculturalism is drawn from those reformists who accept cultural assimilation as a matter of racial reality and common sense. "As most minorities who have attained a measure of socioeconomic success well know, the dominant American culture does not accommodate unique languages, customs, or other minority cultural traits. If a minority expects to succeed in . . . [mainstream America], these legitimate cultural phenomena must be 'suspended,' as it were."[82] Similarly, Glenn Loury sees no logic in a search for a "counter-hegemonic political theory." Loury continues: "What are we to do? Overthrow Kantian ethics? And put what, exactly, in its place? Do we think democratic ideas are bad ideas? . . . Do we think that striving for a racially transcendent, non-particularistic understanding of how we should interact with one another is an unworthy quest? To recognize the flaws of the liberal tradition is one thing; to replace it with something workable is quite another. . . . One cannot throw . . . [the Enlightenment] off because some of the Founding Fathers were themselves duplicitous or hypocritical."[83] Loury insists that, "with due humility, I am a reformer, not an 'abolitionist.' "[84]

Other reformists are more progressive about the American mainstream culture. Joe Feagin, for example, envisions a transcultured mainstream culture. He suggests that transculturalism should be prescribed in a new constitutional order in which all American groups are represented. Cornel West's respect for "cultural hybridization" aligns him with Feagin.[85]

The cultural transition from black to white or mocha contemplated by biculturalism is a subordinating condition that many blacks would find objectionable. Former NBA player Jalen Rose voiced this concern in a much-discussed TV special program, *The Fab Five*, which he produced in March of 2011 and aired on ESPN. The program dealt with his days as one of five black freshman superstar basketball players who won national acclaim at the University of Michigan from 1991 to 1993. Rose claimed that Duke University at that time recruited only black players he considered to be "Uncle Toms." Grant Hill, an African American NBA star who played on the 1992 Duke team that beat Michigan in the Final Four, wrote a *New York Times* op-ed piece responding to Rose's charge: "Jalen seems to change the usual meaning of those very vitriolic words into his own meaning, i.e., blacks from two-parent, middle-class families. . . . To hint that those who grew up in a household with a mother and father are somehow less black than those who did not is beyond ridiculous."[86]

The issue of whether a black person can straddle two cultures—white and black—without "selling out," a major issue in the black culture, was brought to light in dramatic fashion in Jeff Hobbs's book *The Short and Tragic Life of Robert Peace: A Brilliant Young Man Who Left Newark for the Ivy League,* discussed earlier in this chapter. A failed attempt to live in both worlds need not result in death, as it did in the case of Robert Peace. But it can lead to cultural dissonance, as most of the black Yale students interviewed in Hobbs's book experienced.

Biculturalism may portend more racial subordination than it advertises. If blacks were ever to become completely acculturated, there would no longer be a need for cultural way stations, safe harbors, or stepping-stones to mainstream culture. The very notion of cultural identity becomes vitiated as blacks become increasingly acculturated. According to Justice O'Connor in *Grutter,* this should all happen by 2028. Some cultural theorists, such as traditionalist Michael Barone, believe the acculturation process may take longer. He states, "It took 120 years from their initial inrush for the Irish to be fully interwoven into the fabric of American society. For all the mistakes Americans—ordinary people and elites of all races—have made, there is still reason to hope that it will not take as long for the American blacks."[87] Of course, blacks have been here for more than 120 years and it still isn't working. Putting aside that obvious pushback, it seems clear that if hard or soft biculturalism is successful, reformism's main cultural implication may be indistinguishable from that of either traditionalism or critical race theory. In other words, cultural subordination under hard and soft biculturalism replicates cultural subordination under cultural assimilation and transculturalism, respectively. Cultural subordination is determined by what happens in the mainstream culture: it is all about the mainstream.[38]

Limited Separation's Cultural Pluralism

One should not allow the term "limited separation" to preshape his or her opinion about its cultural implications. It may offer the only possible formula for avoiding cultural subordination. As will be seen, the cultural diversity model it suggests is not as radical as one might suppose. Indeed, most integrationists whom I have met do not feel threatened by limited separation. Some rather like what it has to say about diversity because it does not preclude racial integration. A real concern for me, however, is whether it offers a theoretical solution to the problem of cultural subordination.

Limited separation's core principle is that racial solidarity is the best strategy for racial advancement in our post–civil rights society. Given that basic civil rights orientation, limited separatists would seem to envision a form of cultural diversity that respects ethnic traditions not just in private but in public. This is an American mainstream culture that is multifaceted, a mainstream culture that consists of not one but many cultures, many legitimate mainstreams—black, white, Native American, Chinese, Asian Indian, Latino, women, gays, and so on. These cultures are distinct. They are not intended to merge in the mainstream, as is the case with transculturalism or soft biculturalism. Limited separatists do not believe it is possible to blend all cultures into a mythical melting pot, be it cultural assimilation or transculturalism, without forcing one culture on another, in other words, without cultural subordination. I shall refer to the limited-separation model of cultural diversity as *cultural pluralism.*

The only way to avoid cultural subordination, limited separatists would insist, is to allow each group to develop its own mainstream institutions. Each group exercises cultural hegemony over its own institutions. Each group's culture is to be respected, with one important proviso: mutual respect is to be accorded only to the *good* features of a group's culture. "Good" and "authentic" are not the same thing. Thuggery in gangsta rap may qualify as "authentic youth music" in pop culture, but it is not necessarily a good cultural expression. In fact, I believe it is "bad" culture because it promotes dysfunctional, self-defeating, misogynistic, and racist behaviors and values. It restricts rather than affirms life. There is no redeeming value in gangsta rap, nothing therein that saves the individual from evil or error. Similarly, although the minstrel character in blackface was an unmistakably authentic part of pop culture prior to the civil rights movement, it had no redeeming value; it was a "bad" feature of white culture. So too was (and still is) the use of the N-word. It was (and still is) in the minds of most blacks associated with a history of racial oppression or disrespect. Although authentic, each of these cultural expressions is without any redeeming, life-affirming, or freedom-giving value. None, therefore, is entitled to respect. This is how I read cultural pluralism operating through limited separation.[89]

To gain a deeper understanding of how limited separation signals and embraces a particular type of cultural pluralism, it is may be useful to consider how limited separatists approach the identity question. The identity question is fraught with complexity, none more so than the question of African-American identity. Harold Cruse's seminal polemic on black identity, *The Crisis of the Negro Intellectual*, provides an excellent springboard from which to delve into the limited separatists' perspective on the identity question. Still read in black studies and civil rights courses, Cruse begins with the following story:

> In 1940, as one of my first acts in the pursuit of becoming a more "social" being, I joined a YMCA amateur drama group in Harlem. I wanted to learn about theater so I became a stage technician—meaning a handyman for all backstage chores. But the first thing about this drama group that struck me as highly curious was the fact that all the members were overwhelmingly in favor of doing white plays with Negro casts. I wondered why and very naively expressed my sentiments about it. The replies that I got clearly indicated that these amateur actors were not very favorable to the plays about Negro life, although they would not plainly say so. Despite the fact that this question of identity was first presented to me within the context of the program of a small, insignificant amateur drama group, its implications ranged far beyond. A theater group, no matter how small, must have an audience. What did the audience at the Harlem YMCA really think about the group's productions?[90]

Limited separatists would argue that the actors' work did not reflect appropriate aesthetic values. By not focusing on themes that reflect the life experiences of blacks in the community, the actors missed an opportunity to enrich, validate, or bring greater awareness to these experiences. Given the audience's cultural preference, the actors, limited separatists would contend, had a duty to create experiences that acknowledged the life that they lived. While others might applaud the actors' attempts to link African Americans to a larger community through the works of Shakespeare, Samuel Beckett, and other white playwrights, limited separatists would argue that the actors had a responsibility to delve into themes the audience desired—black pride, black culture, and black self-determination. If not black actors, then who?[91]

This view of black identity contrasts sharply with the traditionalists view and brings us to the heart of the cultural diversity question for African Americans. Traditionalists, who start from the premise that race no longer matters, question the utility of race as a descriptive, analytical, or prescriptive concept in our post–civil rights society. They would argue that Ralph Ellison, one of our most celebrated black authors, had it right. He tried to construct an identity as an American rather than as an African American. Most notably in *Invisible Man,* winner of the National Book Award, Ellison argued for an identity independent of race. "[T]he frontier spirit in Oklahoma . . . had fostered in [Ellison] a sense of human possibility that he considered the very essence of American democracy."[92] Ellison was offering a counternarrative not only to Jim Crow racism and the type of black identity it had produced, but also to racial essentialism. He rejected the mind-set of Bigger Thomas, the young black male fictional character in Richard Wright's *Native Son,* who was driven to murder by his own suffering as a victim of a racist society. "Bigger Thomas murders a white girl because the racist society has so imbued him with a fear of being found alone with a white female that his own instinct for survival leads him to kill her, virtually by reflex. Racism so determines Bigger's self that his will is irrelevant."[93] Ellison disdained such essentialism, even positive expressions of racial essentialism, arguing that it oversimplified identity and deprived African Americans of agency.

Cultural pluralism, as conceived by limited separatists, does not deny agency to blacks. It gives blacks the *option and responsibility* to choose or not to choose black identity (a heightened sensibility about racial justice, or black racial sensibility) in whole or in part, systemically or ad hoc for the sake of their individual happiness and worldly success. Under this form of cultural pluralism, African Americans would be able to embrace black identity and not feel that they were doing something untoward, illegitimate, or un-American. The choice is made without accusing whites or the system of being racist. It is made not as a reaction to racism but in the interest of self-actualization.

Clearly, then, this view of black identity is a far cry from "Bigger Thomas–style determinism." Limited separatists do not regard black identity to be a form of racial victimology or individual defeatism. For limited separatists, black identity is positive and personally fulfilling. Black identity creates a kind of psychic bubble in which blacks can find their personalities and hone their talents. To the extent that the American mainstream culture denies blacks the right to be themselves (for racist or nonracist reasons), to the extent that racial subordination is a precondition for racial success in the mainstream, and to the extent that assimilation is not available for all blacks who desire it (as discussed earlier), this psychic bubble may well be justified.

The limited-separatist version of cultural pluralism is very democratic. It gives not only African Americans but other individuals the choice between black identity and other identities. Rachel Dolezal's decision to leave behind her white identity and opt for black identity is a nonissue under cultural pluralism. The former president of the NAACP chapter in Spokane, Washington, need not lie about being black. If cultural pluralism were the prevailing model of cultural diversity in our society, a person who was biologically white, like Dolezal, could become culturally black without raising questions about her authenticity. She would still be white and, hence, not entitled to the institutional resources set aside for biological blacks who have actually experienced racial disadvantage; but she could still live a black lifestyle and, being a civil rights activist, exhibit a heightened sensibility regarding racial injustice. Many white students who attend Historically Black Colleges and Universities (HBCUs) make this transition. In fact, Ms. Dolezal attended Howard University.[94]

Cultural pluralism, then, is predicated upon the limited separatist's complex view of identity. Black identity is not viewed as a temporary condition. It is not regarded as a stepping-stone to a larger white or blended cultural identity, as in the case of biculturalism. Each culture, instead, has a fixed and equal status in American society. There is no real incentive or need to move outside of one's racial or ethnic group, no need to burst the psychic bubble. One can simply remain within her racial or ethnic group, her comfort zone, should one choose to do so. Each racial group is given equal respect and cultural legitimacy within its respective realm or ambit of influence. There is no single cultural canon; there are, instead, many canons. Hence, under this model of cultural diversity, the races mix like a salad: red tomatoes and green cucumbers are distinctly noticeable vegetables in the bowl.

This form of cultural pluralism avoids many conventional criticisms lodged against other forms of "pluralism" or "multiculturalism." For example, it carries no "deeply anti-individualist, anti-voluntarist expectation that individuals . . . [will] naturally accept the cultural, social, and political habits popularly ascribed to their communities of descent, rather than their own associations to the extent that their life-circumstances permitted choices."[95] In contrast, limited separatists' view of cultural pluralism is one that provides individuals with real choice among many identities and operates on the basis of individual self-interest rather than groupthink. In what can only be described as an interesting mixture of mainstream individualism and black identity, limited separatists want blacks to exercise freedom of choice, *freedom to embrace black culture or not.* They do so in service to the *self* rather than in service to racial kinship. Also, limited separatists would argue that what Kwame Appiah writes about "cosmopolitanism" (a cultural theory discussed in note 88) applies with equal force to their version of cultural pluralism: "[H]uman variety matters because people are entitled to the options they need to shape their lives in partnership with others."[96]

Still, I am mainly skeptical of the limited-separatist adaptation of cultural pluralism. The major problem in my view lies not in cultural balkanization (I doubt that the psychic bubble will burst into a bunker mentality, as cultural pluralism is not racially exclusionary) nor in cultural relativism—limited separatists do not "hold all ways of life to be equally good";[97] they accord mutual respect only to positive cultural identities. As successful community building is important to the success of cultural pluralism, blacks will have to generate enough financial capital to sustain communities as economically strong and independent as Little Havana in Miami, Chinatowns that dot the American landscape, casino-rich Indian reservations, and vibrant homosexual communities like the Hillcrest section of San Diego. If an ethnic mainstream is to be viable, it must provide a sustainable alternative to the white middle-class mainstream. People must be able to function well within these alternative mainstream communities, which must in turn be able to effectuate commerce with other mainstream communities. Thus, if black communities cannot develop strong homegrown socioeconomic structures, with or without government financial assistance, the American mainstream for blacks will remain white and middle class by default. Cultural pluralism, therefore, runs the risk of merely replicating biculturalism in spite of its determined effort to avoid cultural subordination.

Resolving Cultural Subordination

Notwithstanding our professed commitment to cultural diversity, cultural subordination is a major factor in our mainstream culture. It is manifested in two distinctly different ways of defining the "melting pot," that quintessentially American cultural ideal. Cultural assimilation, envisioned by the traditionalist norm that race no longer matters, and transculturalism, inspired by the critical race theorist core belief in social transformation, suppress contraposed values that spring from a black racial sensibility. The candidates for suppression include the belief that black is beautiful, that counteracting racism is a matter of some urgency, and that rooting out anti-black racism should be a high priority of the federal and state governments. Transculturalism's progressiveness tends to distract one from racial subordination inherent in its requirement that each group thrown into the cultural mix must surrender some of its identity and, thereby, sublimate its special concerns to the concerns of the new progressive culture. Hence, the issue of anti-black racism might be given less urgency than, say, women's rights, gay marriage, Syrian refugees, or immigration policy in general. How a culture prioritizes its limited resources of time, money, and moral outrage is a critically important determination.

That determination is at the heart of cultural assimilation and transculturalism. Both have legitimate social goals—social cohesion and progressive inclusiveness, respectively—that reflect legitimate post–civil rights norms: the convictions that race neutrality gives blacks the best chance for achieving racial equality (traditionalism), and that changing the relationship between race and power in our culture is an essential condition for racial equality (critical race theory). Assimilationists, in other words, argue that because government-sanctioned racism is no longer a factor in the African American's chances for racial equality, there is no need to revisit the culturally divisive matter of race. We should, instead, focus on matters that ought to unite us culturally. Those things necessarily coalesce around the majoritarian middle—white middle-class values—to which all groups must adapt. Transculturalists, in contrast, begin with the conviction that the social order is constructed in the image of straight white men. That gives these insiders a cultural advantage, which needs to be addressed rather than ignored. Blending all cultural traditions is the best way to dilute that power. Although not necessarily racist, both positions hurt blacks by falsely assuming that blacks and whites (traditionalists) or blacks and outsiders (critical race theory) are similarly situated when in fact *they are not at equal risk,* as I explained more fully earlier in this chapter and in the introduction.

Biculturalism, in my view, is worse. It is not only tainted by the fact that it replicates cultural assimilation (hard biculturalism) or transculturalism (soft biculturalism) in the mainstream, but also by the fact that it gives cultural clearance to racism in the private domain. It is one thing to force people to act in a certain way in their private spaces, which I am not advocating here, but quite another thing to teach certain rules of propriety by which decent people should behave in private, which I am most certainly advocating here. Biculturalism is agnostic regarding totems of intolerance kept in private. Let us take, as an example, the Confederate flag.

"A flag is a symbol—a powerful symbol, reflecting beliefs and values so strongly held that followers are willing to fight and die for them." Public opinion on the Confederate flag is mixed. A 2015 Suffolk University / *USA Today* poll found that "42 percent of respondents thought the

flag was racist and should be removed from state grounds, while 42 percent thought the flag was not racist and represents Southern history."[98]
Soft biculturalism, but not necessarily hard biculturalism or cultural
assimilation, would not permit the flag to fly on government property
or be embedded in a state's flag. Flying the Confederate flag on government grounds or allowing it to be part of the state's flag clashes with
transcultural values of tolerance and antiracism. The flag severely subordinates black dignity and personhood. Blacks are forced to live with a
symbol that came into existence as a statement of white supremacy, an
ignominious part of southern history. The flag is an ongoing slap in the
face to African Americans. But, while soft biculturalism would counsel
removing the flag from public viewing on government property to,
perhaps, a museum where it could be viewed as a historical artifact of
slavery or the Civil War, it would *not* advise against private displays of
the confederate flag, such as in a fraternity house on or off campus. Soft
biculturalism, unlike transculturalism, sanctions ethnic expressions
in private places. The same cultural mechanism that celebrates black
heritage in private respects racist speech in private. As I made clear in
chapter 3, I am not a fan of cultural relativism.[99]

Cultural pluralism is the only nonsubordinating model of cultural
diversity. Shaped by limited separation, this model does not present a
racially subordinating mainstream as it recognizes many mainstreams
rather than a single, dominating one. Yet, I question the practicality of
cultural pluralism for the reasons previously stated. What, then, should
we do?

I do not believe the problem of cultural subordination can be
completely resolved in our culturally diverse society. It can, however, be
alleviated or managed provided that we return to first principles—our
commitment to racial democracy. As I argued earlier in this chapter,
substantive democracy and the American Creed, the raw ingredients of
racial democracy, fuel our commitment to cultural diversity. They
establish the legitimacy of cultural diversity in America today. In a real
sense, they embody the spirit of *Brown*—sustained, unrelenting racial
advancement—in the cultural context. In deference to this pledge, we
ought to pursue the cultural diversity model that engenders the *least*
amount of cultural subordination. In my view, transculturalism

combined with cultural pluralism, wherever possible, offers the least amount of cultural subordination.[100]

Although there is likely to be more racial subordination in transculturalism's blended mainstream (as black concerns are merged with and, hence, diluted by the concerns of other minority groups) than in cultural pluralism's unapologetically black mainstream, it is still less tyrannical than an assimilationist or hard biculturalist mainstream. Transculturalism invites blacks to negotiate with all other social groups which values shall become mainstream values. Thus, even though important black values may not prevail in the marketplace of values, transculturalism gives blacks a fighting chance. Cultural subordination is diminished to the extent that blacks have a chance to fight for black values and know that, should they lose, the matter is never really settled.[101]

To the extent possible, transculturalism and cultural pluralism should work together. The latter must be taken seriously because it comes from a legitimate post–civil rights norm of self-sufficiency and it is the only cultural diversity model that avoids cultural subordination. Unlike transculturalism, cultural pluralism allows black values to take full effect within a mainstream American culture—black face, black mind. Many African Americans would find personal happiness in black communities and institutions that are vibrant and that do not exclude whites or other racial groups. Black folkways are not devalued, marginalized, or diluted in such places. Questions or concerns deemed important to African Americans are given top priority. Just as we as a society find cultural legitimacy in Chinatowns, Little Havanas, Indian reservations, Amish communities, homosexual sections of cities, and single-sex colleges and universities, so too we should find cultural legitimacy in African American communities and institutions. We should respect positive expressions of black identity and racial solidarity, including in black churches that do not exclude white worshippers, in HBCUs that do not exclude white students, and in President Obama's public condemnation of the murder of Trayvon Martin and the arrest of Harvard Professor Henry Louis Gates Jr. for trying to get into his own house. I would, in short, allow cultural pluralism to work in tandem with transculturalism, recognizing all the while that cultural pluralism may take some time to develop, if it develops at all, beyond ad hoc demonstrations.

Higher education is one area in which cultural pluralism and transculturalism can work together. HBCUs are permitted to stand un-diluted alongside predominantly white colleges and universities. Cultural pluralism governs the former, and transculturalism manages race relations in the latter.

Applied to predominantly white colleges and universities, transculturalism would certainly reduce much of the racism and racial subordination that one sees on these campuses. Recent incidents include white hoods worn by students at The Citadel, a military college; white sheets draped over a prominent indoor mural featuring black historical events at the University of Kentucky; racial slurs hurled from cars speeding through campus at the University of Missouri; the confederate flag on hats and shirts worn by students at numerous southern colleges; the defacing of portraits of black professors at Harvard Law School; and the myriad racial threats and insults appearing on social media.

Although these racist acts came in small dosages, they became magnified under a regime of racial subordination. For months and even years, college presidents and other top administrators failed to heed the voices of the black students. The administrators were either racially obtuse, "too busy" with "more important matters," or believed that freedom of expression protected racist expression, not unlike Mark Cuban's view of Donald Sterling's racism. To be sure, there was likely no intent on the part of the administrators to harm black students. But there is a principle of criminal and civil law that states that "a person intends the natural and foreseeable consequences of his voluntary actions."[102] The foreseeable, indeed inexorable, consequences of the administrators' inactions were to diminish the quality of racial inclusion on campus, to freeze black students out of important aspects of campus life, to impede racial advancement.

One racially subordinating administrative action that received much public attention took place at Yale University. In October of 2015, Erika Christakis, a lecturer at the Yale Child Study Center, the associate master of Silliman College (a residential college at Yale University), and the wife of the college's master, raised the very serious matter of free expression in reply to an e-mail from the school's Intercultural Affairs Council admonishing students to think about the racial consequences of the Halloween costumes they select. Student had in fact worn racially offensive costumes to campus events in the past. Christakis wrote in her e-mail, "Is there no room anymore for a child or young person to be a little bit obnoxious, . . . a little bit inappropriate or provocative or, yes, offensive?" In the context of the racially subordinating environment at Yale, the black students who lived in Silliman College, with whom Christakis was in an *in loco parentis* relationship, found the e-mail "jarring and disheartening." They read the e-mail as giving license to racism in their own home. These students needed empathy and validation from the administrators, not a lecture on free speech regarding an e-mail they did not send. But one black student went too far when she confronted the college master on the quad and shouted for him to "step down" for supporting his wife's e-mail. Two wrongs don't make a right.[103]

Black students across the nation have had to deal with racial slurs and racist behavior on their own with little help from college administrators. These incidents have had a harmful impact on their education. Many black students do not feel safe on campus. Others do not sleep well at night, and some do not see the purpose of going to class. One black student at Yale was so distraught by the racial environment that she wondered aloud, "Where do I go to find hope?"

Peter Salovey, president of Yale University, showed great wisdom and leadership when he issued a statement to the Yale community on November 17, 2015, that recognized his own racial subordination. Although it was late in coming, it was greatly welcomed. "Wisdom too often never comes, and so one ought not reject it merely because it comes late."[104] Instead of looking away or suggesting, as the master of Silliman College had, that the main problem on campus was simply a matter of free speech, Salovey confessed, "You have offered me the opportunity to listen to and learn from you—students, faculty, staff, and alumni, from every part of the university." His statement also outlined the measures Yale would take to make the college mainstream culture more racially inclusive, less racially subordinating. These measures included committing $50 million over the next five years to "enhance faculty diversity."[105]

President Salovey's statement strikes what I believe is the right response. But diversity, whether involving the faculty or student body, is only the first step in institutionalizing transcultural values of racial tolerance and understanding. At the very least, support for these values must be embedded in the DNA at Yale and other schools as well.

Knowledge is the lifeblood of colleges and universities. It is also the most effective antidote for racial intolerance and ignorance. Millennials have lots of racial information, thanks to Google, but a dearth of racial knowledge. They have little wisdom about their ethnically diverse experiences. The subject of race is much too complex for millennials to try to learn on their own. In fact, they have been doing a lousy job of self-education. Contrary to popular belief, millennials are quite racist. More than baby boomers, white millennials believe blacks are lazy and unintelligent.[106]

It is the job of colleges and universities to help students develop the knowledge they will need to adapt to a society committed to racial democracy. This can only be done by offering a series of mandatory courses on race and inclusion. All students should be required to take courses on race and inclusion at every college or university that receives federal funds, which is virtually every college and university in the nation. Mandatory courses on race and inclusion will help all students, regardless of race or color, to overcome racial ignorance, the face of racial intolerance. White students will be taught that their sense of entitlement—the conviction that they have "a right to pursue their own individual preferences" or "to act on their own behalf to gain advantage," which they imbibed from their middle-class upbringing (discussed in chapter 3)—does not give them a personal right to say anything that comes to mind and assume it is valid. Just as free expression does not give one the right to yell "Fire!" in a crowded theater or to make sexist remarks to a female co-worker, it does not give one the right to make racist remarks or threats. Students will also learn about the country's inglorious racial history and the impact that history has had on the relationship between race and power in our society today. They will learn that equal treatment is not always fair treatment—that African Americans are not at equal risk with whites or nonblack racial minorities—and that taking a strong stance against racial intolerance, even against one's friends, is the right thing to do. These courses will not only teach students why they should act against intolerance but also *how* to do so effectively, such as by appealing to empathy ("How would you feel if you were the target of intolerance?"), to friendship ("I don't want you to make an ass of yourself"), or to one's personal space ("That's not something I would do" or "you're making me feel uncomfortable"). Simply giving the transgressor a long, hard stare can also be effective. Professors have a role to play as well. They should warn students who make racially derogatory remarks in or out of class under the guise of free speech that their behavior is offensive and contrary to university values.

African American students will also benefit by taking these mandatory courses. The course readings should contain material from which black students can develop coping skills. For example, Martin Luther King Jr.'s famous "Letter from a Birmingham City Jail" was a powerful response to a public statement written by eight white religious leaders of the South who criticized Reverend King's participation in nonviolent demonstrations as "unwise and untimely." King replied, "I am in Birmingham because injustice is here. . . . I cannot sit idly by in Atlanta and not be concerned about what happens in Birmingham. Injustice anywhere is a threat to justice everywhere." Black students should take from this letter the importance of listening and responding to opposing views, however uncomfortable, rather than attempting to shut down discourse. The circumstances under which the letter was written (a cold jail cell) should give perspective to the black student who wonders aloud, "Where do I go to find hope?"[107]

Transcultural values will also help the campus community think through the problem of campus buildings named after controversial historical figures. For example, several structures at Princeton University have been named after Thomas Woodrow Wilson, who was not only president of the United States but also president of Princeton University. Wilson was an unapologetic segregationist. He segregated the federal agencies in Washington, D.C., and not a single black student was admitted to Princeton University during his university presidency. The debate over whether Wilson's name should be removed from Wilson College or the International Affairs School at Princeton should be less about whether historical figures are to be judged by the tenor of the times in which they lived (there were plenty of dissenting voices Wilson could have heeded at the time), than about whether Wilson represents the past that Princeton wants to move beyond or points to the future that Princeton wishes to embrace. These buildings were named during periods of racial oppression in this country. Would they be given the same name if they were being named for the first time today? Is Wilson's legacy something with which all students, faculty, staff, and alumni should identify going forward? Is it a legacy on which the university can build for the future? Does a legacy of racial segregation provide a bridge to racial healing and inclusion in the future?

This discussion might be uncomfortable and even offensive to black students. Forcing black students "to see their personal pain reduced to a PR quagmire" certainly subordinates an important black value. For that reason, the discussion must be conducted in the least subordinating manner possible.[108] This would not be a concern at HBCUs, as black students do not face such challenges on these campuses; hence the importance of the HBCU alternative. But on predominantly white campuses, the discussion is important because it generates the type of knowledge that is essential to transcultural understanding, the values, attitudes, and behaviors that are the necessary conditions for overcoming racial intolerance in culturally diverse settings.

Epilogue

Unrelenting Racial Progress

B eyond the usual coordinates of racism, conventionally defined, and socioeconomic class lies a form of racial inequality that has not been fully studied or developed in scholarly circles or public discussions about the problems African Americans, or blacks, face in our post–Jim Crow society. This form of racial inequality subordinates racial advancement to competing nonracist interests. It disadvantages all blacks, including the rich and famous—Oprah and President Obama—by making it more difficult than it otherwise has to be for blacks to climb out of the abyss of racial degradation wrought by slavery and Jim Crow. Racial degradation strikes at the heart of basic equality; that is, human dignity, equal worth. I call this form of racial inequality racial subordination.

While racial subordination is not racial innocence, a view that puts me at odds with my conservative friends, neither is it racism, a view that disappoints my progressive friends. But always subjecting Supreme Court decisions that disadvantage blacks to the critical apparatus of racism seems not quite right to me. I do, however, see the juridical subordination when the justices take perfectly legitimate normative stances that, in the context of current racial conditions, yield racially harmful results. The Court contributes to racial inequality when it favors state sovereignty over black voting rights, or color blindness over black college

participation. The latter points to the insidious nature of juridical subordination: it is often hidden in the justices' civil rights rhetoric—their
core beliefs about civil rights. Juridical subordination can be found in
the traditionalist justices' (for example, Chief Justice Roberts's and Justice Alito's) seemingly unshakable belief in the racial-omission norm,
and in the reformist justices' (for example, Justices Ginsburg's and Breyer's) equally strong conviction in the racial-integration norm. Justice
Kennedy is adrift, though recently he has set sail more with the reformists than the traditionalists. The justices are caught in the civil rights–era
vortex of racial omission versus racial integration. It is only Justice
Sotomayor, a reformist most of the time, who comes close to recognizing
white hegemony, but only in passing remarks, and it is only Justice
Thomas, mostly a traditionalist, who speaks up for black identity or
solidarity, but only in the context of HBCUs and K–12 public schools.
(The classical-liberal Koch brothers also champion black schools.) If
there is one justice poised to break out of the Court's intellectual paraly-
sis, it is Justice Kagan. She knows this stuff very well, having been dean at
Harvard Law School, one of the centers of out-of-the-box legal analysis.

Racial progress is likewise impeded when the mainstream culture
discounts black racial sensibility. The quickest way for a black professional or executive to lose face within his or her organization, even
among white friends, is to raise a racial issue. Whites are uncomfortable
with race talk. African Americans can no more avoid the topic than they
can change the color of their skin. Within the mainstream culture, the
white view on racial matters typically trumps the black view, from the
standard of beauty (ivory is ranked higher than ebony) to the very legitimate black belief that combating racism is a matter of some urgency,
warranting the government's high priority. Much of the cultural pushback is racism, as in many cases of excessive police force and racial pro-
filing directed toward unarmed, innocent black males; but much of it is
also cultural subordination, specifically, the traditionalist's belief in cultural assimilation (black face, white voice). Cultural subordination can
also come from the critical race theory's belief in transculturalism (black
face, mocha voice) and the reformist's belief in biculturalism (black
face, white or mocha voice). The limited separatist's call for cultural
pluralism (black face, black voice) is the only nonsubordinating model

of cultural diversity that I can find. It may not, however, be within the reach of most African Americans today.

Breaking through the racial glass ceiling is certainly within the reach of morally motivated individuals and institutions—men, women, and institutions of probity and intelligence. First and foremost, the racial barrier must be properly named. Misnomers beget misdiagnoses. Calling it racism or regarding it as racially innocent necessitates a very different type of discourse than what appears in the pages of this book. Racial subordination seems appropriately descriptive to me.

Breaking through the racial glass ceiling does not, in my view, require a new national story—a new version of American exceptionalism or, perhaps, unexceptionalism. Instead, we need only draw upon venerable norms that have given shape to our national aspirations as a virtuous society. In law, the Supreme Court need only demonstrate fealty to *Brown's* spirit of persistent racial advancement. In culture, our mainstream institutions must simply give greater deference to our belief in racial democracy—substantive democracy and the American Creed. Our commitment to racial democracy is very much in sync with the spirit of *Brown*. Both require us not just to acknowledge racial inequality, but to *prioritize racial equality*. Together, they represent good social policy in today's society.

Breaking through the racial glass ceiling, in a word, brings us face-to-face with the reality that racial progress has not been as great as we have wanted to believe. Breaking through involves confronting complex and uncomfortable questions about what we value as Americans. It requires us to be reasonable people, and to pursue reasonable racial goals reasonably.

Appendix A: Diagram of Main Arguments

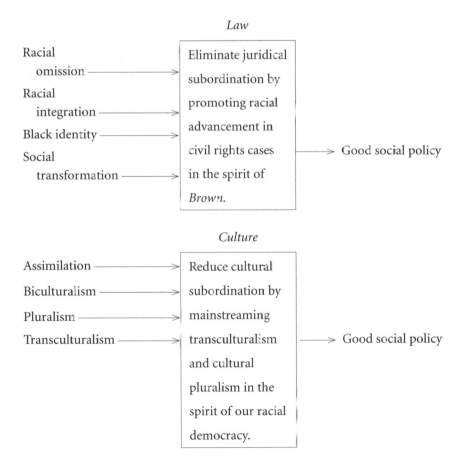

Law

Racial
    omission ──────────▷

Racial
    integration ──────▷

Black identity ───────▷

Social
    transformation ───▷

| Eliminate juridical subordination by promoting racial advancement in civil rights cases in the spirit of *Brown.* |

──▷ Good social policy

Culture

Assimilation ─────────▷

Biculturalism ────────▷

Pluralism ────────────▷

Transculturalism ─────▷

| Reduce cultural subordination by mainstreaming transculturalism and cultural pluralism in the spirit of our racial democracy. |

──▷ Good social policy

Appendix B: Post–Civil Rights Cases That Impede Racial Progress

This appendix provides a sampling of Supreme Court cases not discussed in chapter 2 that demonstrate the Court's dismal proclivity toward impeding racial progress in the post–Jim Crow era. Indeed, Congress has regularly passed bipartisan corrective legislation to overturn the Court's restrictive interpretations of its civil rights laws. In addition to legislation protecting the 1965 Voting Rights Act discussed quite extensively by Ari Berman in *Give Us the Ballot: The Modern Struggle for Voting Rights in America* (New York: Farrar, Straus and Giroux, 2015), Congress has passed legislation in the form of the 1991 Civil Rights Act in response to a number of Supreme Court cases that limited application of the 1964 Civil Rights Act, which is the most important piece of civil rights legislation in the history of our country. Among the cases targeted by the 1991 act are *Patterson v. McLean Credit Union*, 491 U.S. 164 (1988), which held that an employee could not sue for damages caused by racial harassment on the job, because § 1981, which provides that "[a]ll persons . . . shall have the same right . . . to make and enforce contracts . . . as is enjoyed by white citizens," does not apply to conduct that occurs after the formation of a contract and that does not interfere with the right to enforce established contract obligations; *Wards Cove Packing Co. v. Atonio*, 490 U.S. 642 (1989), which placed the burden of persuasion on the plaintiff to disprove the employer's assertion of its business necessity defense in a disparate impact case and which required the plaintiff to identify the particular employment policy or practice that produced the alleged disparate impact regardless of whether such a policy or practice could be isolated in that manner; *Price Waterhouse v. Hopkins*, 490 U.S. 228 (1989), which cut off employer liability in a case involving both permissible and impermissible reasons for discriminatory treatment if the employer could prove that it would have made the same decision even in the absence of the impermissible factor; *Martin v. Wilks*, 490 U.S. 755 (1989), which permitted white firefighters who had not been party to the litigation establishing a consent decree governing hiring and promotion of black firefighters in the Birmingham,

Alabama, Fire Department to bring suit to challenge the decree (a collateral attack), even though they knew, should have known, or were adequately represented by the original parties.

Many pieces of corrective legislation are codified in relative obscure laws known only to lawyers and legal scholars who specialize in civil rights law. See, for example, 29 U.S.C. 794(b), overturning *Grove City College v. Bell*, 265 U.S. 555 (1984), which limited the meaning of "program or activity" for purposes of liability under both Title XI and by extension Title VI. For a discussion of other important corrective legislation, see Roy L. Brooks, Gilbert Paul Carrasco, and Michael Selmi, *The Law of Discrimination: Cases and Perspectives* (New Providence, NJ: LexisNexis, 2011), 564–568, 1272–1275.

Civil rights casebooks are filled with Supreme Court cases that undercut civil rights protections. These cases are collected in casebooks because they are major pronouncements on civil rights law. In addition to the cases just discussed and in chapter 2, some of these cases follow. *Milliken v. Bradley*, 418 U.S. 717 (1974), significantly limits the use of metropolitan desegregation plans to integrate highly segregative inner-city schools. This case along with *Board of Education v. Dowell*, 498 U.S. 237 (1991), and *Freeman v. Pitts*, 503 U.S. 467 (1992), both of which allow school districts that have not achieved full unitary status to stop trying, are considered by many civil rights scholars to be tragic decisions for race relations because they effectively accept racial segregation and thereby constitute abdication of the Supreme Court's role as the arbitrator of racial equality since *Brown I*. *Regents of the Univ. of Cal. v. Bakke*, 438 U.S. 265 (1978), limits racial integration through college admissions. *City of Shaw v. Reno*, 509 U.S. 630 (1993); *Shelby County v. Holder*, 133 S. Ct. 2612, 2631 (2013); and *Alabama Legislative Black Caucus v. Alabama*, No. 13–895, 135 S. Ct. 1257 (2015), made it more difficult to establish effective political representation for blacks in states with a history of restricting the voting rights of blacks. *Richmond v. J. A. Croson*, 488 U.S. 469 (1989), and *Adarand Constructors, Inc. v. Pena*, 515 U.S. 200 (1995), made it difficult for cities to require its contractors to award subcontracts to black businesses. *Missouri v. Jenkins*, 515 U.S. 70, 114 (1995) (Jenkins III), denied the federal courts the authority, absent a showing of segregative intent, to order the state to fund higher teacher salaries that could attract better teachers to inner-city schools. *United States v. Fordice*, 505 U.S. 717 (1992), threatened the existence of HBCUs, prompting Justice Thomas to write separately, "[T]here exists 'sound educational justification' for maintaining historically black colleges as such." *Gratz v. Bollinger*, 539 U.S. 244 (2003), overturned an admission process designed to increase the number of black and Latino students at a prestigious university. But *Grutter v. Bollinger*, 539 U.S. 306 (2003), decided the same day, approved an admission process designed to increase the number of black and Latino students at a prestigious law school. *Parents Involved in Community Schools v. Seattle School District No. 1*, 551 U.S. 701 (2007), squashed integration efforts in de facto segregated school districts. *Schuette v. Coalition to Defend Affirmative Action, Integration, & Immigration Rights & Fight for Equality by Any Means Necessary*, 134 S. Ct. 1623 (2014), required blacks to engage in the arduous process of amending the state constitution to implement state affirmative-action programs. Again, this is just a sampling of the Court's decisions.

These decisions have had a major impact on the black equality interest. In the wake of *Holder,* for example, several states, most in covered jurisdictions, passed laws that effectively limited black voting rights. Many of these restrictions were enacted prior to the 2012 presidential election and were eerily similar to forms of discrimination used during the Jim Crow era to prevent blacks from voting. In a 2012 report, the NAACP detailed the numerous efforts by state governments across the nation, particularly in the South, to disfranchise African Americans. See NAACP Legal Defense & Educational Fund, Inc., & NAACP, *Defending Democracy: Confronting Modern Barriers to Voting Rights in America* (2011), http://naacp.3cdn.net/67065c25be9ae43367_mlbrsy48b.pdf. Although these efforts are executed in the name of politics and are facially neutral, they have a significant disparate impact on blacks. See ibid., at 11–38. Some are clearly targeted toward African Americans, Hispanics, and the poor. See ibid., at 37–38. For a sample of the disfranchisement measures detailed in the NAACP report, see ibid., at 11–13.

Florida and Texas have enacted laws that substantially restrict voter registration drives that work to the detriment of black voters, many of whom rely heavily on these drives to register. In Florida, nearly 20 percent of blacks, more than any other group, register through voter registration drives. See ibid., at 11, citing Letter from League of Women Voters of Florida, Brennan Center for Justice, Democracia USA, & Lawyers' Committee for Civil Rights Under Law to Chris Herren, Chief, Voting Section, Civil Rights Division, U.S. Dep't of Justice 12 (July 15, 2011), https://www.brennancenter. org/sites/default/files/legacy/Democracy/Florida%20Section%205%20comment%20 letter%20-%20FINAL.pdf. Also, many poor blacks register to vote at public assistance agencies (three times more often than poor white voters do). See ibid., at 16, citing U.S. Census Bureau, *Voting and Registration in the Election of November 2008—Detailed Tables,* Table 14, https://www.census.gov/hhes/www/socdemo/voting/publications/p20/ 2008/tables.html. States are required by federal law to provide voter registration services at state public assistance agencies. See National Voter Registration Act (NVRA), Pub. L. 103–131, § 7, 107 Stat. 77, 80, codified as amended at 50 U.S.C. § 20506 (2012). Yet, Louisiana, Georgia, Texas, and other states have failed to comply with the NVRA. See *Defending Democracy,* at 12.

Some states have limited the time and place individuals can register to vote, all to the detriment of blacks. Florida, Ohio, Wisconsin, and Maine have enacted such laws. Ohio, for example, repealed a law that provided a one-week period in which individuals could both register and vote at the same time. The elimination of this law falls disproportionately on black voters, who have used it more than other groups in the past. See *Defending Democracy,* at 12.

Several states have enhanced their eligibility requirements for voting. Alabama, Kansas, and Tennessee have enacted laws that require documentary proof of citizenship before one can register to vote. See ibid. This facially neutral requirement will fall more harshly on older African Americans because many were born in the Jim Crow era, when most blacks were born at home without birth certificates, as they were denied access to hospitals or did not have enough money to pay for a hospital delivery. See ibid., citing *New State Voting Laws: Barriers to the Ballot?* Hearings Before the Subcommittee on the

Constitution, Civil Rights, and Human Rights of the S. Comm. on the Judiciary, 112th Cong., 9 (Sept. 8, 2011) (statement of Ryan P. Haygood, Director, Political Participation Group, NAACP LDF), http://www.naacpldf.org/files/case_issue/Final%20Voting%20 Barriers%20Testimony2C%20September%2012C%202011%20_400__2.pdf. The same result occurs with laws in states like Wisconsin, which lengthen the period of time one must be a resident of the state before becoming eligible to vote. These durational residency requirements disproportionately affect blacks, who tend to move more frequently than whites. See *Defending Democracy*, at 12, citing Paul Taylor et al., Pew Research Center, *American Mobility: Who Moves? Who Stays Put? Where's Home?* 22 (2008), http://www.pewsocialtrends.org/files/2010/10/Movers-and-Stayers.pdf.

The Florida and Iowa legislatures have passed laws that deny the franchise to convicted felons. See *Defending Democracy*, at 26–27. Ex-felons who have served their sentences are permanently denied the right to vote. As African Americans have disproportionately high rates of felony convictions and incarcerations, these laws will disfranchise thousands of black citizens. See ibid., at 12.

Florida, Mississippi, and several other states have taken steps to purge voters from the registration rolls. While the stated purpose of voter purges is to maintain the purity of the lists of eligible voters by removing the names of ineligible individuals, eligible voters are often purged from the lists. See ibid. A ninety-one-year-old war hero, for instance, was stricken from the rolls in Florida. See Greg Allen, *World War II Vet Caught Up in Florida's Voter Purge Controversy*, NPR (May 31, 2013), http://www.npr.org/ sections/itsallpolitics/2012/05/31/154020289/world-war-ii-vet-caught-up-in-floridas-voter-purge-controversy. That state's purging program has been so flawed that twelve thousand voters have been erroneously flagged or purged. See *Defending Democracy*, at 12. Over 70 percent of these voters have been black or Latino. See ibid., citing Wendy Weiser and Margaret Chen, Brennan Center for Justice, *Recent Voter Suppression Incidents* 2 (2008), http://brennan.3cdn.net/e827230204c5668706_pom6b54jk.pdf.

Florida, Georgia, Ohio, Tennessee, and West Virginia passed legislation that substantially reduced the opportunities for early voting. The period for early voting was cut almost in half, from fourteen to eight days, in Florida. Again, this facially neutral move falls more heavily on blacks than whites, as blacks are more likely than whites to use the early voting process. See ibid. Although only 13 percent of the Florida electorate, blacks accounted for 22 percent of the early voters therein during the 2008 general election. See ibid., citing Letter from NAACP LDF to Chris Herren, Chief, Voting Section, Civil Rights Division, U.S. Dep't of Justice, 4 (June 17, 2011), http://naacpldf.org/files/ case_issue/2011-06-17%20LDF%20joint%20statement%20to%20AG%20regarding%20 Florida%20election%20laws%20.PDF.

Finally, several states have passed laws requiring voters to present a government-issued photo ID at the polls on election day. Among these states are Alabama, Texas, Mississippi, South Carolina, Kansas, Rhode Island, Tennessee, and Wisconsin. See ibid., at 12–13. These laws have a tremendous disfranchisement effect on the American people, as 11 percent of voting-age citizens, approximately 22.9 million people, do not have a government-issued photo ID. See ibid., at 13, citing Brennan Center for Justice, *Citizens*

Without Proof: A Survey of Americans' Possession of Documentary Proof of Citizenship and Photo Identification 3 (2006), http://www.brennancenter.org/page/-/d/download_ file_39242.pdf. They are especially devastating for blacks, as 25 percent of black voting-age citizens (over 6 million people) do not possess a valid government-issued photo ID. See ibid.

The NAACP report also highlights federal and state attempts to weaken the Voting Rights Act of 1965. See ibid., at 39–40. Sections 2 and 5 are the most important provisions of the act. Many of these facially neutral voting measures smack of voting techniques used throughout the South during the Jim Crow era to deny the right to vote or to reduce the voting power of blacks.

Notes

Introduction

1. Cuban stated his position in different ways in numerous interviews at the time. For example, in an interview on ESPN, he stated, "What Donald said was wrong. It was abhorrent. There's no place for racism in the NBA, any business I'm associated with, and I don't want to be associated with people who have that position.... But at the same time, that's a decision I make. I think you've got to be very, very careful when you start making blanket statements about what people say and think, as opposed to what they do. It's a very, very slippery slope.... But regardless of your background, regardless of the history they have, if we're taking something somebody said in their home and we're trying to turn it into something that leads to you being forced to divest property in any way, shape or form, that's not the United States of America. I don't want to be part of that." Tim MacMahon, "Cuban Not in Favor of Booting Sterling," ESPN, April 29, 2014, http://espn.go.com/nba/story/_/id/10854381/mark-cuban-dallas-mavericks-rails-donald-sterling-not-favor-kicking-owner (accessed April 16, 2016). For similar statements, see, e.g., Chuck Schilken, "Mark Cuban on Donald Sterling: 'People Are Allowed to Be Morons,'" *Los Angeles Times*, April 29, 2014, http://www.latimes.com/sports/sportsnow/la-sp-sn-mark-cuban-donald-sterling-20140429-story.html (accessed April 16, 2016); Nicki Jhabvala, "Mark Cuban Talks Donald Sterling, Admits His Own Prejudices," *Denver Post*, May 22, 2014, http://blogs.denverpost.com/nuggets/2014/05/22/mark-cuban-talks-donald-sterling-admits-prejudices/10717 (accessed April 16, 2016). Sterling's association with the NBA ended with the sale of the Los Angeles Clippers to former Microsoft CEO Steve Ballmer for $2 billion. The sale closed after a California court ruled that Sterling's wife, Shelly, was legally authorized to sell the team on behalf of the Sterling Family Trust. See Ken Berger, "Sale of Clippers to Steve Ballmer Closes; Donald Sterling Out," CBS Sports, August 12, 2014, http://www.cbssports.com/nba/writer/ken-berger/24657297/

sale-of-clippers-to-steve-ballmer-closes-donald-sterling-out (accessed April 16, 2016); "Shelly Sterling Can Proceed with Sale," ESPN, July 29, 2014, http://espn.go.com/los-angeles/nba/story/_/id/11277942/judge-rules-donald-sterling-attempt-block-sale-los-angeles-clippers (accessed April 16, 2016); "Donald Sterling Banned for Life from NBA and Fined 2.5 Million for Racist Rant," YouTube, April 29, 2014, https://www.youtube.com/watch?v=gnr7wnRoh6U (accessed April 16, 2016).

2. See, e.g., Richard Delgado & Jean Stefancic, *Critical Race Theory: An Introduction*, 2nd ed. (New York: NYC Press, 2012); Eduardo Bonilla-Silva, *Racism Without Racist: Color-blind Racism and the Persistence of Racial Inequality in the United States*, 3rd ed. (Lanham, MD: Rowman & Littlefield, 2009); Roy L. Brooks, *Structures of Judicial Decision Making from Legal Formalism to Critical Race Theory*, 2nd ed. (Durham, NC: Carolina Academic Press, 2005), pt. 2. Critical race theory, delinked from racism, is included in the broader perspective presented in this book. See chapters 2 and 4.

3. Ta-Nehisi Coates, "This Town Needs a Better Class of Racist," *Atlantic*, May 1, 2014, http://www.theatlantic.com/politics/archive/2014/05/This-Town-Needs-A-Better-Class-Of-Racist/361443 (accessed September 1, 2015). See also Ta-Nehisi Coates, *Between the World and Me* (New York: Spiegel & Grau, 2015). I would position racial subordination between intentional and unintentional discrimination. It is less egregious than many acts of intentional discrimination because of the absence of an invidious animus, but more glaring than unintentional discrimination because of the awareness of racial harm prior to taking action. The true unintentional discriminator has no awareness of the racial harm at the time of the decision to act, and is made aware of it only after the facially neutral factor has been put into play, e.g., a requirement that male employees cannot wear beards. Under current law, racial subordination is not actionable as either intentional (or "disparate treatment") discrimination or unintentional ("disparate impact") discrimination. It is not the former because the harmful treatment took place not "because of" race but rather "in spite of" race. Furthermore, the perpetrator is protected from legal liability if he has "a legitimate, nondiscriminatory reason" for taking the racially harmful action, which in the case of Mark Cuban is the right to privacy or protection of private property. Similarly, racial subordination is not actionable as unintentional discrimination because it would have to be proven, through time-consuming statistical analysis, that application of the racially neutral factor (e.g., the right to privacy) has a disproportionate impact on blacks. And, if proven, there is still no liability if the disparate impact serves a "business necessity" and is the "least discriminatory alternative" available. Too often the legal community gets lost in a parallel universe of its own creation. Taking racial subordination out of these weeds, as I endeavor to do in this book, allows us to focus on the big picture and not allow the tail to wag the dog. See Texas Department of Housing & Community Affairs v. Inclusive Communities Project, Inc., 135 S. Ct. 2507 (2015); Wards Cove Packing Company, Inc. v. Atonio, 490 U.S. 642 (1989); Texas Department of Community Affairs v. Burdine, 450 U.S. 248 (1981). See generally Roy L. Brooks, Gilbert Paul Carrasco, and Michael Selmi, *The Law of Discrimination: Cases and Perspectives* (New Providence, NJ: LexisNexis, 2011).

4. James Baldwin, "Many Thousands Gone," in *Notes of a Native Son* (Boston: Beacon Press, 1984), 24. For additional commentary, see Watson Branch, "Reparations for Slavery: A Dream Deferred," *San Diego International Law Journal* 3 (2002): 177, 182.

5. Nicolas C. Vaca, *The Presumed Alliance: The Unspoken Conflict Between Latinos and Blacks and What It Means for America* (New York: Rayo, 2004), 13 (quoting Toni Morrison). A well-known study of discrimination against African Americans by immigrants of color was reported in the New York taxi industry, wherein most of the taxicab drivers are immigrants from Asia, the Middle East, and Africa. See Thomas J. Lueck, "No Fare; New York's Cabbies Show How Multi-Colored Racism Can Be," *New York Times,* November 7, 1999, section 4 (Week in Review). According to my female students from Nigeria, Nigerian women are told by their parents not to date or marry an African American. "Black immigrants are in general faring better economically than blacks born in the U.S." Monica Anderson, "6 Key Findings About Black Immigration to the U.S.," Pew Research Center, Fact Tank, April 9, 2015, http://www.pewresearch.org/fact-tank/2015/04/09/6-key-findings-about-black-immigration/ (accessed March 22, 2016).

6. Amita Kelly, "WATCH: Black GOP Senator Says He's Been Stopped by Police 7 Times in a Year," NPR, Politics, July 14, 2016, http://www.npr.org/2016/07/14/485995136/watch-black-gop-senator-says-hes-been-stopped-7-times-by-police-in-a-year (accessed July 31, 2016).

7. Joe R. Feagin, "Documenting the Costs of Slavery, Segregation, and Contemporary Racism: Why Reparations Are in Order for African Americans," *Harvard BlackLetter Law Journal* 20 (2004): 49.

8. Americans are inoculated against the unique plight of African Americans when all racial minorities are placed under a single conceptual umbrella. See Orlando Patterson, "Race and Diversity in the Age of Obama," *New York Times Book Review,* August 16, 2009, 23; Jennifer Lee and Frank Bean, *The Diversity Paradox: Immigration and the Color Line in Twenty-First Century America,* ppb. ed. (New York: Russell Sage Foundation, 2012); Wendy Wang, "Interracial Marriage: Who Is 'Marrying Out'?" Pew Research Center, Fact Tank, June 12, 2015, http://www.pewresearch.org/fact-tank/2015/06/12/interracial-marriage-who-is-marrying-out (accessed March 24, 2016). For a longitudinal study of capital deficiencies in black America, see Roy L. Brooks, *Racial Justice in the Age of Obama* (Princeton, NJ: Princeton University Press, 2009), app., figs. 1–100. The wage differential between college-educated black and white males has actually *increased* since 1972. See ibid., fig. 38. For an excellent discussion of black identity in today's society, see Baker and Simmons, *The Trouble with Post-Blackness.*

9. The Altarum Institute and the W. K. Kellogg Foundation (WKKF) released a report in 2013 detailing the economic impact of racism and the benefits of advancing racial equity. Conducted in collaboration with scholars from Johns Hopkins, Brandeis, and Harvard Universities, the study concluded that racial bias cost the United States almost $2 trillion in 2013. "We found that, if the average incomes of minorities were raised to the average incomes of whites, total U.S. earnings would increase by 12%, representing nearly $1 trillion today. By closing the earnings gap through higher productivity, gross domestic product (GDP) would increase by a comparable percentage, for an increase of $1.9 trillion today. The earnings gain would translate into $180 billion in additional corporate profits, $290 billion in additional federal tax revenues, and a potential reduction in the federal deficit of $350 billion, or 2.3% of GDP. When projected to 2030 and 2050,

the results are even more startling. . . . Closing the earnings gap by 2030 would increase GDP by 16%, or more than $5 trillion a year. Federal tax revenues would increase by over $1 trillion and corporate profits would increase by $450 billion. By 2050, closing the gap would increase GDP by 20%. This is roughly the size of the entire federal budget, and a higher percentage than all U.S. healthcare expenditures." Ani Turner, "The Business Case for Racial Equity," W. K. Kellogg Foundation, October 24, 2013, http://www.wkkf.org/resource-directory/resource/2013/10/the-business-case-for-racial-equity (accessed March 22, 2016). See also Ani Turner, "The Business Case for Racial Equity in Michigan." W. K. Kellogg Foundation, June 11, 2015, https://www.wkkf.org/news-and-media/article/2015/05/the-business-case-for-racial-equity-in-michigan-report-released (accessed March 24, 2016). It is not surprising, then, that a UCLA study found that in the years from 2011 to 2015, "movies make more when half their casts are non-white." Ryan Nakashima, "UCLA: Movies Make More Money When Half Cast Is Non-White," *San Diego Union-Tribune,* February 26, 2016, C1, http://abcnews.go.com/Entertainment/wireStory/ucla-diversely-cast-films-box-office-37190303 (accessed March 24, 2016). Although no one has conducted a similar study of racial subordination, it would seem that racial subordination only adds to the overall cost that racial disadvantage exacts on businesses and the economy.

David Von Drehle has written a series of insightful articles on anger and riots in black communities following several police killings of unarmed blacks. See, e.g., "Black Lives Matter. This Time the Charge Is Murder," *Time,* April 26, 2015, 24; "America, 2015: What Has Changed. What Hasn't. The Roots of a Riot," *Time,* May 11, 2015, 34. The statistics on police killings by race are incomplete at best. According to Jim Bueermann, a former police chief and president of the Police Foundation, a nonprofit organization based in Washington, D.C., "These shootings are grossly underreported." Bueermann's organization is dedicated to improving law enforcement. "385 People Shot, Killed by Police So Far This Year," *San Diego Union-Tribune,* May 31, 2015, A21. Indeed, an analysis by the *Washington Post* found that fatal police shootings overall happen "at twice the rate the FBI is reporting." Ibid. The available statistics show that although more whites are killed by police than blacks, the percentage of black deaths is greater than the percentage of white police killings. For example, the Justice Department's Bureau of Justice Statistics reports that more than 2,900 arrest-related deaths involving law enforcement occurred between 2003 and 2009, averaging about 420 deaths a year during the seven-year period. Blacks were about four times as likely to die while under the control of law enforcement (in custody or while being arrested) than whites. BJS Arrest-Related Deaths 2003–2009, https://docs.google.com/spreadsheets/d/1Tx7gUUqFgd2wLYVd161uuR6bnnfEz4Ouo7PYqa6aHKE/edit#gid=0 (accessed March 22, 2016). Relying on data found in the FBI's Supplementary Homicide Report, ProPublica reports, "The 1,217 deadly police shootings from 2010 to 2012 captured in the federal data show that blacks, age 15 to 19, were killed at a rate of 31.17 per million, while just 1.47 per million white males in that age range died at the hands of police." Ryan Gabrielson, Ryann Grochowski Jones, and Eric Sagara, "Deadly Force, in Black and White: A ProPublica Analysis of Killings by Police Shows Outsize Risk for Young Black Males," ProPublica, October 10, 2014, http://

www.propublica.org/article/deadly-force-in-black-and-white (accessed June 12, 2015). The statistics not only tend to underreport police killings but they do not narrow the range of the analysis by age or population difference, as ProPublica, the public-interest Web site for journalism, attempts to do. Nor do the statistics indicate whether the victims were armed or unarmed, the latter of which is the main concern of African Americans. In an effort to get better data, the *Washington Post* conducted a study of every police killing for the first five months of 2015. It focused on killings by shootings as opposed to killings by other means, such as stun guns. "Using interviews, police reports, local news accounts and other sources, [the paper] . . . tracked more than a dozen details about each killing, . . . including the victim's race, whether the person was armed and the circumstances that led to the fatal encounter." It found, inter alia, that "at least 385 people [were] shot and killed by [the] police nationwide. . . . About half the victims were white, half minority. But the demographics shifted sharply among the unarmed victims, two-thirds of whom were black or Hispanic. Overall, blacks were killed at three times the rate of whites or other minorities when adjusted by the population of the census tracts where the shooting occurred. . . . Forty-nine had no weapons, while the guns wielded by 13 others turned out to be toys. . . . The dead ranged in age from 16 to 83. Eight were children younger than 18. . . . About half of the time, police were responding to people seeking help with domestic disturbances and other complex social situations. A homeless person behaving erratically. A boyfriend threatening violence. . . . Although police are authorized to use deadly force only when they fear for their lives or the lives of others, less than 1% of the 385 police killings resulted in an officer being charged with a crime." "385 People Shot, Killed by Police So Far This Year," *San Diego Union-Tribune*, May 31, 2015, A21.

Finally, the Department of Justice engaged in a yearlong study of the Baltimore Police Department in the wake of the Freddie Gray death. Gray was a twenty-five-year-old black man who died on April 19, 2015, from injuries to his spinal cord sustained while being transported in a police van by six Baltimore police officers. Gray was arrested for allegedly possessing an illegal switchblade. His death triggered protests and riots in Baltimore. After a medical examiner ruled that Gray's death was a homicide, three of the police officers were charged with manslaughter and lesser crimes. They were subsequently acquitted, and prosecutors decided to drop criminal charges against the remaining three officers. See "Freddie Gray Case Ends with No Convictions of Any Police Officers," *New York Times*, July 27, 2016, http://www.nytimes.com/interactive/2015/04/30/us/what-happened-freddie-gray-arrested-by-baltimore-police-department-map-timeline.html (accessed August 10, 2016). Notwithstanding the outcome of these trials, the Department of Justice's report concluded that the Baltimore Police Department had a "longstanding and systemic" practice of targeting blacks and violating their civil rights. The report found that the police department engaged in "a pattern or practice" of discrimination against African Americans, including making stops, searches, and arrests in violation of the Fourth Amendment's prohibition against unreasonable searches and seizures, retaliating against the exercise of free speech guaranteed by the First Amendment, and using excessive force routinely. These practices, the report stated, were "driven by systemic deficiencies in the BPD's policies, training, supervision, and accountability structures that failed to equip officers with the tools they need to police effectively and within the bounds of federal law." The report highlighted pedestrian stops. In the period from 2010 to 2015, Baltimore police officers made more than 300,000 recorded stops. Of these stops, 410 involved people who were stopped at least 10 times. Within this group, 95% were African American, one of whom had been stopped 30 times in less than four years and never criminally charged. "Unnecessarily violent" stops were common, as was using the N-word. See "Justice Department Announces Findings of Investigation into Baltimore Police Department," United States Department of Justice, Office of Public Affairs, Justice News, August 10, 2016, https://www.justice.gov/opa/pr/justice-department-announces-findings-investigation-baltimore-police-department (accessed August 10, 2016); Kevin Rector, "Following Justice Dept. report, Rawlings-Blake: 'We have to heal our city,'" Freddie Gray Case Trials, *Baltimore Sun*, August 10, 2016, http://www.baltimoresun.com/news/maryland/baltimore-city/bs-md-ci-doj-report-released-20160810-story.html (accessed August 10, 2016). One wonders whether anything short of massive dismissals of police officers in the department will resolve the problem in Baltimore. In other words, is it possible to change a bad cop into a good cop?

10. Touré, "How to Talk to Young Black Boys About Trayvon Martin," *Time*, April 2, 2012, 17. Those who criticize Touré's post-blackness would likely applaud his moment of affirming blackness. See Houston A. Baker and K. Merinda Simmons, eds., *The Trouble with Post-Blackness* (New York: Columbia University Press, 2015).

11. Damon Tweedy, *Black Man in a White Coat: A Doctor's Reflection on Race and Medicine* (New York: Picador, 2015), 132.

12. Kareem Abdul-Jabbar, "Kareem Abdul-Jabbar: How to Tell if You're a Racist Like Donald Sterling," *Time*, May 5, 2014, http://time.com/87024/kareem-abdul-jabbar-why-donald-sterling-does-not-think-he-is-racist/ (accessed February 20, 2016).

13. "Significantly more African-Americans (70%) report that they prefer bigger government compared with the total population (46%), who are much more divided on the issue (43% prefer smaller government)." Neha Sahgal and Greg Smith, "A Religious Portrait of African-Americans," Pew Research Center, January 30, 2009, http://www.pewforum.org/2009/01/30/a-religious-portrait-of-african-americans (accessed March 2, 2016).

14. John Lewis, "Time to Restore Voting Rights Act," *San Diego Union-Tribune*, February 22, 2014, B9. In 1991, Congress enacted a new Civil Rights Act for the purpose of overturning a number of Supreme Court decisions handed down in the 1980s. For a more detailed discussion, see, e.g., Brooks, Carrasco, and Selmi, *The Law of Discrimination*, 434.

15. Oliver Wendell Holmes, *The Common Law*, ed. Mark DeWolfe (Cambridge, MA: Belknap Press of Harvard University Press, 1963), 5.

16. Thurgood Marshall, "Reflections on the Bicentennial of the United States Constitution," *Harvard Law Review* 101 (1987): 1, 5.

17. Zachary Roth, "Voting Rights in Danger One Year After Shelby County Supreme Court Ruling," MSNBC, June 25, 2014, http://www.msnbc.com/msnbc/voting-rights-danger-one-year-after-shelby-county-supreme-court-ruling (accessed February 20, 2016).

18. See Zachary Roth, "93-Year-Old Black Man Disenfranchised by Alabama Voter ID Law," MSNBC, June 3, 2014, http://www.msnbc.com/msnbc/voter-id-law-disenfranchises-93-year-old-black-man (accessed February 20, 2016). William Barber, *The Third Reconstruction: Moral Mondays, Fusion Politics, and the Rise of a New Justice Movement* (Boston: Beacon Press, 2016); Ari Berman, *Give Us the Ballot: The Modern Struggle for Voting Rights in America* (New York: Farrar, Straus and Giroux, 2015). For a more detailed discussion, see appendix B in this book.

19. Dating back to the early 1980s, gifted thinkers, structuralists, and behaviorialists alike have attempted to explain why the pace of socioeconomic progress for African Americans could be so slow after the demise of de jure segregation and discrimination in the 1960s and early 1970s. Scholars such as Derrick Bell, Thomas Sowell, Joe Feagin, Orlando Patterson, Shelby Steele, William Julius Wilson, Stephan and Abigail Thernstrom, Cornel West, Glenn Loury, Skip Gates, Michael Eric Dyson, Thomas Shapiro, Richard Delgado and Jean Stefancic, Ellis Cose, Dinesh D'Souza, John McWhorter, Herna Vera, Melvin Sikes, Eric Yamamoto, Eileen O'Brien, Tommy Shelby, Eduardo Bonilla-Silva, George Lipsitz, Michelle Alexander, and Ta-Nehisi Coates, to name but a few, have focused on external and internal factors. They have, for example, looked at racism (individual and institutional, conscious and unconscious, and what Joe Feagin calls "frontstage" and "backstage," such as Donald Sterling's racist remarks), seismic shifts in the economy (from urban to suburban centers of employment, from smokestack to high-tech jobs), failing public schools, broken families, teenage pregnancy, black-on-black crime, racial discrimination in our criminal justice system, and other racial or class barriers within the context of what can be called the "socioeconomic race problem"—financial, human, and social capital disparities between black and white Americans. Where scholars have considered the socio-legal and sociocultural race problems, they have treated them entirely as problems of racism. There has been very little, if any, attempt to view these problems from the perspective of racial subordination as defined and applied here. The most important law book by a critical race theorist, first published in 1973, remains Derrick Bell, *Race, Racism, and American Law,* 6th ed. (Boston: Aspen Publishers, 2008). See also Dorothy A. Brown, *Critical Race Theory: Cases, Materials, and Problems,* 2nd ed. (St. Paul, MN: Thomson/West, 2007). The prolific Joe Feagin has coauthored a wonderful book on President Obama's racist treatment in the American mainstream culture. See Adia Harvey-Wingfield and Joe Feagin, *Yes We Can? White Racial Framing and the Obama Presidency,* 2nd ed. (New York: Routledge, 2013).

Chapter 1. The Spirit of *Brown*

1. For a discussion of post–Jim Crow civil rights theories and socioeconomic conditions facing blacks, see Roy L. Brooks, *Racial Justice in the Age of Obama* (Princeton: Princeton University Press, 2009). Prior to *Bakke,* blacks made the most racial progress ever, save for emancipation, especially in earnings at all educational levels (high school to postgraduate education) and in college participation, even slightly exceeding the white percentage, *without* negatively impacting white progress in any appreciable way. See

ibid., app., figs. 30–36, 55–60. As Judge Constance Baker Motely, who as a young NAACP lawyer worked on the *Brown* case, has remarked, *Brown* gave constitutional status to group rights: "Group rights, thus, became substantively as well as procedurally a distinct, new area in constitutional adjudication." Constance Baker Motley, *Equal Justice Under the Law: An Autobiography* (New York: Farrar, Straus and Giroux, 1998), 111.

2. By Lincoln's second inauguration, the purpose of the war had changed for the North from a war to save the Union to one to end slavery. Union soldiers returning from the South had reported the horrors of slavery to their fellow citizens. Many soldiers reenlisted. See generally James M. McPherson, *For Cause and Comrades: Why Men Fought in the Civil War* (New York: Oxford University Press, 1997). The defeated South was forced to accept emancipation, at least on paper, as a condition for rejoining the Union. A similar transformation took place in "free" states. For example, "Illinois, so notorious for antiblack racism before the war and anti-emancipation legislation during the war, repealed its 'Black Laws' in 1865 and was the first state to ratify the new Thirteenth Amendment." Allen C. Guelzo, *Lincoln's Emancipation Proclamation: The End of Slavery in America* (New York: Simon & Schuster, 2004), 232–233. Guelzo argues that at the time of his death, Lincoln believed in racial equality, and the nation through the enactment of the Reconstruction Amendments had followed him to that position. See ibid., 250. I would argue that this is true, but only on paper, hence the Reconstruction laws. Yet I do concede that this was quite an achievement relative to what was on paper prior to the Civil War.

Section 1 of the Thirteenth Amendment abolishes slavery in the United States, and section 2 gives Congress the power to enforce section 1 through legislation. U.S. Const. amend. XIII, §§ 1, 2. Section 1 of the Fourteenth Amendment declares, "All persons born or naturalized in the United States, and subject to the jurisdiction thereof, are citizens of the United States and of the state wherein they reside. No state shall make or enforce any law which shall abridge the privileges or immunities of citizens of the United States; nor shall any state deprive any person of life, liberty, or property, without due process of law; nor deny to any person within its jurisdiction the equal protection of the laws." Section 5 of the Fourteenth Amendment gives Congress the power to enforce the Fourteenth Amendment through legislation. U.S. Const. amend. XIV, §§ 1, 5. Section 1 of the Fifteenth Amendment declares that a citizen may not be denied the right to vote based on race, color, or previous condition of servitude. Section 2 gives Congress the power to enact legislation to enforce section 1. U.S. Const. amend. XV, §§ 1, 2.

Article 5 of the Constitution details the amendment process described in the text. The enactment of a statute is cumbersome but not as difficult as the amendment process. Before passed into law, statutes are bills. Bills may originate in either the House of Representatives or the Senate, and a representative or senator must sponsor the bill. Next, a committee is assigned to review the bill. If the committee releases the bill, it is voted on by members of the congressional house in which it originated. If the bill passes by a simple majority, the bill then moves to the other congressional house, where it is reviewed by another committee and voted upon if released by that committee. If the bill passes by a simple majority in that house, members of both the Senate and House of

Representatives work together to create the final bill by fixing differences in the versions of the bill passed by each house. The final product is again voted on by members of the House of Representatives and the Senate. If passed by a simple majority in both houses, the bill is sent to the president, who may sign the bill into law or veto it within ten days. "The Legislative Process," U.S. House of Representatives, http://www.house.gov/content/learn/legislative_process/ (last visited February 9, 2015). See also Charles W. Johnson, "How Our Laws Are Made," H.R. Doc. No. 108-93 (2003).

Congress enacted several Reconstruction-era criminal and civil statutes. One of the most important criminal statutes was Title 18, U.S.C., § 241, which offered some protection to African Americans who were being intimidated and attacked by white supremacist groups primarily in the South. Section 241 made it illegal for two or more people to "conspire to injure, oppress, threaten, or intimidate any person" for exercising a federal right. The punishment for violating section 241 included monetary fines and up to ten years in prison, or life imprisonment if the criminal act resulted in death. See Enforcement Act of 1870, §§ 4–6, 16 Stat. 140, 141–142 (codified as amended at 18 U.S.C. § 241 [2012]). Congress also enacted Title 18 U.S.C. § 242, which prohibited a person from willfully depriving any person in any state, territory, commonwealth, or district of any rights, privileges, or immunities secured or protected by the Constitution or federal laws. Those who violated section 242 faced jail time and/or fines. 18 U.S.C. § 242 (2012). In United States v. Price, 383 U.S. 787, 805–806 (1966), the Supreme Court held that the defendant sheriff and his coconspirators could be convicted under 18 U.S.C. § 241 for depriving three victims of their federal rights not to be deprived of life or liberty without due process when the sheriff released the victims from jail in the middle of the night, which allowed the coconspirators to kill them. See generally Roy L. Brooks, Gilbert Paul Carrasco, and Michael Selmi, *The Law of Discrimination: Cases and Perspectives* (New Providence, NJ: LexisNexis, 2011), 744 for a discussion of sections 241 and 242.

As to civil statutes, Congress passed section 1 of the Civil Rights Act of 1866, which provided that every person born in the United States, regardless of race or color, has the same right within the United States to make and enforce contracts, sue and be sued, give evidence in court, inherit, purchase, sell, lease, convey real and personal property, and receive full and equal benefit of all laws and proceedings as are enjoyed by white citizens. Act of April 9, 1866, ch. 31 § 1, 14 Stat. 27 (reenacted by the Enforcement Act of 1870, Act of May 31, 1870, ch. 114, §§ 16 & 18, 16 Stat. 140, 144). Section 1 of the Act of 1866 was codified and slightly amended in 42 U.S.C. § 1981 (2012). Additionally, the Civil Rights Act of 1866 gave all citizens the same right to "inherit, purchase, lease, sell, hold, and convey real and personal property." These protections were codified in 42 U.S.C. § 1982. Act of April 9, 1866, ch. 31, 14 Stat. 27 (reenacted by Enforcement Act of 1870, ch. 114, § 18, 16 Stat. 140, 144 (1870) (codified as amended at 42 U.S.C. § 1982 [2012]). See Brooks, Carrasco, and Selmi, *The Law of Discrimination,* 289. Title 42 U.S.C. § 1983 originated as section 1 of the 1871 Civil Rights Act, which was passed three years after the Fourteenth Amendment was enacted. Ibid., 849. Section 1983, as it is commonly known today, provides a civil remedy for persons deprived of their rights. The statute states that "[e]very person who, under color of any statute, ordinance, regulation, custom, or usage, of any State or Territory or the District of Columbia, subjects, or causes to be subjected, any citizen of the United States or other person within the jurisdiction thereof to the deprivation of any rights, privileges, or immunities secured by the Constitution and laws, shall be liable to the party injured in an action at law, suit in equity, or other proper proceeding for redress. . . ." 42 U.S.C. § 1983 (2012). Congress also enacted section 1985(3) as part of the 1871 Civil Rights Act. Section 1985(3) allows for the recovery of damages from persons who conspired to deprive "any person or class of persons of equal protection of the laws, or of equal privileges and immunities under the law." 42 U.S.C. § 1985(3) (2012). See also Roy L. Brooks, "Use of the Civil Rights Acts of 1866 and 1871 to Redress Employment Discrimination," *Cornell Law Review* 62 (1977): 258, 258–266 (discussing the history and implementation of 42 U.S.C. §§ 1983, 1985(3), and 1981). Congress did not stop there. For example, it also enacted the Civil Rights Act of 1875, which prohibited racial discrimination in juries, schools, transportation, and public accommodations. Civil Rights Act of 1875, ch. 114, 18 Stat. 335 (1875). For a discussion on the legislative history of the Civil Rights Act of 1875, see Aderson Bellegarde François, "The Brand of Inferiority: The Civil Rights Act of 1875, White Supremacy, and Affirmative Action," *Howard Law Journal* 57 (2014): 573.

3. Lawrence Goldstone, *Inherently Unequal: The Betrayal of Equal Rights by the Supreme Court, 1865–1903* (New York: Walker, 2011), 12. See, e.g., Jason Sokol, *All Eyes Are Upon Us: Race and Politics from Boston to Brooklyn* (New York: Basic Books, 2014), xxii–xxvi (arguing that northerners supported high-achieving blacks individually but opposed civil rights for blacks collectively).

4. 98 Eng. Rep. 499, 510 (K.B. 1772). For further discussion of Lord Mansfield's opinion, see, e.g., Steven M. Wise, *Though the Heavens May Fall: The Landmark Trial That Led to the End of Human Slavery* (Boston: Da Capo Press, 2005), 179–182.

5. See, e.g., Alfred W. Blumrosen and Ruth G. Blumrosen, *Slave Nation: How Slavery United the Colonies & Sparked the American Revolution* (Naperville, IL: Sourcebooks, 2005), 11–12; A. Leon Higginbotham Jr., *In the Matter of Color: Race and the American Legal Process: The Colonial Period* (New York: Oxford University Press, 1978), 313–368.

6. 60 U.S. 393, 408 (1856).

7. For further discussion, see Blumrosen and Blumrosen, *Slave Nation*, 249–251. One of the best analyses of the case remains Don E. Fehrenbacher, *The Dred Scott Case: Its Significance in American Law and Politics* (New York: Oxford University Press, 1978).

8. Between 1875 and 1954, the year that Brown v. Board of Education was decided, the Supreme Court issued a few positive civil rights decisions. See, e.g., Strauder v. West Virginia, 100 U.S. 303, 310 (1880) (holding unconstitutional West Virginia's statute that categorically excluded African Americans from serving on juries purely based on their race); Powell v. Alabama, 287 U.S. 45, 71, 73 (1932) (reversing the criminal convictions and death sentences of nine African American males convicted of rape and holding that a trial court's failure to give defendants charged with capital offenses reasonable time to secure a lawyer or to appoint effective counsel violated the due-process clause of the Fourteenth Amendment).

9. United States v. Cruikshank, 92 U.S. 542 (1875); United States v. Cruikshank, 25 F. Cas. 707, 707 (Circuit Court District Louisiana 1874). The number of dead African Americans is reported in Goldstone, *Inherently Unequal*, 89. But see Charles Lane, *The Day Freedom Died: The Colfax Massacre, the Supreme Court, and the Betrayal of Reconstruction* (New York: Henry Holt, 2008), 265, estimating that between sixty-two and eighty-one African Americans were killed in the Colfax Massacre.

10. See *Cruikshank*, 92 U.S. at 542, 554, 559. Howard notes that "The record does not indicate that William Cruikshank or his companions were men of means yet the defense team numbered in its ranks John A. Campbell, architect of the butchers' *Slaughterhouse* argument and former member of the Supreme Court, and David Dudley Field, brother of then sitting Justice Stephen Field. Money raised from Klan sympathizers . . . probably also paid for the lawyers defending Cruikshank and his codefendants." John R. Howard, *The Shifting Wind: The Supreme Court and Civil Rights from Reconstruction to Brown* (New York: State University of New York Press, 1999), 100. The Enforcement Act of 1870 was a bulwark for the Fourteenth and Fifteenth Amendments. It sought to ensure that Reconstruction laws were respected, by criminally sanctioning persons who conspired to interfere with another citizen's federally guaranteed rights. Goldstone, *Inherently Unequal*, 91. The Enforcement Act of 1870 was one of several statutes designed to implement the Reconstruction Amendments both criminally and civilly. See Xi Wang, "The Making of Federal Enforcement Laws, 1870–1872," *Chicago-Kent Law Review* 70 (1995): 1013, 1022–1032.

11. See *Cruikshank*, 92 U.S. at 554, 549. Specifically, the Court wrote, "The fourteenth amendment prohibits a State from depriving any person of life, liberty, or property, without due process of law; but this adds nothing to the rights of one citizen as against another. It simply furnishes an additional guaranty against any encroachment by the States upon the fundamental rights which belong to every citizen as a member of society." Ibid., at 554. But see Wilson R. Huhn, "The Legacy of Slaughterhouse, Bradwell, and Cruikshank in Constitutional Interpretation," *Akron Law Review* 42 (2009): 1051, 1074–1078 (arguing that the Fourteenth Amendment was, in fact, intended to apply to acts of discrimination committed by private individuals). See generally "The Evolution of the State Action Doctrine and the Current Debate," *Harvard Law Review* 123 (2010): 1255, 1255–1258, for a discussion of state action doctrine's development.

12. See *Cruikshank*, 92 U.S. at 555–556. See also 551–552 (stating that the right to assemble was not created by the First Amendment, and the First Amendment only protects against congressional interference on that right); ibid., 553 (stating that the right to bear arms was not created by the Second Amendment, which, in any event, only protects citizens from federal encroachment).

13. See Douglas Linder, *Lynching in America: Statistics, Information, Images*, University of Missouri, Kansas City, http://law2.umkc.edu/faculty/projects/ftrials/shipp/lynchingyear.html (accessed February 2, 2015) (reporting the high volume of black lynchings that occurred, especially in the 1890s).

14. See United States v. Reese, 92 U.S. 214, 221, 215–217 (1875). See also 238–239 (Clifford, J., with whom Hunt, J., joins, dissenting). In response to the North's

Reconstruction efforts, many southern states adopted poll taxes, which required eligible voters to pay a fee in order to vote. Poll taxes were used to prevent African Americans and poor whites from voting. David Schultz and Sarah Clark, "Wealth v. Democracy: The Unfulfilled Promise of the Twenty-Fourth Amendment," *Quinnipiac Law Review* 29 (2011): 375, 386–391. Kentucky was a slave state that remained loyal to the Union during the Civil War. About sixty thousand Kentucky residents served in the Union Army, whereas thirty thousand joined the Confederate Army. Despite its loyalty to the North, "pro-Union white sentiment [in Kentucky] was neither opposed to slavery nor supportive of black rights." Howard, *The Shifting Wind*, 105.

15. See *Reese*, 92 U.S. at 216–217.

16. See ibid. at 217–218, 220–221. The Court noted that if the interference with voting rights was not motivated by race, color, or previous condition of servitude, Congress had no power to punish. Ibid., 218.

17. Ibid., 241 (Clifford, J., with whom Hunt, J., joins, dissenting). The importance of *Reese* was reflected in the fact that decisions in more than forty cases were suspended pending the Court's decision. Howard, *The Shifting Wind*, 107.

18. "The impact of *Cruikshank* and *Reese* was immediate, practical, and devastating. The 1876 presidential election was months away." Howard, *The Shifting Wind*, 109. In 1874, almost one thousand cases were filed in the South alleging violations of the Enforcement Acts. In 1875, after both *Reese* and *Cruikshank* were decided, that number fell to about two hundred suits. Ibid.

19. Civil Rights Cases, 109 U.S. 3, 9. (1883).

20. Ibid. One of the five plaintiffs did not report his race. That plaintiff brought suit against the Grand Opera House in New York "for denying to another person, whose color is not stated, the full enjoyment of the accommodations of the theater. . . ." Ibid., 4. See also Howard, *The Shifting Wind*, 126–127, reporting that one plaintiff, Mr. William R. Davis, a twenty-six-year-old African American man, had purchased tickets to the opera knowing he would not be admitted. He wanted to test the opera house's discriminatory policy, much like Homer Plessy would later test Louisiana's public transportation laws. Howard also notes, "The cluster of suits that became the *Civil Rights Cases* illuminated the meaning of racial caste distinctions in the everyday lives of blacks and whites. . . . It was a case which also went to the feeling and tone of everyday life for blacks." Ibid., 125–127.

21. Ibid., 24.

22. Ibid., 9, 11, 19, 20–21, 24–25.

23. Ibid., 26, 34, 35, 43, 58–59 (Harlan, J., dissenting).

24. Ibid., 46–47, 49–50, 52, 59–59. Section 2 of article IV of the United States Constitution is known as the Privileges and Immunities Clause. It provides that "[t]he Citizens of each State shall be entitled to all Privileges and Immunities of Citizens in the several States." U.S. Const. art. IV, § 2.

25. Civil Rights Cases, 109 U.S. at 61. See Goldstone, *Inherently Unequal*, 128–129. Following the *Civil Rights Cases* decision, over two thousand whites and blacks gathered in Washington, D.C., at a protest where Frederick Douglass spoke. Howard, *The Shifting Wind*, 131.

26. Plessy v. Ferguson, 163 U.S. 537, 541–542, 550–551 (1896). The statute stated "that all railway companies carrying passengers in their coaches in this state, shall provide equal but separate accommodations for the white, and colored races, by providing two or more passenger coaches for each passenger train, or by dividing the passenger coaches by a partition so as to secure separate accommodations: provided, that this section shall not be construed to apply to street railroads. No person or persons shall be permitted to occupy seats in coaches other than the ones assigned to them, on account of the race they belong to." Ibid., 540 Violators would be charged twenty-five dollars or imprisoned for up to twenty days. Ibid., 541. Goldstone reports that the railway conductor and police deputy involved had agreed to take part in the incident, and that Plessy was removed peacefully from the railway car. Goldstone, *Inherently Unequal*, 159. In Rosa Parks and Jim Haskins, *Rosa Parks: My Story* (New York: Dial Books, 1992). 115–118, Rosa Parks recalls the famous civil rights incident in 1955 when she, an African American woman, was arrested after refusing to give her seat to a white bus rider. For a more detailed analysis of Plessy v. Ferguson, see Brooks, Carrasco, and Selmi, *The Law of Discrimination*, 34–35.

27. *Plessy*, 163 U.S. at 544.

28. Ibid., 542–544, 551–552, 558. See also Howard, *The Shifting Wind*, 148 (detailing how the majority opinion followed sociologist William Graham Sumner's proposition that the law cannot alter culture, and thus the Fourteenth Amendment must not be construed as doing so).

29. *Plessy*, 163 U.S. at 559.

30. Ibid., 555–559, 562–566. See, e.g., Michael Stokes Paulsen, "The Worst Constitutional Decisions of All Time," *Notre Dame Law Review* 78 (2003): 995, 100 (declaring that Plessy v. Ferguson and Dred Scott v. Sanford are "among the many obvious rivals for the title of worst constitutional decision of all time"); Jamal Greene, "The Anticanon," *Harvard Law Review* 125 (2011): 379, 380 (referring to Plessy v Ferguson and Dred Scott v. Sanford as stock answers to the question of "What is the worst Supreme Court decision?"). As we shall see in the next chapter, Justice Harlan's opinion contains other language to which critical race theorists often point in making an important observation about the deficiency of the racial-omission norm.

31. Williams v. Mississippi, 170 U.S. 213, 213–214, 225 (1898). See also Charles L. Zelden, *The Battle for the Black Ballot* (Lawrence: University Press of Kansas, 2004), 18 (describing how many southern states enacted literary tests, poll taxes, and grandfather clauses in the early 1900s in an effort to prevent blacks from voting and serving on juries).

32. *Williams*, 170 U.S. at 214, 217, 220–221. The voter registration law also included residency requirements and prohibited citizens who had been convicted of certain crimes from registering. Ibid., at 220–221. After Mississippi enacted its new voting requirements, less than 9,000 out of the 147,000 voting-age blacks voted in elections. Zelden, *The Battle for the Black Ballot*, 18.

33. *Williams*, 170 U.S. at 220.

34. Ibid., at 221.

35. Ibid., at 223–225. See also Angela Behrens, Jeff Manza, and Christopher Uggen, "Ballot Manipulation and the 'Menace of Negro Domination': Racial Threat and Felon Disenfranchisement in the United States, 1850–2002," *American Journal of Sociology* 109 (2003): 559, 569 (arguing that the Court was aware disfranchisement laws were aimed to inhibit blacks from voting by targeting " 'the alleged characteristics of the negro race' " while allowing laws to target "both 'weak and vicious white men as well as weak and vicious black men' ").

36. Giles v. Harris, 189 U.S. 475, 482–488 (1903). The pre-1903 voting registration criteria included residency requirements and poll taxes. It excluded from eligibility "insane persons" and people who had been convicted of certain crimes. Finally, it allowed men who were veterans, descendants of veterans, or "of good character and who understand the duties and obligations of citizenship under a republican form of government" to register to vote. Unsurprisingly, the pre-1903 voter registration laws were "practically administered . . . [to] let in all whites and [keep] out a large part, if not all, of the blacks," so African Americans would not be assured lifelong voting rights. Ibid., at 483. Under the post-1903 scheme, a person seeking to register to vote either had to pass a literacy test, own forty acres of land, or have substantial real and personal property upon which they had paid three hundred dollars in state taxes the previous year. Ibid., at 482–483.

37. Ibid., at 486–487. See also Howard, *The Shifting Wind,* 164 (explaining how the Court's opinion "gratuitously ridicule[d] the plaintiffs and their claims. . . . If the law was a fraud how could they ask to be its beneficiary, but if it were not a fraud, as implied by a demand to be put on the rolls it created, why would they complain about being excluded by its operation.").

38. *Giles,* 189 U.S. at 494 (Harlan, J., dissenting).

39. Missouri ex rel. Gaines v. Canada, 305 U.S. 337 (1938); McLaurin v. Oklahoma State Regents for Higher Education, 339 U.S. 637 (1950); Sweatt v. Painter, 339 U.S. 629 (1950).

40. Missouri ex rel. Gaines v. Canada, 305 U.S. 337, 343 (1938).

41. Ibid.

42. Ibid., at 346.

43. Ibid., at 350.

44. For further discussion, see Sherman P. Willis, "Bridging the Gap: A Look at the Higher Education Cases Between *Plessy* and *Brown,*" *Thurgood Marshall Law Journal* 30 (2004): 1, 5–12.

45. See Gong Lum v. Rice, 275 U.S. 78, 84 (1927) (finding a failure to allege Chinese petitioner was denied the right to attend a "colored school"); Cumming v. Board of Education, 175 U.S. 528, 545 (1899) (petitioner did not allege that school district failed to establish and maintain a high school for "colored children" out of existing funds).

46. McLaurin v. Oklahoma State Regents for Higher Education, 339 U.S. 629, 637, 640 (1950).

47. Ibid., at 241.

48. Ibid.

49. Ibid., at 632.

50. "It is fundamental that these cases concern rights which are personal and present. This Court has stated unanimously that 'The State must provide (legal education) for (petitioner) in conformity with the equal protection clause of the Fourteenth Amendment and provide it as soon as it does for applicants of any other group.'" Ibid., at 635 (quoting Sipuel v. Board of Regents, 332 U.S. 631, 633 [1948]). See also 640–642.

51. Ibid., at 636.

52. Brown v. Board of Education, 347 U.S. 483, 492 (1954). The attack on separate but equal was first lodged at the district court level in one of the four cases consolidated in *Brown*, Briggs v. Elliott, 342 U.S. 350 (1952), when the NAACP, with some prodding from a sympathetic trial judge, Judge Julius Waties Waring, changed its litigation strategy against separate but equal from an attack on the equality part of the equation (equalized facilities) to an attack on the separation part (segregation is immoral and inherently unequal). See Richard Kluger, *Simple Justice: The History of* Brown v. Board of Education *and Black America's Struggle for Equality* (New York: Knopf, 2004), 304. Kluger's book may be the best book written about the *Brown* case. There is a bit of a controversy as to how the NAACP's litigation strategy changed. In his memoir, *A Matter of Law: A Memoir of Struggle in the Cause of Equal Rights* (New York: New Press, 2005), Robert L. Carter, claims that the original complaint in *Briggs* stated a frontal attack on the separate-but-equal doctrine, that the group's litigation strategy had changed from tangible to intangible inequality. Based on my review of the original filing papers, I must side with Richard Kluger's account. The complaint in *Briggs* focuses on tangible inequality, e.g., "failing to or refusing to provide such transportation to Negro children" and "maintaining public facilities for Negro children . . . which are in every respect inferior to [as opposed to separate from] those maintained for white students." Complaint at 9–10, ¶¶ 2–5, Henry Briggs, Jr. v. The Board of Trustees for School District Number 22, Clarendon County, South Carolina, United States District Court for Eastern District of South Carolina, Civil Action No. 2505, filed May 17, 1950. Although the amended complaint continues to make reference to the "facilities," it also avers that "the policy, custom, practice and usage of defendants in refusing to allow infant plaintiffs, and other Negro children to attend elementary and secondary public schools in Clarendon County, South Carolina which are maintained and operated exclusively for white children is a violation of the equal protection of the laws as guaranteed under the Fourteenth Amendment to the Constitution. . . ." Complaint at 12, ¶¶ 2–3, Henry Briggs, Jr. v. R. W. Elliott, United States District Court for Eastern District of South Carolina, Civil Action No. 2657, filed December 22, 1950.

53. *Brown*, 347 U.S. at 494.

54. Robert Carter, "The Warren Court and Desegregation," *Michigan Law Review* 67 (1968): 237, 246–247.

55. Judge Pollak's quote appears in *Simple Justice*, "About the Book," richard-kluger.com, http://www.richardkluger.com/AboutSimpleJustice.htm (accessed May 25, 2015). In my view, the definitive account of the *Brown* decision remains Richard Kluger's book, *Simple Justice: The History of* Brown v. Board of Education *and Black America's Struggle for Equality* (New York: Knopf, 1976).

56. Dennis Hevesi, "Louis H. Pollak, Civil Rights Advocate and Federal Judge, Dies at 89," *New York Times,* May 12, 2012, http://www.nytimes.com/2012/05/13/us/louis-pollak-judge-and-civil-rights-advocate-dies-at-89.html?_r=0.

57. For a discussion, see, e.g., Roy L. Brooks, *Rethinking the American Race Problem* (Berkley: University of California Press, 1990), 28. Gunnar Myrdal was a Swedish Nobel-laureate economist and sociologist who headed a large-scale study of racial relations in the United States funded by the Carnegie Institution and documented in his seminal book, *An American Dilemma: The Negro Problem and Modern Democracy* (New York: Harper & Brothers, 1944). That book described the problem of race in the United States as "an America Dilemma" because of the obvious conflict between the high ideals of freedom and equality embedded in our founding documents and continuously espoused by our leaders, which Myrdal called the "American Creed," and the regime of cruelty and humiliation visited upon blacks under the separate-but-equal doctrine, or Jim Crow. The materialists play down the impact Myrdal's book had on the *Brown* Court.

58. Derrick Bell, "Brown v. Board of Education: Forty-Five Years After the Fact," *Ohio Northern University Law Review* 26 (2000): 171, 179–180 (citing brief for the United States as amicus curiae). See Mary L. Dudziak, "Desegregation as a Cold War Imperative," *Stanford Law Review* 41 (1988): 61, 111–112.

59. See e.g., Richard Delgado, "Explaining the Rise and Fall of African American Fortunes: Interest Convergence and Civil Rights Gains," *Harvard Civil Rights–Civil Liberties Law Review* 37 (2002): 369, 369–376 (book review); Mary L. Dudziak, *Cold War Civil Rights: Race and the Image of American Democracy* (Princeton: Princeton University Press, 2002), 48–79.

60. Nor is the materialistic view inconsistent with the Myrdalian view. Clearly, the justices could have been motivated by both materialistic (bringing the country into a new, postwar order) and idealistic (living up to the American Creed) considerations, the latter of which could include atonement for a shameful judicial course of conduct in racial relations. For other views regarding the meaning of *Brown,* see, e.g., Martha Minow, *In Brown's Wake: Legacies of America's Educational Landmark* (New York: Oxford University Press, 2010); Jack M. Balkin, ed., *What Brown v. Board of Education Should Have Said: The Nation's Top Legal Experts Rewrite America's Landmark Civil Rights Decision* (New York: NYU Press, 2002).

61. *Brown,* 347 U.S. at 493.

62. Ibid., partially quoting the lower court and citing the doll test. The doll test is cited in a famous footnote 11 of the Court's opinion. *Brown,* 347 U.S. at 493, n. 11. For a more detailed discussion of the Clarks' work and legacy, see "Segregation Ruled Unequal, and Therefore Unconstitutional," *American Psychological Association,* July 2007, http://www.apa.org/research/action/segregation.aspx (accessed July 28, 2016). For the *Plessy* Court's view of the black perspective on the segregation statute, see Plessy v. Ferguson, 163 U.S. 537, 550 (1896). *Brown* does not expressly overrule *Plessy.* Why the Court did not do so is a mystery to civil rights scholars. Judge Constance Baker Motley thought that it might be because the Court "did not want to render a decision that would remove

the legal props for racial segregation in all areas of public life at once." Motley, *Equal Justice Under the Law,* 108. A go-slow approach is certainly consistent with the Court's "with all deliberate speed" directive given in Brown v. Board of Education of Topeka (*Brown II*), 349 U.S. 294 (1955).

Chapter 2. Juridical Subordination

1. See, e.g., Roy L. Brooks, *Rethinking the American Race Problem* (Berkeley: University of California Press (1990), 25 (sources cited therein).

2. For a discussion of cases and statutes that implement the racial-omission and racial-integration norms, see, e.g., Roy L. Brooks, Gilbert Paul Carrasco, and Michael Selmi, *The Law of Discrimination: Cases and Perspectives* (New Providence, NJ: Lexis-Nexis, 2011).

3. See, e.g., Fisher v. Univ. of Tex. at Austin, 138 S. Ct. 2411 (2013); Parents Involved in Cmty. Schs. v. Seattle Sch. Dist. No. 1, 551 U.S. 701 (2007); Gratz v. Bollinger, 539 U.S. 244 (2003); Grutter v. Bollinger, 539 U.S. 306 (2003); Adarand Constructors, Inc. v. Pena, 515 U.S. 200 (1995); City of Richmond v. J. A. Croson, Co., 488 U.S. 469 (1989); Regents of the Univ. of Cal. v. Bakke, 438 U.S. 265 (1978). See generally Brooks, Carrasco, and Selmi, *The Law of Discrimination,* 1323–1401; Kathleen M. Sullivan and Gerald Gunther, *Constitutional Law,* 15th ed. (New York: Foundation Press, 2004), 667–769.

4. See Civil Rights Act of 1964, Pub. L. No. 88-352, 78 Stat. 241 (1964) (codified as amended in 42 U.S.C. §§ 2000e–2000e-15); Voting Rights Act of 1965, Pub. L. No. 89-110, 79 Stat. 437 (1965) (codified as amended at 52 U.S.C. §§ 10101–10508); Fair Housing Act of 1968, Pub. L. No. 90-284, 82 Stat. 81 (1968) (codified as amended at 42 U.S.C. §§ 3601–3619); Title I, Civil Rights Act of 1964, Pub. L. No. 88-352, tit. 1, 78 Stat. 241, 241–242 (codified as amended at 42 U.S.C.A. § 10101 [West 2015]); Title II, Civil Rights Act of 1964, Pub. L. 88-352, tit. 2, 78 Stat. 241, 243–246 (codified at 42 U.S.C. §§ 2000a–a-6 [2012]); Title IV, Civil Rights Act of 1964, Pub. L. No. 88-352, tit. 4, 78 Stat. 241, 246–249 (codified at 42 U.S.C. §§ 2000c–c-9 [2012]); Title VII, Civil Rights Act of 1964, Pub. L. No. 88-352, tit. 7, 78 Stat. 241, 253–266 (codified at 42 U.S.C. §§ 2000e–2000e-17 [2012]). See Roy L. Brooks, "Use of the Civil Rights Acts of 1866 and 1871 to Redress Employment Discrimination," *Cornell Law Review* 62 (1977): 258, 259 (discussing the 1972 Amendments); Hazelwood School District v. United States, 433 U.S. 299, 309 (1977) ("Racial discrimination by public employers was not made illegal under Title VII until March 24, 1972.").

5. For Title VII law, see, e.g., Johnson v. Transp. Agency of Santa Clara County, 480 U.S. 616 (1987) (voluntary); Local 28, Sheet Metal Workers' Int'l. Association v. EEOC, 478 U.S. 421 (1986) (involuntary). See generally Brooks, Carrasco, and Selmi, *The Law of Discrimination,* 1203–1234. For the 1965 Voting Rights Act, see, e.g., Shaw v. Reno, 509 U.S. 630 (1993); Miller v. Johnson, 515 U.S. 900 (1995). Although jurisdictions may continue to take race into account when drawing election districts, the Supreme Court requires a strong justification if racial considerations predominate over traditional districting principles. See Alabama Legislative Caucus v. Alabama, 135 S. Ct. 1257, 1260–1261 (2015). In Shelby County v. Holder, 133 S. Ct. 2612, 2631 (2013), the Court held that § 4(b)

of the Voting Rights Act was unconstitutional as it applied an outdated formula to determine which states and counties were covered entities under § 5 of the act. See generally Brooks, Carrasco, and Selmi, *The Law of Discrimination,* 557–678. Affirmative action under the 1968 Fair Housing Act has taken place in the form of "access" quotas designed to increase minority participation in housing, as opposed to "ceiling" quotas used to regulate the racial composition of a housing complex. The latter is typically referred to as "racial occupancy controls" or "managed integration." See, e.g., United States v. Starrett City Assocs., 840 F.2d 1096, 1101–1102 (2nd Cir. 1988), *cert. denied,* 488 U.S. 946 (1988); South-Suburban Housing Center v. Greater South-Suburban Board of Realtors, 935 F.2d 868, 871, 882–883, 899 (7th Cir. 1991). See generally Brooks, Carrasco, and Selmi, *The Law of Discrimination,* 282–336, 318–320.

6. See, e.g., Texas Department of Housing & Community Affairs v. Inclusive Communities Project, Inc., 135 S. Ct. 2507 (2015); Raytheon Co. v. Hernandez, 540 U.S. 44, 52–53 (2003); McDonald v. Santa Fe Trail, Co., 427 U.S. 273, 278 (1976).

7. See, e.g., Fisher v. University of Texas at Austin, 133 S. Ct. 2411 (2013); Parents Involved in Community Schools. v. Seattle Sch. Dist. No. 1, 551 U.S. 701 (2007); Johnson v. California, 543 U.S. 499 (2005); Gratz v. Bollinger, 539 U.S. 244 (2003); Grutter v. Bollinger, 539 U.S. 306 (2003). See also Adam Winkler, "Fatal in Theory and Strict in Fact: An Empirical Analysis of Strict Scrutiny in the Federal Courts," *Vanderbilt Law Review* 59 (2006): 793, 802–805. But see Adarand Constructors v. Pena, 515 U.S. 200, 237 (1995) (majority expresses the "wish to dispel the notion that strict scrutiny is 'strict in theory, but fatal in fact' ").

8. See Adarand Constructors, Inc., 515 U.S. at 227 ("[A]ll racial classifications, imposed by whatever federal, state, or local governmental actor, must be analyzed by a reviewing court under strict scrutiny. In other words, such classifications are constitutional only if they are narrowly tailored measures that further compelling governmental interests."); *Fisher,* 133 S. Ct. at 2422 (Thomas, J., concurring) (internal citations omitted) ("Under strict scrutiny, all racial classifications are categorically prohibited unless they are 'necessary to further a compelling governmental interest' and 'narrowly tailored to that end.'); Grutter v. Bollinger, 539 U.S. at 326 ("[Strict scrutiny] means that such classifications are constitutional only if they are narrowly tailored to further compelling governmental interests."). See also Brooks, Carrasco, and Selmi, *The Law of Discrimination,* 1197–1318; Sullivan and Gunther, *Constitutional Law,* 667–769.

9. See, e.g., Philip Dray, *At the Hands of Persons Unknown: The Lynching of Black America* (New York: Modern Library, 2002); Sherrilyn A. Ifill, "Creating a Truth and Reconciliation Commission for Lynching," *Law & Inequality* 21 (2003): 263, 282–286; William H. Chafe, Raymond Gavins, and Robert Korstad, eds., *Remembering Jim Crow: African Americans Tell About Life in the Segregated* South (New York: New Press, 2001); Charles S. Mangum Jr., *The Legal Status of the Negro* (Chapel Hill: University of North Carolina Press, 1940).

10. These views are collected in Roy L. Brooks, *Racial Justice in the Age of Obama* (Princeton, NJ: Princeton University Press, 2009), xii, 125–183; Roy L. Brooks, "The Crisis of the Black Politician in the Age of Obama," *Howard Law Journal* 52 (2010): 699, 727–731.

11. Brooks, *Racial Justice in the Age of Obama*, 1–34.

12. Parents Involved in Community Schools v. Seattle Sch. Dist. No. 1, 551 U.S. 701, 743, 748 (2007).

13. See George F. Will, "Why Civil Rights No Longer Are Rights," *San Diego Union-Tribune*, March 10, 2005, B12. See also Schuette v. Coalition to Defend Affirmative Action, Integration & Immigration Rights & Fight for Equality by Any Means Necessary (BAMN), 134 S. Ct. 1623 (2014); Fisher v. Univ. of Tex. at Austin, 133 S. Ct. 2411 (2013); Grutter v. Bollinger, 539 U.S. 306 (2003); City of Richmond v. J. A. Croson, 488 U.S. 469 (1989); Adarand Constructors, Inc. v. Pena, 515 U.S. 200 (1995). Two traditionalist scholars state the traditionalists position most succinctly when they argue that too much attention is being given to the race issue. Larry Alexander and Maimon Schwarzchild, "Race Matters," *Constitutional Commentaries* 29 (2013): 31.

14. Adarand Constructors, Inc. v. Pena, 515 U.S. 200, 241 (1995) (Thomas, J., concurring).

15. Glenn C. Loury, *The Anatomy of Racial Inequality* (Cambridge, MA: Harvard University Press, 2004), 144.

16. President Barack Obama's cultural weakness was on full display when he was severely rebuked by the media for seeing racism in the arrest of a renowned black Harvard professor, Henry Louis Gates, by a white police officer, Sgt. James Crowley of the Cambridge, MA, Police Department. See Helene Cooper, "Obama Criticizes Arrest of Harvard Professor," *New York Times*, July 22, 2009, http://www.nytimes.com/2009/07/23/us/politics/23gates.html?_r=0 (accessed February 16, 2016); Toby Harnden, "Barack Obama's Support Falls Among White Voters," *Telegraph*, August 2, 2009, http://www.telegraph.co.uk/news/worldnews/barackobama/5961624/Barack-Obamas-support-falls-among-white-voters.html (accessed February 16, 2016); Michael A. Fletcher and Michael D. Shear, "Obama Voices Regret to Policeman," *Washington Post*, July 25, 2009, http://www.washingtonpost.com/wp-dyn/content/article/2009/07/24/AR2009072400451.html (accessed February 16, 2016); Krissah Thompson and Cheryl W. Thompson, "Officer Tells His Side of the Story in Arrest of Harvard Scholar," *Washington Post*, July 24, 2009, http://www.washingtonpost.com/wp-dyn/content/article/2009/07/23/AR2009072301073.html (accessed February 16, 2016). Reformists point to other evidence that race still matters. See, e.g., Stuart Elliot, "Vitriol Online for Cheerios Ad with Interracial Family," *New York Times*, May 31, 2013, http://www.nytimes.com/2013/06/01/business/media/cheerios-ad-with-interracial-family-brings-out-internet-hate.html (accessed February 16, 2016); Leslie Houts Pica and Joe R. Feagin, *Two-Faced Racism: Whites in the Backstage and Frontstage* (New York: Routledge, 2007). The DOJ report on Ferguson is published as, "Investigation of the Ferguson Police Department," U.S. Department of Justice, March 4, 2015, https://www.justice.gov/sites/default/files/opa/press-releases/attachments/2015/03/04/ferguson_police_department_report.pdf (accessed February 22, 2016). See also James B. Comey, "Hard Truths: Law Enforcement and Race," FBI, February 12, 2015, http://www.fbi.gov/news/speeches/hard-truths-law-enforcement-and-race (accessed February 22, 2016). On the matter of black-on-black crime versus white-on-white crime, see Brooks, *Racial Justice in the Age of Obama*, 32–33. ("In 2002, for example, 74.5% of violent crimes perpetrated

against African Americans were committed by other African Americans. In that same year, however, 72.6% of violent crimes perpetrated against whites were committed by other whites.") For further discussion of how race still matters, see ibid., 37–53.

17. Loury, *The Anatomy of Racial Inequality*, 121.

18. On average, de facto segregated schools are "inferior in terms of the quality of their teachers, the character of the curriculum, the level of competition, average test scores, and graduation rates." Brenna Lermon Hill, "A Call to Congress: Amend Education Legislation and Ensure That President Obama's 'Race to the Top' Leaves No Child Behind," *Houston Law Review* 51 (2014): 1177, 1184 (quoting Gary Orfield and Chungmei Lee, "The Civil Rights Project, Historic Reversals, Accelerating Resegregation, and the Need for New Integration Strategies," Civil Rights Project, UCLA, August 2007, http://civilrightsproject.ucla.edu/research/k-12-education/integration-and-diversity/historic-reversals-accelerating-resegregation-and-the-need-for-new-integration-strategies-1/orfield-historic-reversals-accelerating.pdf.

19. Sonia Sotomayor, *My Beloved World* (New York: Alfred A. Knopf, 2013), 191. Justice Sotomayor quotes Cornel West, *Race Matters* (Boston: Beacon Press, 2001), in her dissenting opinion in Schuette v. Coalition to Defend Affirmative Action, Integration & Immigration Rights & Fight for Equality by Any Means Necessary (BAMN), 134 S. Ct. 1623, 1676 (2014) (Sotomayor, J., dissenting).

20. See Brooks, *Racial Justice in the Age of Obama*, 73–74.

21. See Robert L. Carter, *A Matter of Law: A Memoir of Struggle in the Cause of Equal Rights* (New York: New Press, 2005), 156–157, 172; Constance Baker Motley, *Equal Justice Under the Law: An Autobiography* (New York: Farrar, Straus and Giroux, 1998), 119. Testimony before the United States Senate indicated that perhaps a majority of African American principals and teachers did lose their jobs. See Kevin D. Brown, "Review: Robert L. Carter, *A Matter of Law*," *Vermont Law Review* 31 (2007): 925, 939. See also Roy L. Brooks, *Structures of Judicial Decision Making from Legal Formalism to Critical Theory*, 2nd ed. (Durham, NC: Carolina Academic Press, 2005), 285n13 (sources cited therein); Alvis V. Adair, *Desegregation: The Illusion of Black Progress* (Lanham, MD: University Press of America, 1984); Harrell R. Rogers Jr. and Charles S. Bullock III, *Law and Social Change: Civil Rights Laws and Their Consequences* (New York: McGraw-Hill, 1972), 94–97; David G. Carter, "Second-Generation School Integration Problems for Blacks," *Journal of Black Studies* 13 (1982): 175, 175–188; Derrick Bell, *And We Are Not Saved: The Elusive Quest for Racial Justice* (New York: Basic Books, 1987), 102, 109 (citing Brief of Amicus Curiae Nat'l. Educ. Assoc., United States v. Georgia, 445 F.2d 303 [5th Cir. 1971] [No. 30–338] (providing empirical data on burden borne by black teachers, administrators, and students because of school integration); James E. Blackwell, *The Black Community: Diversity and Unity*, 2nd ed. (New York: Harper & Row, 1985), 158–160; Harold Cruse, *Plural but Equal: A Critical Study of Blacks and Minorities and America's Plural Society* (New York: William Morrow, 1987), 22. In addition to school closings, many of the integrated schools experienced "second generation resegregation"—i.e., segregation within these schools—with the overplacement of black students in slow-learner, such as "educable mentally retarded," classes and white students in advanced classes. See Brooks, *Rethinking the American Race Problem*, 77.

22. United States v. Fordice, 505 U.S. 717, 729 (1992).

23. Ibid., 748 (Thomas, J., concurring).

24. Missouri v. Jenkins, 515 U.S. 70, 114 (1995) (*Jenkins III*) (Thomas, J., concurring). Some civil rights scholars see implicit racism in *Brown*'s assertion that separate is inherently unequal. See, e.g., Kevin Brown, "Has the Supreme Court Allowed the Cure for De Jure Segregation to Replicate the Disease?" *Cornell Law Review* 78 (1992): 1, 4–6. In a subsequent article, Professor Brown states, "I am one who firmly believes that what allowed Chief Justice Earl Warren to produce an opinion that all the justices of the Supreme Court could agree upon was the notion that segregation damaged only black people. Thus, I think the social science evidence was necessary because it allowed Warren to garner unanimous support for his opinion striking down segregation. As insulting to blacks as I find Warren's opinion in *Brown* fifty years later, my deep and long reflections of twenty years as a law professor assures me that striking down segregation, even at this cost, was a tremendous bargain for black people." Kevin Brown, "Review: Robert L. Carter, *A Matter of Law*", 925, 948.

25. The Court's decision denying certiorari in the case is reported in an article written by Peter Applebone. Peter Applebone, "Equal Entry Standards May Hurt Black Students in Mississippi," *San Diego Union-Tribune*, April 24, 1996, A10.

26. Plessy v. Ferguson, 163 U.S. 537, 559 (1896) (Harlan, J., dissenting).

27. Richard Delgado and Jean Stefancic, *Critical Race Theory: An Introduction* (New York: New York University Press, 2001), 3.

28. Jerry L. Anderson, "Law School Enters the Matrix: Teaching Critical Legal Studies," *Journal of Legal Education* 54 (June 2004): 201, 210.

29. See, e.g., Derrick Bell, *Race, Racism, and American Law*, 2nd ed. (Boston: Little, Brown, 1980); *And We Are Not Saved: Faces at the Bottom of the Well: The Permanence of Racism* (New York: Basic Books, 1992); "Who's Afraid of Critical Race Theory," *University of Illinois Law Review* (1995): 893.

30. Robert Jensen, "White Privilege Shapes the U.S.: Affirmative Action for Whites Is a Fact of Life," *Baltimore Sun,* July 19, 1998, http://articles.baltimoresun.com/1998-07-19/news/1998200115_1_white-privilege-unearned-white-action-for-whites.

31. Richard Delgado, "Recasting the American Race Problem," *California Law Review* 79 (1991): 1389, 1394 (reviewing Brooks, *Rethinking the American Race Problem*).

32. See Brooks, *Racial Justice in the Age of Obama,* 89–108.

33. Carter, *A Matter of Law,* 199. See also Robert L. Carter, "The Warren Court and Desegregation," *Michigan Law Review* 67 (1968): 237; Lewis Steel, "A Critic's View of the Warren Court—Nine Men in Black Who Think White," *New York Times,* October 13, 1968.

34. See, e.g., Bell, *Race, Racism, and American Law; And We Are Not Saved; Faces at the Bottom of the Well;* "Who's Afraid of Critical Race Theory?" 893.

35. See Ari Berman, *Give Us the Ballot: The Modern Struggle for Voting Rights in America* (New York: Farrar, Straus and Giroux, 2015); Jeffrey Rosen, "Rights Unraveled: A Narrative History of the Continuing Efforts to Weaken the Voting Rights Act of 1965," *New York Times Book Review,* August 30, 2015, 14.

36. Obergefell v. Hodges, 135 S. Ct. 2584, 2612 (2015) (Roberts, CJ, dissenting). Justice Holmes's famous aphorism can be found in his seminal book on Anglo-American law. See Oliver Wendell Holmes, *The Common Law*, ed. Mark DeWolfe Howe (Cambridge: Belknap Press of Harvard University Press, 1963), 5.

37. Robinson v. Shell Oil Co., 519 U.S. 337 (1997).

38. Robinson v. Shell Oil Co., 70 F.3d 325, 331 (4th Cir. 1995).

39. Philip P. Frickey, "Revisiting the Revival of Theory in Statutory Interpretation: A Lecture in Honor of Irving Younger," *Minnesota Law Review* 84 (1999): 199, 215.

40. See Brooks, *Racial Justice in the Age of Obama*, 76–77.

41. Ricci v. DeStefano, 129 S. Ct. 2658 (2009). After each examination, the New Haven Civil Service Board (CSB), an unelected body, certifies a ranked list of applicants who passed the test. Under the city's charter, the authority doing the hiring must fill each vacancy by choosing one candidate from the top three scorers on the list. This is called the "rule of three." Of the seventy-three candidates who completed the lieutenant examination (forty-three whites, nineteen blacks, and fifteen Hispanics), thirty-four candidates passed (twenty-five whites, six blacks, and three Hispanics). Eight lieutenant positions were vacant at the time of the examination. Based on the rule of three, this meant that the top ten candidates were eligible for an immediate promotion to lieutenant. All ten were white. Subsequent vacancies would have allowed at least three black candidates to be considered for promotion to lieutenant. Of the forty-one candidates who completed the captain examination (twenty-five whites, eight blacks, and eight Hispanics), twenty-two candidates passed (sixteen whites, three blacks, and three Hispanics). Because seven captain positions were vacant at the time of the examination, nine candidates were eligible for an immediate promotion (seven whites and two Hispanics), based on the rule of three. Ibid., 2665–2671, 2692 (Ginsburg, J., dissenting). The fact that the city discarded the disparate test results indicates that it would have not given the test in the first place had it known about its consequences. For further analysis of disparate impact discrimination, see Texas Department of Housing & Community Affairs v. Inclusive Communities Project, Inc., 135 S. Ct. 2507 (2015).

42. Ricci v. DeStefano, 129 S. Ct. at 2674. "The racial adverse impact here was significant." Ibid., 2677.

43. Under current Title VII law, the condition of adverse effects by itself only establishes a prima facie case of disparate impact liability. Liability is established only if either "the examinations were not job related and consistent with business necessity, or if there existed an equally valid, less discriminatory alternative that served the City's needs but that the City refused to adopt." Justice Kennedy relied on the record as the basis for his ruling that the examinations were job related and consistent with business necessity. He provided several reasons in support of his ruling. First, IOS, an Illinois company hired by the city to develop and administer the exams, devised the written exam "after painstaking analyses of the captain and lieutenant positions." They assembled a pool of thirty assessors who were from outside Connecticut and possessed superior rank to the lieutenant and captain positions being tested. Within this pool of assessors, they "made sure that minorities were overrepresented." Second, IOS

test-designed the questions by observing lieutenants and captains perform their duties and by drawing the questions from sources approved by the fire department. Third, Vincent Lewis, who was the only outside witness that not only had appeared before the CSB but also had reviewed the exams in any detail and had any firefighting experience, stated that the "questions were relevant for both exams." Fourth, Christopher Hornick, who was the only other witness who had seen any part of the examinations and who was one of IOS's competitors, stated that the examinations "appea[r] to be . . . reasonably good" and "recommended that the CSB certify the results." Ibid., 2667–2672. Justice Kennedy also found that there was no strong basis in evidence supporting the contention that an equally valid, less discriminatory alternative existed. He ruled that "respondents have produced no evidence to show that the 6o/40 weighting was indeed arbitrary." Justice Kennedy acknowledged that other ways to weight the tests exist, but concluded that the record presented no evidence that different weighting "would be an equally valid way to determine whether candidates possess the proper mix of job knowledge and situational skills to earn promotions." Justice Kennedy in addition dismissed the respondents' argument that the city could have changed its interpretation of the "rule of three" to produce less discriminatory results. While it is true that had the city employed a "banding" technique and four black and one Hispanic candidate would have become eligible for officer positions, this technique was not available to the city because, "Had the City reviewed the exam results and then adopted banding to make the minority test scores appear higher, it would have violated Title VII's prohibition of adjusting test results on the basis of race." Ibid., 2680. An employer may, however, consider and act to remedy an exam's *potential* racial impact "during the test-design stage," the majority wrote. Ibid., 2667–2672.

44. Adarand Constructors, Inc. v. Pena, 515 U.S. 200, 241 (1995) (Thomas, J., concurring).

45. There are, however, aspects of the Court's opinion that might give some traditionalists pause. The Court holds that race can be considered in the construction of employment examinations—the city could have taken into account the potential racial impact "during the design of the exam"—and when there is "a strong basis in evidence" that it would be liable under the effects test if it takes no action. Consistent with these race-conscious rulings, the Court also recognizes the legitimacy of using an overrepresentation of minority incumbent lieutenants and captains ("minorities were overrepresented") in analyzing the exam during its design phase. For core traditionalists, those rulings prescribe too much race consciousness in derogation of the racial-omission tenet. Even though benign (or rather because they are benign), race-conscious governmental policies or practices place blacks in a negative light, albeit different from invidious race-conscious policies. With these reservations, traditionalists would probably not find juridical subordination in the *Ricci* Court's opinion.

46. *Ricci*, 129 S. Ct. at 2690 (Ginsburg, J., dissenting). In addition, a reformist would probably note the Court's procedural unfairness. The Court announces a new legal standard and does not give the city an opportunity to show that it can satisfy that standard. In other words, the strong-basis-in-evidence standard was promulgated by the

Court for the very first time in this case. Yet the Court does not remand the case to give the city an opportunity to address the new legal standard. This is bad judicial form, especially because the Court uses the standard *against* the city. What this suggests is that the Court is hell-bent on ruling against the city. As a consequence, blacks are denied employment opportunities. It seems that the Court only wants it one way, that it wants "just us" rather than justice. Justice Ginsburg makes a similar charge against the Court. She accuses the Court of underestimating New Haven's legitimate fear of losing a disparate-treatment suit. See ibid., 2702–2703. Justice Ginsburg further says of the Court's reasoning, "Like the chess player who tries to win by sweeping the opponent's pieces off the table," she wrote of the majority opinion, "the court simply shuts from its sight the formidable obstacles New Haven would have faced." Ibid., 2706.

47. Justice Ginsburg's dissenting opinion provides technical legal arguments that directly challenge the legal reasoning made by the Court; i.e., the Court's belief that the examinations were a business necessity and that an equally valid and less discriminatory examination was not available. Justice Ginsburg essentially makes four large points that reformists could easily own. First, she argues that the written examination was insufficient to satisfy the job-related/business-necessity defense. "Successful fire officers, the City's description of the position makes clear, must have the '[a]bility to lead personnel effectively, maintain discipline, promote harmony, exercise sound judgment, and cooperate with other officials.' . . . These qualities are not measured by written tests." Justice Ginsburg cited numerous precedents in support of her position: "Courts have long criticized written firefighter promotion exams for being 'more probative of the test-taker's ability to recall what a particular text stated on a given topic than on his firefighting or supervisory knowledge and abilities' (citing Vulcan Pioneers, Inc. v. New Jersey Department of Civil Service.) . . . A fire officer's job, courts have observed, 'involves complex behaviors, good interpersonal skills, the ability to make decisions under tremendous pressure, and a host of other abilities—none of which is easily measured by a written, multiple choice test' (citing Firefighters Inst. for Racial Equality v. St. Louis)." Ibid., 2704. The argument, therefore, is that a written test, regardless of whether it is neutrally constructed, is not sufficient to satisfy the job-related/business-necessity standard, because the skills required to be an adequate firefighter are not measurable by this type of test.

One could argue, on the other hand, that a written test might be important in assessing the skills or knowledge of someone commanding a firefighting unit. The following is an example of a written test question given to firefighters:

> After an explosion in the living room of a residential home, a couch and the floor beneath it are found to be severely damaged. While the windows are blown out and one of the walls slightly caved in, most of the furniture in the room is only moderately damaged. These circumstances suggest that the damage was caused by:
>
> A) a high order concentrated explosion from some material such as dynamite
>
> B) a diffuse explosion resulting from the ignition of a volatile liquid

C) a low order concentrated explosion, probably from a homemade
bomb
D) a gas leak in the basement
E) gasoline on the couch

See "Free 50 Question Practice Firefighter Exam," Don McNea Fire School, 2016, http://
www.fireprep.com/free_50_question_firefighter_p.html (accessed March 3, 2016).

Second, Justice Ginsburg found that the examination in question may not have
been facially neutral after all. It may have been constructed in a racially biased manner.
Citing one expert, Janet Helms, a professor of counseling psychology at Boston College,
Justice Ginsburg observed that "two-thirds of the incumbent fire officers who submitted
job analyses to IOS during the exam design phase were Caucasian. . . . The heavy reliance on job analyses from white firefighters may thus have introduced an element of
bias." Alternatively, this may have been a situation where unbiased whites simply operated out of their cultural perspective, a perspective that was oblivious to a black perspective on designing tests (e.g., assessment centers, discussion to come). Just because most
of the test designers were white doesn't mean that they were racist. *Ricci*, 129 S. Ct. at
2693–2694 (Ginsburg, J., dissenting).

Third, Justice Ginsburg points to the statements made by Christopher Hornick,
whose credibility the Court questioned, in support of her belief that an equally valid,
less discriminatory evaluation process was available to the city. Hornick, an exam-design
expert with more than two decades of relevant experience, informed the CSB that "an
assessment center process, which is essentially an opportunity for candidates . . . to demonstrate how they would address a particular problem as opposed to just verbally saying
it or identifying the correct option on a written test," was a more valid and less discriminatory way to test candidates than the 60/40 written/oral examination structure.
Even though, as the Court noted, Hornick ultimately recommended that the CSB should
certify the examination results, he was emphatic that "a person's leadership skills,
command presence, their interpersonal skills, their management skills, their tactical
skills could have been identified and evaluated in a much more appropriate way." Justice
Ginsburg notes that "it is unsurprising that most municipalities do not evaluate their
fire officer candidates as New Haven does. Although comprehensive statistics are scarce,
a 1996 study found that nearly two-thirds of surveyed municipalities used assessment
centers ('simulations of the real world of work') as part of their promotion processes."
The prevalence of the use of assessment centers by other municipalities, their reliability,
and their minimized adverse impact justify their validity as an equally valid, less
discriminatory alternative measuring process. Ibid., 2693–2694, 2703–2705 (Ginsburg, J.,
dissenting).

Finally, and perhaps most importantly, Justice Ginsburg points to the Court's
failure to take note of the city's racial makeup and racial history. New Haven is about
60% African American and Hispanic, and has a long history of racial discrimination in
the fire department. At the time the examinations were given, only 22% of the command
structure in the fire department was minority. Blacks had brought antidiscrimination
lawsuits against the fire department in the past. Justice Ginsburg believed that the city's

racial makeup and racial history were very relevant because they give context to the city's mind-set in throwing out the test results. The defendant's state of mind is the most important element regarding the intent test, which is the legal theory on which the plaintiffs brought the action *sub judice*. Ibid., 2690–2691 (Ginsburg, J., dissenting).

48. Ibid.

49. Justice Alito's rather negative portrayal of one of the black leaders, which African Americans would regard as a racial slap-down (see ibid. at 2684–2686), is put in broader perspective by Justice Ginsburg; see ibid., 2690n1.

50. Ibid. at 2667.

51. As I have discussed quite extensively in these note, Justice Ginsburg provides technical legal arguments that could sustain a reformist decision in this case. For the limited separatist result, the Court would have to employ the three-prong test rather than the strict scrutiny test. The interplay between both tests is highlighted in the next case.

52. See Fisher v. University of Texas, 579 U.S. (2016) (*Fisher II*); Fisher v. University of Texas, 133 S. Ct. 2411 (2013) (*Fisher I*); Grutter v. Bollinger, 539 U.S. 306 (2003); Hopwood v. Texas, 78 F.3d 932 (1996); Nikole Hannah-Jones, "What Abigail Fisher's Affirmative Action Case Was Really About," ProPublica, June 23, 2016, https://www .propublica.org/article/a-colorblind-constitution-what-abigail-fishers-affirmative-action-case-is-r (accessed June 28, 2016).

53. See *Fisher II*, 579 U.S. (slip op., at 3–6, 15–18) (Kennedy, J.).

54. Ibid., at 15 (internal citations omitted).

55. Ibid., at 1 (Thomas, J., dissenting) (internal citations omitted).

56. Parents Involved in Community Schools v. Seattle School District No. 1, 551 U.S. 701 (2007) (Roberts, CJ.)

57. Brooks H. Spears, "'If the Plaintiffs Are Right, Grutter Is Wrong': Why Fisher v. University of Texas Presents an Opportunity for the Supreme Court to Overturn a Flawed Decision," *University of Richmond Law Review* 46 (2012): 1113, 1138.

58. *Fisher II*, 579 U.S. (slip op. at 1) (Thomas, J., dissenting).

59. Ibid., at 3–4 (Alito, J., dissenting).

60. Joshua P. Thompson and Damien M. Schiff, "Divisive Diversity at the University of Texas: An Opportunity for the Supreme Court to Overturn Its Flawed Decision in *Grutter*," *Texas Review of Law & Politics* 15 (2011): 437, 486.

61. See Brooks, *Racial Justice in the Age of Obama*, app., 126, figs. 30–44, 55–60.

62. Leslie Yalof Garfield, "Adding Colors to the Chameleon: Why the Supreme Court Should Have Adopted a New Compelling Governmental Interest Test for Race-Preference Student Assignment Plans," *Kansas Law Review* 56 (2008): 277, 279.

63. See Ann Millott Killenbeck, "Bakke, With Teeth? The Implications of Grutter v. Bollinger in an Outcomes-Based World," *Journal of College and University Law* 36 (2009): 1, 60; Daniel Kiel, "An Ounce of Prevention Is Worth a Pound of Cure: Reframing the Debate About Law School Affirmative Action," *Denver University Law Review* 88 (2011): 791, 792.

64. *Fisher II*, 579 U.S. (slip op. at 3–4) (Alito, J., dissenting).

65. Ibid., at 15 (Kennedy, J.).

66. Derrick Bell, "Diversity's Distractions," *Columbia Law Review* 103 (2003): 1622, 1622. The critical race theory position on affirmative action was famously stated in Charles Lawrence and Mari J. Matsuda, *We Won't Go Back: Making the Case for Affirmative Action* (New York: Houghton Mifflin, 1997).

67. Maurice C. Daniels and Cameron Van Patterson, "(Re)considering Race in the Desegregation of Higher Education," *Georgia Law Review* 46 (Spring 2012): 521.

68. Mark T. Terrell, "Bucking *Grutter*: Why Critical Mass Should Be Thrown off the Affirmative-Action Horse," *Texas Journal on Civil Liberties & Civil Rights* 16 (2011): 233, 261, 262.

69. Bell's interest-convergence thesis is sometimes seen as a prescription for redressing white hegemony. The thesis holds that interest convergence between outsiders and insiders is the only way racial progress is made in this country. If interest convergence is descriptively correct, then whites would have to benefit from affirmative action as well as blacks if the Court is to sustain affirmative action. But Bell and other critical race theorists believe that true civil rights reform cannot be predicated on interest convergence. Interest convergence is a weak response to white hegemony to the extent that it only allows for the creation of civil rights laws that benefit whites and blacks equally. Equal treatment means the racial differential will largely remain unchanged. Where is the racial progress in that? White hegemony can only be overcome by using socially transformative legal measures, which in the case of affirmative action would certainly entail racial quotas. Given that, affirmative action for critical race theorists would be sustainable as an egalitarian, or moral, response to white hegemony rather than as a by-product of interest convergence. See Derrick A. Bell, Jr., "Brown v. Board of Education and the Interest-Convergence Dilemma," *Harvard Law Review* 93 (1980): 518.

70. Blacks made the most racial progress relative to whites in the post–civil rights era during the heyday of affirmative action, which was in the mid- to late 1970s. In some instances, black advances slightly exceeded white advances without negatively impacting white progress in any appreciable way. In other words, whites continued to gain during this time as well. In my book, *Racial Justice in the Age of Obama*, I point to government data that show comparable income at all educational levels, from high school dropouts to postgraduates (app., figs. 30–36), and a black college participation rate that was slightly higher than the white college participation rate at the height of affirmative action (app., figs. 55–60). Hispanics did even better. But in all cases, white income and college participation did not fall correspondingly. Hence, affirmative action was greatly beneficial for blacks and Hispanics and did not unnecessarily prejudice the wages or educational interests of whites. So what happened? In 1978, the Supreme Court in Regents of the University of California v. Bakke, 438 U.S. 265, outlawed the use of racial quotas in college admissions and thus signaled a general indisposition toward affirmative action across the board, not just in higher education.

71. Motley, *Equal Justice Under the Law,* 111

72. In *Mismatch: How Affirmative Action Hurts Students It's Intended to Help, and Why Universities Won't Admit It* (New York: Basic Books, 2012), Professor Richard

Sander and journalist Stuart Taylor advance an argument against affirmative action that Justice Thomas picked up in his concurring opinion in *Fischer I*. The authors argue that the mismatch between the academic index (typically comprising test scores and GPA) of an affirmative-action student (usually a black or Hispanic student) and the college, university, or law school the student attends hurts this student academically and professionally. Mismatched students are hurt because they earn lower grades and class rankings, fail to graduate, become disaffected, and, in the case of law school graduates, fail the bar exam and fail to land the big-money jobs in large law firms. The solution, according to the authors is "cascading," i.e., mismatched students should move down to lower-tier schools, especially HBCUs, that fit their academic indexes. Most of the authors' support for this thesis comes from black/white data sets. Beyond agreeing with the basic proposition that too much of an academic differential is bad for any student, I would argue that the authors clearly fail in their attempt to use the academic performance of affirmative-action students as a basis for ending affirmative action in higher education. Providing few institution-specific data, the authors' statistical arguments are necessarily generalized. They also make no attempt to differentiate between black and Hispanic students who are and are not affirmative-action students. They assume, stereotypically, that all black and Hispanic students are beneficiaries of affirmative action. Viewing the authors' evidence in its most favorable light, their analysis is woefully insufficient to sustain their arguments for ending affirmative action in undergraduate or law-school education. The authors base their argument regarding undergraduate education primarily on the percentage of black students versus white students who switch out of STEM (science, technology, engineering, and mathematics) majors, the generalized statistic that affirmative-action students graduate in the lower quarter of their class, and the post–Proposition 209 (the 1996 state initiative that ended affirmative action in California's public universities) increase in black applications to all UC schools as well as an increase in the black graduation rate at UCLA. I simply demur to the claim regarding STEM majors, because universities report that up to 80% of entering college students express uncertainty about their major, even after declaring it, and over 50% of college students change their major at least once. The latter number is higher in STEM majors when one factors out premed students who tend not to switch out. Based on the authors' metric, over 50% of college students are failures. Equally important to this demurrer, the authors employ a rather perverse tactic: they use statistics from a tiny subset (STEM majors) as a predicate for assessing the value of affirmative action for the entire set (the whole undergraduate curriculum, including the humanities, social science, arts, and business). The authors cite a study that finds "in virtually all selective schools . . . where racial preferences in admissions is practiced, the majority of [affirmative action] students end up in the lower quarter of their class." Again, I demur; for it is also true today, as it has been since the early 1990s, that the vast majority (conservatively about 80%) of black students who matriculate at the nation's top fifty institutions of higher education graduate—e.g., since the year 2000, from 92% to 95% at Harvard, 90% to 93% at Princeton, and 87% to 89% at Yale—and that they graduate at twice the 42% national average for black students, and higher than the 62% national average for white students.

Furthermore, the black graduation rate at elite schools is much higher than that at HBCUs, the authors' schools of choice for blacks, where the graduation rate has been as low as 7% at some schools. Finally, the black graduation rate has at times been *higher* than the white graduation rate at several elite schools (e.g., at Wellesley, 92% black, 90% white, and at Mount Holyoke, 82% black, 78% white). By the authors' own metric, any student who graduates in the lower quarter of her class is a failure. But isn't it all about graduating? Even assuming, *arguendo,* the validity of the mismatch theory for lower-tier schools, that does not justify eliminating affirmative action in the top fifty colleges and universities where it is working so well. While there has been a post–Prop 209 increase in black applications to all UC schools, there is no evidence that even begins to substantiate the authors' claim that the increase in applications is due to the passage of Prop 209. And while there has been a post–Prop 209 increase of 15% in the black graduation rate at UCLA (but not at Berkeley), there has been a concomitant decrease of 20% in the actual number of black graduates from UCLA. The authors fail to engage the fact that the black graduation rate at Berkeley (70%) and UCLA (73%), neither of which have affirmative-action admissions policies, is lower than the black graduation rate at other elite schools, such as the Ivies, that do practice affirmative action. Finally, a report, not cited by the authors, notes an increase in overall black graduation from the UC schools since the passage of Prop 209. This report also notes, however, that the increase comes from the lower-tier UC schools. Admissions, enrollment, and graduation numbers are way down (as much as by 50%) at the state's flagship schools. Simply put: the post–Prop 209 statistics do not support the authors' claim that affirmative action hurts its beneficiaries. The statistics, in fact, prove just the opposite. The authors' argument that affirmative action hurts black and Hispanic law students is also without merit. Again, they primarily rely on statistics relating to black students, arguing that affirmative action reduces black learning in law schools, which, in turn, reduces the number of blacks who can pass the bar exam, which, in turn, reduces the number of black lawyers. Yes, black law graduates underperform on the bar exam, but the authors have a hard time connecting that fact to affirmative action when they also note that "Blacks were much less likely to pass the bar exam than were whites with the same academic index coming out of college." To see the connection, the authors ask the reader to make several assumptions, such as that black and white applicants with identical academic indicators always matriculate at different schools as opposed to attending the same school or similarly ranked schools. The authors purport to have conducted a study that shows that grades are more important than law-school prestige in landing big-paying jobs. Yet every law student knows this to be untrue. In fact, *The Wall Street Journal* once noted a postrecession study that concluded that "the name of your school matters a lot" when it comes to salaries. The main flaw in the author's argument lies in their assumption that a successful legal career is measured by bar passage on the first attempt. Many successful lawyers, judges, politicians, and legal scholars, such as Supreme Court Justice Benjamin Cardozo, former Republican California governor and U.S. senator Pete Wilson, Democratic California governor Jerry Brown, former secretary of state and presidential candidate Hilary Clinton, Senator Edward Kennedy, and former Harvard Law professor and dean of Stanford Law School Kathleen Sullivan failed the bar exam on their first attempt yet went on to have stellar professional careers, as have most blacks who eventually pass the bar. Also, the notion that working in a large law firm for a high salary is the chief indicator of a successful legal career is a rather myopic view of what counts as a successful legal career. Many law school graduates simply do not want to work in a large firm; nor are they highly motivated by money. What about job satisfaction? This is especially true for women and minorities. Exhibit A: the career paths chosen by Justice Sonia Sotomayor (assistant district attorney) and President Barack Obama (community organizer). Finally, the authors do not engage studies that predict lawyer success based on both academic and nonacademic factors. In the end, the authors are not big fans of diversity. They believe that corporations and other institutions use diversity as a proxy for racial preferences. For a more detailed discussion of these and other criticisms of the book, see Roy L. Brooks, "Helping Minorities by Ending Affirmative? A Review of *Mismatch: How Affirmative Action Hurts Students It's Intended to Help, and Why Universities Won't Admit It*," *Georgetown Journal of Law & Modern Critical Race Perspectives* 6 (2014): 69 (sources cited therein).

73. Recall that to pass constitutional scrutiny under the three-prong test, HBCUs must serve a "good end," meaning they must have a racially compensatory purpose, must not deny admissions to nonblacks. and must only do so when not doing so would cause the school to lose its identity as a black institution of higher education. HBCUs satisfy the first prong because they provide an educational alternative to white universities within the state, most especially the public institutions, that reject many black applicants, creating a problem of black underrepresentation in colleges. While there are many reasons white universities reject black applicants, one reason is the lingering effects of slavery and Jim Crow, which have relegated black students to poor performing K–12 public schools. HBCUs are more responsive to such racialized conditions than white colleges and universities are; they know how to educate racially subordinated students. Beyond that, HBCUs are important assets to the black community. HBCU graduates include entrepreneurs, lawyers, judges, scientists, engineers, doctors, dentists, and entertainers. Martin Luther King Jr., Oprah, Tom Joyner, Spike Lee, Common, Alice Walker, Toni Morrison, Colbert King (Pulitzer Prize winner), Evelynn Hammonds (Harvard physics professor), and Tommie Shelby (Harvard philosophy professor) all came out of HBCUs. Thousands of other HBCU graduates have also made significant contributions to our society. HBCUs certainly establish the second prong. Nonblacks are routinely admitted to these schools. In fact, the valedictorian of the class of 2008 at Morehouse, arguably the most prestigious HBCU, was white. Joshua Packwood, who turned down an Ivy League scholarship, holds that distinction. Finally, HBCUs are so overwhelmingly black, there is very little chance they will ever trigger the third prong. Because HBCUs can easily satisfy the three-prong test, limited separatists would find them to be constitutional under the Equal Protection Clause.

74. We want our courts to give us laws that are stable yet do not stand still. We want our courts to be free of politics yet responsive to the needs of the nation. We want our courts to respect the will of the people yet protect minorities from tyrannical ma-

jorities. We want our courts to make moral decisions yet avoid basing decisions on sub-
jective moral beliefs. We want our courts to follow extant rules of law yet achieve justice
in the end. We want our courts to lead us to higher ground yet avoid social conflict.
We want our courts to respect other branches of government yet not hesitate to step
in when they cease being democratic. Many hands, indeed, tug at the judicial robe.
This is not new in Anglo-American law. Going back to the very beginning of Western
civilization, the Greeks saw equity as a "rectification" of law that was "defective owing
to its universality." The tension between law and equity recurs today in continuous
clashes between two broad methods of judicial decision-making: the logical method
and the policy method. The logical method is "the search for justice disciplined by prior
rules," while the policy method is "the search for justice disciplined by what comes
before the case (precedent, community norms, and existing institutional arrangements)
and by what comes after the case (the consequences decision in the case will have on
a particular community)." Roy L. Brooks, *Structures of Judicial Decision Making from
Legal Formalism to Critical Race Theory*, 2nd ed. (Durham, NC: Carolina Academic
Press, 2005), 5, 183.

What, then, is the source of legal legitimacy for my solution to juridical subordination? One might suppose it is legal realism. Not I. Legal realism is one of several
expressions of the policy method. It was part of my formal legal education at Yale
Law School, so engagingly captured by Laura Kalman, in *Legal Realism at Yale, 1927–1960*
(Chapel Hill: University of North Carolina Press, 1986). Karl Llewellyn insisted that legal
realism is less a school of thought than a collection of diverse perspectives. For example,
while some scholars, including Nicola Lacey in her essay "The Path Not Taken: H. L. A.
Hart's Harvard Essay on Discretion," *Harvard Law Review* 127 (2013): 636, argue that legal realism sees "legal rules not as normative standards but rather as predictions of official behavior," ibid., 643, others, such as Brian Leiter, most recently in "Legal Realism
and Legal Doctrine," *University of Pennsylvania Law Review* 164 (2015): 1975, argue
that legal realists "do not reject the idea that judges decide cases in accordance with
normative standards of some kind. . . . : What the Legal Realists teach us is that too often
the doctrine that courts invoke is not really the normative standard upon which they
really rely." Ibid., 1975. The entire issue 7 of this volume of the law review is devoted
to legal realism. In "Rethinking Legal Realism: Toward a Naturalized Jurisprudence,"
Texas Law Review 76 (1997): 267, Leiter begins his effort to bring legal realism out of its
nominalist shadow.

If legal realism simply minimizes the importance of rules in deciding cases (the
policy method trumps the logical method), then most judges today are legal realists. But
in my view, legal realism means more than that. It has a core set of beliefs that are both
descriptive and prescriptive. Descriptively, legal realism asserts that when one looks at
how judges actually decide difficult cases, one sees that law is less a body of rules than
a set of facts giving rise to competing normative stances. In such "hard cases" law is
policy—the elaboration and enforcement of policy. The judge "reacts to the underlying
policies in the case, . . . and uses the rules to provide ex post facto 'legal' rationales for
her policy choices. 'Judgment for the plaintiff,' runs the old anecdote of Marshall;

'Mr. Justice Story will furnish the authorities.'" Brooks, *Structures of Judicial Decision Making*, 89. In her memoir, *Equal Justice Under the Law*, Judge Constance Baker Motley, the only female lawyer on the NAACP team of lawyers that litigated *Brown*, notes that she learned as a student at Columbia Law School that "national policy is established as much by a Supreme Court decision on a major constitutional issue as by a law enacted by Congress. After the Supreme Court's decision in *Plessy*, segregation became national policy." Ibid., 95. Judge Richard Posner, who is arguably our greatest living scholarly jurist, notes in *Divergent Paths: The Academy and the Judiciary* (Cambridge, MA: Harvard University Press, 2016) that legal rules do not decide hard cases. Indeed, as we have seen, the racial-omission and racial-integration norms have had more to do with deciding civil rights cases than syllogism or doctrinal niceties. Prescriptively, legal realism calls for judges to exercise their considerable discretion in favor of progressive ends. Judges could go in a nonprogressive direction, such as in Bush v. Gore, 531 U.S. 98 (2000), but I doubt we would place such judicial activism in the tradition of Jerome Frank or Charles Black. Indeed, Justice Scalia's originalism—which gives a decidedly conservative bent to the Framers' "meaning" of constitutional riddles such as "due process" and "equal protection"—could not sustain the decision in *Brown* itself. Legal realism is not coextensive with nominalism.

My solution to the problem of juridical subordination, the spirit of *Brown*, is certainly progressive but not in a legal realist way. The judge has less discretion to disregard precedent (*Brown*) than what is typically described by legal realists. Under my regime, the judge is required to follow a well-established precedent—have a *felt duty* to respect *Brown*—unless it has an exceedingly important reason not to. The exceedingly important justification also makes the application of the *Brown* standard less certain than in what H. L. A. Hart called the "noble dream" theories of judicial decision-making, such as purely deductive reasoning in legal formalism. That judicial technique sees "unrealistically regarded legal standards as determining clear results in all cases." Lacey, "The Path Not Taken," 643. See H. L. A. Hart, "American Jurisprudence Through English Eyes: The Nightmare and the Noble Dream," *Georgia Law Review* 11 (1977): 969. Thus, I am moved less by legal realism than by legal process, whose core aspiration is that legal problems should be resolved as coherently and as rationally as possible through processes and criteria that preexist the decision—"reasoned elaboration from existing arrangements." A court moves off or against governing rules based on *ex ante* standards of institutional decision-making (e.g., other rules, history, and public policies) that promote the social good. The spirit of *Brown*, as I have attempted to show in chapter 1, is an extant judicial or constitutional policy that promotes the public good. It is my belief that when the Supreme Court proceeds therefrom, it acts with legal legitimacy as it is not treating the judicial power as a discretionary power but as a more limited power— the power of reasoned elaboration. The Supreme Court is exemplifying the principle of "reasonable persons pursuing reasonable purposes reasonably." Brooks, *Structures of Judicial Decision Making*, 133.

H. L. A. Hart, the "radical positivist," conceded in an unpublished essay titled "Discretion," that, similar to process theory, judicial discretion based not on the judge's "whim" but on grounds "deserving of rational approval" can be fully consistent with the rule of law. Hart saw "discretion [as] *part of law*, to be *perfected*, rather than [as] an obstacle associated with the rule not of law but of men." Geoffrey C. Shaw, "H. L. A. Hart's Lost Essay: Discretion and the Legal Process School," *Harvard Law Review* 127 (2013): 666, 669, 724 (emphasis in original). However, as Nicola Lacey, Hart's biographer, explains, this "commonsense" view of law was antithetical to Hart's positivism developed both before and after the lost essay. Accepting the notion that discretion, even as a long-standing institutional practice, can be a source of legal legitimacy, would compromise Hart's "idea that law's normativity derives entirely from the rule of recognition." Lacey, "The Path Not Taken," 650. Even Shaw ultimately downplays the significance of the lost essay: "Hart's [theory] was a pre-*Brown* theory of judicial discretion composed in a post-*Brown* world. Hart did not attempt to state the precise conditions under which courts can rightly overturn the commands of electoral majorities." Shaw, "H. L. A. Hart's Lost Essay," 726. Most tellingly, Hart's fragmentary thoughts about judicial discretion, written in the midst of an intellectually intense visit to Harvard Law School dominated by process scholars, were never fully developed in his seminal writing, *The Concept of Law* (New York: Oxford University Press, 1961). The lost essay was finally published in 2013. See H. L. A. Hart, "Discretion," *Harvard Law Review* 127 (2013): 652. However, it was actually found years earlier by Professor Anthony Sebok, who referred to it in his book *Legal Positivism in American Jurisprudence* (New York: Cambridge University Press, 1998), 169n232.

Chapter 3. Race and Culture

1. Samuel R. Lucas and Marcel Paret, "Law, Race, and Education in the United States," *Annual Review of Law and Social Science* 1 (2005): 203, 203–204. Laura Gomez concurs, noting that, racial classification turns not on what one feels or on how one identifies racially, but on what others allow one to do. Laura E. Gomez, "Understanding Law and Race as Mutually Constitutive," *Journal of Scholarly Perspectives* 8.1 (2012): 47, 50.

2. Angela Ards, "In the Twinkling of an Eye," *Black Issues Book Review*, July/August 2005, 23 (quoting Gladwell).

3. See David Matthews, *Ace of Spades: A Memoir* (New York: Henry Holt, 2007), 64–66, 158–160, 163–165.

4. Bliss Broyard, "Half and Half," *New York Times Book Review*, February 11, 2007, 6. See generally Bliss Broyard, *One Drop: My Father's Hidden Life—A Story of Race and Family Secrets* (Boston: Little, Brown, 2008).

5. Arnold Rampersad, *Ralph Ellison: A Biography* (New York: Alfred A. Knopf, 2007), 197.

6. James Hebert, "1 After 1: In Pop Culture, Who or What Is No. 1 Changes in a Flash," *San Diego Union-Tribune*, October, 9, 2006, D1. See Peter Keepnews, "Culture's Ambassador," *New York Times Book Review*, June 6, 2010, 29, reviewing Harvey G. Cohen, *Duke Ellington's America* (Chicago: University of Chicago Press, 2010). See also Lisa E. Davenport, *Jazz Diplomacy: Promoting America in the Cold War Era* (Jackson, MS: University Press of Mississippi, 2013), 90. Both high and pop culture should be accounted for as Stefan

Kanfer does in his analysis of a major cultural figure. "The image and reputation of Humphrey Bogart would be expected to run through popular culture. But rather unexpectedly, they worked their way into high culture as well." Stefan Kanfer, *Tough Without a Gun: The Life and Extraordinary Afterlife of Humphrey Bogart* (New York: Vintage Books, 2011), 218.

Unlike the counterculture of the 1960s, pop culture does not directly challenge high culture. High culture and pop culture do in fact coexist. The counterculture, in contrast, opposed both high and pop culture. As chronicled in such seminal works as Charles A. Reich's *The Greening of America* and Theodore Roszak's *The Making of a Counter Culture,* the counterculture was a sustained attack on "technocracy," the hegemonic cultural imperative of the mainstream culture, both high and pop culture. Roszak defined "technocracy" as "that society in which those who govern justify themselves by appeal to technical experts who, in turn, justify themselves by appeal to scientific forms of knowledge." Theodore Roszak, *The Making of a Counter Culture: Reflections on the Technocratic Society and Its Youthful Opposition* (Berkeley: University of California Press, 1995), 8. Technocracy, then, is a regime of experts—e.g., Tim Cook at Apple, Bill Gates at Microsoft, and Mark Zuckerberg at Facebook—whose authority is derived from the reliance upon rationality, scientific process, and reason as the final arbiters of truth and human organization. The influence of technocracy reaches all forms of life. As Roszak observed, technocracy represents an "era of social engineering in which entrepreneurial talent broadens its province to orchestrate the total human context which surrounds the industrial complex. Politics, education, leisure, entertainment, culture as a whole, the unconscious drives, and even protest against the technocracy itself: all these become the subjects of purely technical scrutiny and of purely technical manipulation." Ibid.

Christina Ribbhagen elaborates on Roszak's concept of "technocracy," writing in "What Makes a Technocrat? Explaining Variation Thinking Among Elite Bureaucrats," *Public Policy and Administration* 26.1 (2011), "First, a technocrat believes that technics must replace politics and defines his own role in apolitical terms. A technocrat believes in rationality and in problem solving using a strict scientific approach. Second, the technocrat is skeptical and even hostile towards politicians and political institutions. A technocrat makes decisions on a firm basis of technical knowledge; political values and preferences are considered irrelevant since all questions can be reduced to technique. Third, the technocrat is fundamentally unsympathetic to the openness and equality of political democracy. Since information and knowledge can solve societal problems, it is not necessary that the government listen to the people and be responsive, since the people are not experts. This view of policy making has been characterized as 'technocratic dictatorship.' Fourth, the technocrat believes that social and political conflict is, at best, misguided, and, at worst, contrived. Since there is a right answer to each problem, a technocrat will not understand negotiations between different positions on a question, or will at least believe that differences can be resolved once the misinformed obtain proper information and gain an accurate understanding of the problem. Fifth, 'the technocrat rejects ideological or moralistic criteria, preferring to debate policy in practical, "pragmatic" terms' when analy[z]ing public issues. Answers are not found in 'emotional simplifications' but through social and scientific knowledge. The right question to ask is not 'is it right' (morally or doctrinally) but rather 'will it work'? Finally, sixth, in terms of values, the technocrat is strongly committed to technological progress and material productivity; he is less concerned about distributive questions of social justice. Efficiency, rather than distributive justice, is a primary goal." Ibid., 23.

Opposition to the authoritarianism of technocratic regimes, Roszak argued, largely originated from the youth of the 1960s "because of the passivity of the adult generation." Roszak, *The Making of a Counter Culture,* 22. The youth of today, of course, are heavily invested in technology. With groups like the Occupy Wall Street movement and individuals like Ralph Nader who believe that runaway technology threatens society, the counterculture today has a smaller presence in our society. But the counterculture at full strength certainly threatens competing cultures deeply invested in technology. The counterculture seeks, as Reich maintains, a "new consciousness," a "bloodless revolution" against the values that technology has thrust upon society. Charles A. Reich, *The Greening of America* (New York: Random House, 1970), 3. Similar to the German concept of *Kultur* (particularly its emphasis on the spiritual and emotional life of the community, of placing "individual genius and self-expression against stifling bureaucracy" and scientific knowledge and rationalism, to borrow from Adam Kuper), the counterculture prescribes nothing less than a fundamental restructuring of the American culture writ large. There is no coexistence between the counterculture and mainstream culture, whether high culture or pop culture. For a general discussion of culture, see, e.g., Adam Kuper, *Culture: The Anthropologists' Account* (Cambridge, MA: Harvard University Press, 1999), 6. See, e.g., William W. Zellner, *Countercultures: A Sociological Analysis* (New York: St. Martin's Press, 1995); Christina Ribbhagen, "What Makes a Technocrat?"; Ruth Benedict, *Patterns of Culture* (Boston: Houghton Mifflin, 1989); Josef Joffe, "The Perils of Soft Power: Why America's Cultural Influence Makes Enemies Too," *New York Times Magazine,* May 14, 2006, 15.

7. Bart Landry, *The New Black Middle Class* (Berkeley: University of California Press, 1987), x. Scholars today continue to reference Landry's rigorous analysis, as I did when I last wrote about the topic. See Roy L. Brooks, *Rethinking the American Race Problem* (Berkeley: University of California Press, 1990), 34–36. The consensus is clear: "'Middle Class' is a notoriously elusive category based on a combination of socioeconomic factors (mostly income, occupation, and education) and normative judgments (ranging from where people live, to what churches or clubs they belong to, whether they plant flowers in their gardens)." Mary Patillo, *Black Picket Fences: Privilege and Peril Among the Black Middle Class,* 2nd ed. (Chicago: University of Chicago Press, 2013), 14.

8. Karyn R. Lacy, *Blue-Chip Black: Race, Class, and Status in the New Black Middle Class* (Berkeley: University of California Press, 2007), 2. See also Patrick Sharkey, "Spatial Segmentation and the Black Middle Class," *American Journal of Sociology* 119 (2014): 903.

9. See Tami Luhby, "Typical American Family Earned $53,657 Last Year," CNN Money, American Opportunity, September 16, 2014, http://money.cnn.com/2015/09/16/news/economy/census-poverty-income (accessed July 30, 2016). See Catherine Rampell, "Defining the Middle Class," *New York Times,* Economix, September 14, 2012, http://

economix.blogs.nytimes.com/2012/09/14/defining-middle-class (accessed December 3, 2015). On the endangered middle class, see, e.g., Teresa A. Sullivan, Elizabeth Warren, and Jay Lawrence Westbrook, *The Fragile Middle Class: Americans in Debt* (New Haven, CT: Yale University Press, 2000); Elizabeth Warren and Amelia Warren Tyagil, *The Two-Income Trap: Why Middle-Class Parents Are (Still) Going Broke*, ppb. ed. (New York: Basic Books, 2016).

10. Barbara Ehrenreich, *Fear of Falling: The Inner Life of the Middle Class* (New York: Pantheon Books, 1989), 15.

11. Burton J. Bledstein, *The Culture of Professionalism: The Middle Class and the Development of Higher Education in America* (New York: W. W. Norton, 1978), 4.

12. Joseph Epstein, *Snobbery: The American Version* (Boston: Houghton Mifflin, 2002), 131. See Aundra Saa Meroe, "Democracy, Meritocracy, and the Uses of Education," *Journal of Negro Education* 83.4 (2014): 485, 485–498; Annette Lareau and Elliot B. Weininger, "Class and Transition to Adulthood," in *Social Class: How Does It Work?* ed. Annette Lareau and Dalton Conley (New York: Russell Sage Foundation, 2008), 127–131; Jennifer L. Hochschild, *Facing Up to the American Dream: Race, Class, and the Soul of the Nation* (Princeton: Princeton University Press, 1995), 159–160; Joseph L. DeVitis and John Martin Rich, *The Success Ethic, Education, and the American Dream* (New York: State University of New York Press, 1996), 83; Lois Weis, ed., *Class, Race, & Gender in American Education* (Albany: State University of New York Press, 1988), 311.

13. Malcolm Gladwell, *Outliers: The Story of Success* (New York: Little, Brown, 2008), 102–105. See Michèle Lamont, *The Dignity of Working Men: Morality and the Boundaries of Race, Class, and Immigration* (New York: Russell Sage Foundation, 2009), 31. See also Annette Lareau, *Unequal Childhoods: Class, Race, and Family Life* (Berkeley: University of California Press, 2011).

14. Gladwell, *Outliers*, 108; Elliot Currie, *The Road to Whatever: Middle Class Culture and the Crisis of Adolescence* (New York: Metropolitan Books, 2008), 68–88. See Shahid Alvi, Hannah Scott, and Wendy Stanyon, "We're Locking the Door: Family Histories in a Sample of Homeless Youth," *Qualitative Report* 15.5 (2010): 1210, 1210–1211.

15. Christopher Lasch, *The True and Only Heaven: Progress and Its Critics* (New York: W. W. Norton, 1991), 458. See also 192, 486. Though somewhat off point, it is worth noting that Charles Murray argues that because of the financial excesses of Wall Street, disdain toward the upper class now extends beyond the middle class. Charles Murray, *Coming Apart: The State of White America 1960–2010* (New York: Crown Forum, 2012), 194–196. See Jeffrey A. Becker, *Ambition in America: Political Power and the Collapse of Citizenship* (Lexington: University Press of Kentucky, 2014), 116. Indeed, disdain toward the upper class extends to their allies in Congress, the political establishment, as so dramatically demonstrated by Donald Trump's 2016 primary election victories over such Republican political insiders as Jeb Bush and, on the other side, by Bernie Sanders's many primary election victories over Democratic insider Hillary Clinton. See, e.g., Philip Elliott, "The Brief: Why Would Democrats Vote For Trump? It's All About Trade," *Time,* March 21, 2016, 15.

16. Epstein, *Snobbery,* 38.

17. Epstein, *Snobbery*, 38–43; Jeff Torlina, *Working Class: Challenging Myths About Blue-Collar Labor* (Boulder: Lynne Rienner Publishers, 2011), 4; Forrest Wickman, "Working Man's Blues: Why Do We Call Manual Laborers *Blue Collar?*" *Slate*, May 1, 2012, www.slate.com/articles/business/explainer/2012/05/blue_collar_white_collar_why_do_we_use_these_terms_.html (accessed March 11, 2016). But see Dennis Gilbert, *The American Class Structure in an Age of Growing Inequality*, 6th ed. (Belmont, CA: Thomson Wadsworth, 2003), 18 (diverging from the traditional use of manual labor to distinguish classes). "To be more precise, middle class persons tend to work either with people or with data. Their occupational positions, as opposed to those in the working class, are delineated by the extent to which they interact with others and by the degree to which they manipulate information." Ibid. See Melvyn L. Fein, *Human Hierarchies: A General Theory* (Piscataway, NJ: Transaction Publishers, 2012), 240–242.

18. Sullivan, Warren, and Westbrook, *The Fragile Middle Class*, 21. See also Karen McCormack, "Credit and Credibility: Homeownership and Identity Management in the Midst of the Foreclosure Crisis," *Sociological Quarterly* 55.2 (2014): 261.

19. "Inside the Middle Class: Bad Times Hit the Good Life," Pew Research Center, April 9, 2008, http://www.pewsocialtrends.org/2008/04/09/inside-the-middle-class-bad-times-hit-the-good-life (accessed December 14, 2015); Mark Chaves, *American Religion: Contemporary Trends* (Princeton: Princeton University Press, 2011), 51; W. Bradford Wilcox, Andrew J. Cherlin, Jeremy E. Uecker, and Matthew Messel, "No Money, No Hunny, No Church: The Deinstitutionalization of Religious Life Among the White Working Class," *Research in Sociology of Work* 23 (2012): 227, 229; Murray, *Coming Apart*, 200–208; Michael Ariens, "What Hath Faith Wrought?" *Journal of Law and Religion Book Review* 24 (2008/2009): 195, 197–198, reviewing Robert F. Cochran, *Faith and Law: How Religious Traditions from Calvinism to Islam View American Law* (New York: New York University Press, 2008). For a very good discussion of homosexuality and religion, see Patrick Allitt, *Religion in America Since 1945: A History* (New York: Columbia University Press, 2003), 231–241; Robert Booth Fowler, "The Roman Catholic Church in 'Protestant' America Today," *Forum* 11.4 (2014): 721–742.

20. "The Decline of Marriage and Rise of New Families," Pew Research Center, November 18, 2010, www.pewsocialtrends.org/files/2010/11/pew-social-trends-2010-families.pdf (accessed December 13, 2015).

21. "The Generation Gap and the 2012 Election," Pew Research Center, November 3, 2011, www.people-press.org/files/legacy-pdf/11-3-11%20Generations%20Release.pdf (accessed December 13, 2015).

22. See Elizabeth Mendes, Lydia Saad, and Kyley McGeeney, "Stay-at-Home Moms Report More Depression, Sadness, Anger," Gallup, May 18, 2012, www.gallup.com/poll/154685/Stay-Home-Moms-Report-Depression-Sadness-Anger.aspx (accessed December 13, 2015). On the feminist belief that women can work and be mothers at the same time, see Eileen Patten and Kim Parker, "A Gender Reversal on Career Aspirations: Young Women Now Top Young Men in Valuing High-Paying Career," Pew Research Center, Social Trends, April 19, 2012, 1–2, www.pewsocialtrends.org/files/2012/04/Women-in-the-Workplace.pdf (accessed December 13, 2015). See also Caitlin Friedman

and Kimberly Yorio, *Happy at Work, Happy at Home: The Girl's Guide to Being a Working Mom* (New York: Broadway Books, 2009); Linda Mason, *The Working Mother's Guide to Life: Strategies, Secrets, and Solutions* (New York: Three Rivers Press, 2002); "The Decline of Marriage and Rise of New Families," 69 (reporting that "the public has been more inclined to believe that a working mother can do just as good a job with her children as a stay-at-home mother"). But see Anne-Marie Slaughter, "Why Women Still Can't Have it All," *Atlantic*, July/August 2012, 84–102. While Slaughter's article brought a great deal of attention to the issue, the idea that women cannot "have it all" was not new. See, e.g., Rebecca Korzec, "Working on the Mommy-Track: Motherhood and Women Lawyers," *Hastings Women's Law Journal* 8 (Winter 1997): 117. On the participation rate of mothers in the labor force, see Cohn, D'Vera, Gretchen Livingston, and Wendy Wang, "After Decades of Decline, a Rise in Stay-at-Home Mothers," Pew Research Center, April 8, 2014, http://www.pewsocialtrends.org/2014/04/08/after-decades-of-decline-a-rise-in-stay-at-home-mothers/ (accessed December 13, 2015); "The Decline of Marriage and Rise of New Families," ii–iii, 68. See also Sheryl Sandberg, *Lean In: Women, Work, and the Will to Lead* (New York: Random House, 2013). In 1971, one household wage earner had more purchasing power than the two-wage-earner household had in 2001. See Warren and Tyagil, *The Two-Income Trap.*

23. Lasch, *The True and Only Heaven,* 484.

24. Charles Vert Willie and Richard J. Reddick, *A New Look at Black Families* (Walnut Creek, CA: Rowman & Littlefield Publishers, 2003), 55–56. "Education has always been a vital route toward upward mobility." Hephzibah V. Strmic-Pawl and Phyllis K. Leffler, "Black Families and Fostering of Leadership," *Ethnicities* 11.2 (2011): 139, 159. Susan Toliver reports that middle-class African Americans "firmly attested to having been encouraged in their educational pursuits by their parents, especially their mothers. . . . They attributed their greater success to the fact that they are 'self-starters'—they are hardworking; aggressive; highly motivated; personally driven; committed to excellence; desirous of success." Susan D. Toliver, "Critical Perspectives on Black Family Theory: A Revised ABC-X Model for Understanding Black Family Stress and Black Family Strengths," *European Scientific Journal* 1 (2015): 380, 395.

25. Lacy, *Blue-Chip Black,* 2. See also Patillo, *Black Picket Fences,* ix.

26. See Leland Ware and Theodore J. Davis, "Ordinary People in an Extraordinary Time: The Black Middle-Class in the Age of Obama," *Howard Law Journal* 55 (2012): 533, 539.

27. Lacy, *Blue-Chip Black,* 3. Afro-Caribbeans living in London exhibit similar signaling traits as African Americans in the United States. See Nicola Rollock, David Gilborn, Carol Vincent, and Steven Ball, "The Public Identities of the Black Middle Classes: Managing Race in Public Spaces," *Sociology* 45.6 (2011): 1078, 1086–1089.

28. Lacy, *Blue-Chip Black,* 14, 94. "Language and accent were regarded as central tools that enabled black middle class respondents to signal their class status to white others." Nicola Rollock et al., "The Public Identities of the Black Middle Classes," 1086–1089.

29. Ware and Davis, "Ordinary People in an Extraordinary Time," 539. Lacy, *Blue-Chip Black,* 93–110. Rollock et al., "The Public Identities of the Black Middle Classes," 1086–1089.

NOTES TC PAGES 80–84

30. Rollock et al., "The Public Identities of the Black Middle Classes," 1086–1089. See Nicole Arlette Hirsch and Anthony Abraham Jack, "What We Face: Framing Problems in the Black Community," *Du Bois Review: Social Science Research on Race* 9.1 (2012): 133. Devan Carbado and Mitu Gulati similarly argue that racial judgments are often based not only on one's color but also on one's behavior; i.e., stereotypes based on how one dresses or speaks, how one styles one's hair, politics, friends, and demeanor. See Devon W. Carbado and Mitu Gulati, *Acting White? Rethinking Race in "Post-Racial" America* (New York: Oxford University Press, 2013).

31. Houston A. Baker, *Betrayal: How Black Intellectuals Have Abandoned the Ideals of the Civil Rights Era* (New York: Columbia University Press, 2008), 9. See Cornel West and Christa Buschendorf, *Black Prophetic Fire* (Boston: Beacon Press, 2014).

32. Touré, "Visible Young Man," *New York Times Book Review,* May 3, 2009, 1, reviewing Colson Whitehead, *SAG Harbor* (New York: Doubleday, 2009). See also Touré and Michael Eric Dyson, *Who's Afraid of Post-Blackness? What It Means to Be Black Now* (New York: Free Press, 2011); Ytasha L. Womack, *Post Black: How a New Generation Is Redefining African American Identity* (Chicago: Lawrence Hill Books, 2010). I would challenge the notion that Kanyé is "post-black," especially considering lyrics such as "[a]s long as I'm in Polo smiling, they think they got me / But they would try to crack me if they ever see a black me." Kanyé West, "Gorgeous," *My Beautiful Dark Twisted Fantasy* (Def Jam Records, 2010). See Ralph Ellison, *Invisible Man* (New York: Vintage Books, 1947, 1952).

33. *Black Families in Crisis: The Middle Class,* ed. Alice F. Coner-Edwards and Jeanne Spurlock (New York: Brunner/Mazel, 1988), 6; "Optimism About Black Progress Declines: Blacks See Growing Values Gap Between Poor and Middle Class," Pew Research Center, November 13, 2007, 3, www.pewsocialtrends.org/files/2010/10/Race-2007.pdf (accessed March 3, 2016); Harry T. Edwards, "The Journey from *Brown v. Board of Education* to *Grutter v. Bollinger*: From Racial Assimilation to Diversity," *Michigan Law Review* 102 (2004): 944, 947. See also Lori Latrice Martin, "Strategic Assimilation or Creation of Symbolic Blackness: Middle-Class Blacks in Suburban Contexts," *Journal of African American Studies* 14.2 (2010), 234, 238; ibid.

34. Landry, *The New Black Middle Class,* 141; Robert C. Smith and Richard Seltzer, *Race, Class and Culture: A Study in Afro-American Mass Opinion* (Albany: State University of New York Press, 1992), 54, table 3.5. See Patillo, *Black Picket Fences,* 2.

35. Touré, "How to Talk to Young Black Boys About Trayvon Martin," *Time,* April 2, 2012, 17.

36. Smith and Seltzer, *Race, Class and Culture,* 51, table 3.4, 52. See also Patillo, *Black Picket Fences,* 2. Raymond Brock-Murray finds similar results among college students. See Raymond Brock-Murray, "Comparing Racial Identity, Acculturative Stress, and Feelings of Alienation in African-American College Attendees and Non-Attendees," *Seton Hall University Dissertations and Theses (ETDs),* Paper 334, 2010, http://scholarship.shu.edu/cgi/viewcontent.cgi?article=1334&context=dissertations (accessed March 2, 2016).

37. Smith and Seltzer, *Race, Class and Culture,* 29. See also 45; Bart Landry and Kris Marsh, "The Evolution of the New Black Middle Class," *Annual Review of Sociology* 37 (2011): 373, 388; Charles Vert Willie and Richard J. Reddick, *A New Look at Black*

Families, 5th ed. (Walnut Creek, CA: Rowman & Littlefield Publishers, 2003), 57. See also Lori Latrice Martin, "Strategic Assimilation or Creation of Symbolic Blackness: Middle-Class Blacks in Suburban Contexts," *Journal of African American Studies* 14.2 (2010): 234. A Pew study shows that "nearly eight-in-ten (79%) African-Americans say the government should do more to help the needy, even if it means going deeper into debt," compared to 62% of the total population. Neha Sahgal and Greg Smith, "A Religious Portrait of African-Americans," Pew Research Center, January 30, 2009, http://www.pewforum. org/2009/01/30/a-religious-portrait-of-african-americans (accessed March 2, 2016).

38. Smith and Seltzer, *Race, Class and Culture,* 69–70, table 3.9.

39. See "Partisan Polarization Surges in Bush, Obama Years Trends in American Values: 1987–2012," at section 8: "Values About Immigration and Race," 89, Pew Research Center, U.S. Politics & Policy, June 4, 2012, http://www.people-press.org/2012/06/04/ partisan-polarization-surges-in-bush-obama-years/ (accessed March 2, 2016).

40. Brooks, *Rethinking the American Race Problem,* 143–144; Roy L. Brooks, "Cultural Diversity: It's All About the Mainstream," *Monist* 95.1 (2012): 17, 19.

41. Langston Hughes, "The Negro Mother," in *The African American Book of Values,* ed. Steven Barboza (New York: Doubleday, 1998), 552–553.

42. Ibid., 552.

43. Brooks, *Rethinking the American Race Problem,* 145. See Barboza, *The African American Book of Values,* 553.

44. Maya Angelou, "Voices of Respect," in Barboza, *The African American Book of Values,* 822–823.

45. Lamont, *The Dignity of Working Men,* 2, 10, 23. Being a member of the working class is "like running on a treadmill that keeps increasing in speed. You have to go faster and faster just to stay in place. Or, as a factory worker said many years ago, 'You can work 'til you drop dead, but you won't get ahead' " (interview with Bob Herbert of *The New York Times,* who has built a career on studying the working class). Diana Kendall, *Framing Class: Media Representations of Wealth and Poverty in America,* 2nd ed. (Lanham, MD: Rowman & Littlefield Publishers, 2011), 122, 157–162.

46. Michael Zweig, ed., *What's Class Got to Do With It? American Society in the Twenty-First Century* (Ithaca, NY: Cornell University Press, 2004), 141.

47. Lamont, *The Dignity of Working Men,* 2–3, 20, 26; Torlina, *Working Class,* 23–25. See Kristen Lucas, "The Working Class Promise: A Communicative Account of Mobility-Based Ambivalences," (2011), Papers in Communication Studies, Paper 12, Communication Studies Department, University of Nebraska-Lincoln, http:// digitalcommons.unl.edu/commstudiespapers/12 (accessed November 15, 2015), noting at 353 that "The social construction of working class is accomplished through communicating four core values: a) work ethic, b) provider orientation, c) the dignity of all work and workers, and d) humility." See also Melvyn L. Fein, *Human Hierarchies: A General Theory* (Piscataway, NJ: Transaction Publishers, 2012). But see Murray, *Coming Apart,* 168–188, 272–273. Murray suggests that all white males, including working-class white males, became less industrious between 1960 and 2010 because more men did not participate in the labor force and fewer men worked forty or more hours a week. In this

same period, more women have joined the workforce and nearly the same amount of women work forty or more hours a week.

48. Lamont, *The Dignity of Working Men*, 26. See Fein, *Human Hierarchies*; Harold R. Kerbo, *Social Stratification and Inequality: Class Conflict in Historical, Comparative, and Global Perspective*, 4th ed. (Boston: McGraw-Hill, 2000), 230–231.

49. Lamont, *The Dignity of Working Men*, 26. See generally Annette Lareau, *Unequal Childhoods*. But see Torlina, *Working Class*, 79–81, 184–185. Torlina challenges the "sacred idea" that society is arranged in a social ladder that places the middle class above the working class, because many blue-collar workers "viewed the social-class hierarchy in horizontal terms, with class positions occupying separate spheres—neither necessarily superior nor inferior to each other." Torlina contends that the hierarchical social ladder structure "may actually promote inequality . . . [r]ather than reflect inequality" between classes.

50. Lamont, *The Dignity of Working Men*, 30–31; Torlina, *Working Class*, 64; Joseph A. Kahl, *The American Class Structure* (New York: Rinehart, 1957), 208. See Lareau, *Unequal Childhoods*.

51. Lamont, *The Dignity of Working Men*, 19. See also Jeff Torlina, *Working Class*, 63–64.

52. Lamont, *The Dignity of Working Men*, 30, 34; Bret E. Carroll, ed., *American Masculinities: A Historical Encyclopedia* (Thousand Oaks, CA: Sage Publications, 2003), 71–73. See Joan C. Williams, "The Class Culture Gap," in *Facing Social Class: How Societal Rank Influences Interaction*, ed. Susan Fiske and Hazel Rose Markus (New York: Russell Sage Foundation, 2012), 39, 47. See also Lareau, *Unequal Childhoods*. The majority of stay-at-home mothers have little education, or the family cannot afford the high cost of child care. See Rose M. Kreider and Diana B. Elliott, *Historical Changes in Stay-at-Home Mothers: 1969 to 2009*, 4, 19–20, U.S. Census Bureau, Fertility and Family Statistics Branch, Paper Presented at American Sociological Association 2010 annual meeting, https://www.census.gov/hhes/families/files/ASA2010_Kreider_Elliott.pdf (accessed August 2, 2015). In accord, D'Vera Cohn, Gretchen Livingston, and Wendy Wang, "After Decades of Decline, a Rise in Stay-at-Home Mothers," Pew Research Center, Social Trends, April 8, 2014, http://www.pewsocialtrends.org/2014/04/08/after-decades-of-decline-a-rise-in-stay-at-home-mothers/ (accessed August 2, 2015) (49% of working mothers have a high school diploma or less).

53. Lamont, *The Dignity of Working Men*, 32–34. See also Williams, "The Class Culture Gap," 42.

54. Lamont, *The Dignity of Working Men*, 35–36.

55. Elizabeth Warren, *A Fighting Chance* (New York: Picador, 2014), 60, 69.

56. See Murray, *Coming Apart*, 132–134, 189–199, 273–275; Lamont, *The Dignity of Working Men*, 36. See Warren and Tyagi, *The Two-Income Trap*.

57. Lamont, *The Dignity of Working Men*, 22, 36–37. Murray, *Coming Apart*, 194.

58. Lamont, *The Dignity of Working Men*, 39–40; W. Bradford Wilcox, Andrew J. Cherlin, Jeremy E. Uecker, and Matthew Messel, "No Money, No Hunny, No Church," 227, 227–229; Murray, *Coming Apart*, 205–208, 275.

59. Lamont, *The Dignity of Working Men,* 43.

60. Ibid., 44.

61. Ibid., 22, 37. See Lareau, *Unequal Childhoods.*

62. Lamont, *The Dignity of Working Men,* 20.

63. Lois Weis and Michelle Fine, "Narrating the 1980s and 1990s: Voices of Poor and Working-Class White and African American Men," *Anthropology & Education Quarterly* 27.4 (December 1996): 500–502. See also 493–516. The study on nepotism is reported at Andrew P. Collins, "Code 3: Investigation Calls Out LA Fire Department for Rampant Nepotism," http://code3.jalopnik.com/investigation-calls-out-la-fire-department-for-rampant-1651020183/+jasontorch (accessed March 15, 2016). For a report on Trump's voters, see, e.g., Daniel White, "Nearly 20% of Trump Fans Think Freeing the Slaves Was a Bad Idea," *Time,* February 24, 2016, http://time.com/4236640/donald-trump-racist-supporters (accessed March 19, 2016).

64. Lamont, *The Dignity of Working Men,* 52–53.

65. Ibid., 41. In accord, Sahgal and Smith, "A Religious Portrait of African-Americans"—79% of African Americans say religion is very important in their lives as opposed to 56% of all other Americans.

66. Lamont, *The Dignity of Working Men,* 42. In Sahgal and Smith, "A Religious Portrait of African Americans." See Nicole Arlette Hirsch and Anthony Abraham Jack, "What We Face," 139. ("They believed that racist stereotypes translate into unfair treatment and hold African Americans back. . . . 'We are considered like the boogey-man.' When asked to expand on what it means to be a boogeyman, he said, 'The big Black guy, it's like [the] stereotype. . . . He's Aggressive.' ").

67. Lamont, *The Dignity of Working Men,* 47. In accord, Sahgal and Smith, "A Religious Portrait of African Americans."

68. Lamont, *The Dignity of Working Men,* 34.

69. Ibid., 47. See also Bige Saatcioglu and Julie L. Ozanne, "Moral Habitus and Status Negotiation in Marginalized Working Class Neighborhood," *Journal of Consumer Research* 40 (2013): 692, 694.

70. Lamont, *The Dignity of Working Men,* 49–51.

71. Thom Hartmann, *Screwed: The Undeclared War Against the Middle Class—and What We Can Do About It* (San Francisco: Berrett-Koehler Publishers, 2006), 9–10. See James Carville and Stan Greenberg, *It's the Middle Class, Stupid!* (New York: Blue Rider Press, 2012), 27–28.

72. William A. V. Clark, *Immigrants and the American Dream: Remaking the Middle Class* (New York: Guilford Press, 2003), 6.

73. Carville and Greenberg, *It's the Middle Class, Stupid!*

74. The black values were discussed in the section of the chapter titled, "Middle-Class Racial Differences."

Chapter 4. Cultural Subordination Through Cultural Diversity

1. To read about the event, see "San Diego Datebook," *San Diego Union-Tribune,* May 23, B5.

2. Eugene Robinson, *Disintegration: The Splintering of Black America* (New York: Doubleday, 2010), 4, 5.

3. John McWhorter, *Authentically Black: Essays for the Black Silent Majority* (New York: Gotham Books, 2003).

4. Cornel West, *Race Matters* (Boston: Beacon Press, 2001), 38.

5. Interview by Tavis Smiley, February 17, 2016, PBS, Tavis Smiley Archives, www.pbs.org/kcet/tavissmiley/archive/200602/20060217_transcript.html (accessed April 21, 2016; hard copy of interview on file with author). For a broader discussion of Shelby's views, see Tommie Shelby, *We Who Are Dark: The Philosophical Foundations of Black Solidarity* (Cambridge, MA: Harvard University Press, 2005). For a discussion of black and other group identities within an international context, see Michael S. Merry, *Equality, Citizenship, and Segregation* (New York: Palgrave Macmillan, 2013).

6. Robinson, *Disintegration,* 10–11.

7. In a candid speech, FBI director James Comey acknowledged the existence of widespread racial bias in law enforcement. He also observed that "many people in our white-majority culture have unconscious racial biases and react differently to a white face than a black face." Brent Staples, "F.B.I. Director James Comey on How Everyone's a Little Bit Racist," *New York Times,* Taking Note, February 12, 2015, http://takingnote.blogs.nytimes.com/2015/02/12/f-b-i-director-james-comey-on-how-everyones-a-little-bit-racist/?action=click&contentCollection=Politics&module=RelatedCoverage&region=argin alia&pgtype=article (accessed June 12, 2015). See Michelle Alexander, *The New Jim Crow: Mass Incarceration in the Age of Colorblindness,* rev. ed. (New York: New Press, 2011).

8. See, e.g., "African American Perspectives," The Progress of a People, Library of Congress, October 19, 1998, http://memory.loc.gov/ammem/aap/aapexhp.html (accessed July 8, 2015); Steven Barboza, ed., *The African American Book of Values* (New York: Doubleday, 1998), 21–62, 217–246, 322–379, 559–612, 745–789, 795–829; Roy L. Brooks, *Rethinking the American Race Problem* (Berkeley: University of California Press, 1992), 40; Francis Terrell and Sandra L. Terrell, "Effects of Race of Examiner and Cultural Mistrust on the WAIS Performance of Black Students," *Journal of Consulting and Clinical Psychology* 49.5 (1981): 750, 750–751. The Pew Research Center reports that 62% of blacks and only 22% of whites believe that society should do everything possible to improve the conditions of blacks and other racial minorities, including giving blacks preferential treatment. "Partisan Polarization Surges in Bush, Obama Years Trends in American Values: 1987–2012," at section 8: "Values About Immigration and Race," Pew Research Center, U.S. Politics & Policy, June 4, 2012, http://www.people-press.org/2012/06/04/partisan-polarization-surges-in-bush-obama-years/ (accessed July 8, 2015). The Pew Research Center is replete with reports on the black/white divide in this country. See, e.g., Monica Anderson, "Vast Majority of Blacks View the Criminal Justice System as Unfair," Pew Research Center, August 12, 2014, http://www.pewresearch.org/fact-tank/2014/08/12/vast-majority-of-blacks-view-the-criminal-justice-system-as-unfair (accessed July 8, 2015). Black values have also been recorded in books (e.g., the aforementioned *African American Book of Values,* the "bible of black values") and poems (e.g., Maya Angelou's *Still I Rise* [1978], in the words of the "Black National Anthem" sung at NAACP conferences

and local gatherings of African Americans, in the themes imprinted on stoles or sashes worn by black graduates from Columbia University to Thurgood Marshall College of UC San Diego, in Kwanzaa celebrations, and in more informal sources (e.g., conversations with family and friends and discussions at those repositories of wisdom in the black community: black barber shops and beauty shops). See also Tim Wise, *Dear White America: Letter to a New Minority* (San Francisco: City Lights Books, 2012), 11.

9. Interview by Tavis Smiley, February 17, 2016.

10. Joyce Carol Oates, *The Sacrifice* (New York: Ecco/HarperCollins, 2015) is a fictional retelling of the Brawley story. A fifteen-year-old African American living in Wappingers Falls, New York, Brawley gained fame (or infamy) in 1987 when she claimed that a group of white men, including a local police officer and prosecutor, brutally gang-raped her. Brawley's story turned out to be an elaborate hoax, for which she was sued for defamation by one of the men she accused. See Mark Memmott, "15 Years Later, Tawana Brawley Has Paid 1 Percent of Penalty," NPR, August 5, 2013, http://www.npr.org/sections/thetwo-way/2013/08/05/209194252/15-years-later-tawana-brawley-has-paid-1-percent-of-penalty (accessed July 29, 2016).

11. "Black Girl Magic Flashback: Watch the Lupita Nyong'o Speech Heard Around the World," *Essence,* February 28, 2014, http://www.essence.com/2014/02/27/lupita-nyongo-delivers-moving-black-women-hollywood-acceptance-speech (accessed July 8, 2015). See "Black Beauty Not Valued on International Scale," Black Girl Wondering and Praying, March 2, 2012, https://blacknotwhitedippedinchocolate.wordpress.com/2012/03/02/black-beauty-not-valued-on-international-scale (accessed June 1, 2015).

12. Claudia Rankine, *Citizen: An American Lyric* (Minneapolis, MN: Graywolf Press, 2014). For the online uproar over this book, see Sheryl Estrada, "Serena Williams, New York Times and Body Image," DiversityInc, July 15, 2015, http://www.diversityinc.com/news/serenawilliams-new-york-times-and-body-image (accessed December 8, 2015). For a discussion of white values that transcend class, see, e.g., Wise, *Dear White America.*

13. One poll taken in 2015 showed that 57% of whites and 18% of blacks "think that people talk too much about race." Similarly, 18% of whites compared to 49% of blacks "think that Americans do not talk enough about race." Peter Moore, "Whites, Blacks Divided on Whether We Talk About Race Too Much or Not Enough," YouGov, March 18, 2015, https://today.yougov.com/news/2015/03/18/whites-blacks-divided-whether-we-talk/ (accessed July 8, 2015). Two white law professors write that it is "obsession with race that is America's more consequential 'race problem' today." Larry Alexander and Maimon Schwarzschild, "Race Matters," *Constitutional Commentary* 29 (2013): 31.

14. Aharon Barak, "A Judge on Judging: The Role of the Supreme Court in a Democracy," *Harvard Law Review* 116 (2002): 16, 39. Justice Barak sits on the Supreme Court of Israel. See generally Ronald Dworkin, *A Bill of Rights for Britain* (London: Chatto & Windus, 1991).

15. In his seminal book on race and American democracy, Gunnar Myrdal writes more fully, "These ideals of the essential dignity of the individual human being, of the fundamental equality of all men, and of certain inalienable rights to freedom, justice, and a fair opportunity represent to the American people the essential meaning

of the nation's early struggle for independence. In the clarity and intellectual boldness of the Enlightenment period these tenets were written into the Declaration of Independence, the Preamble of the Constitution, the Bill of Rights and into the constitutions of the several states. The ideals of the American Creed have thus become the highest law of the land." Gunnar Myrdal, *An American Dilemma: The Negro Problem and Modern Democracy* (New York: Harper & Brothers, 1944), 4–5.

16. Janny Scott and David Leonhardt embellish their point by reference to an interesting analogy: "Everyone is dealt four cards, one from each suit: education, income, occupation and wealth, the four commonly used criteria for gauging class. Face cards in a few categories may land a player in the upper middle class. At first, a person's class is his parents' class. Later, he may pick up a new hand of his own; it is likely to resemble that of his parents, but not always. Bill Clinton traded in a hand of low cards with the help of a college education and a Rhodes scholarship and emerged decades later with four face cards. Bill Gates, who started off squarely in the upper middle class, made a fortune without finishing college, drawing three aces." Janny Scott and David Leonhardt, "Class Matters: Shadowy Lines That Still Divide," *New York Times*, May 15, 2005, http://www.nytimes.com/2005/05/15/us/class/shadowy-lines-that-still-divide.html?_ r=0 (accessed December 8, 2015). Even the children of undocumented aliens are given opportunities, such as a free public education. See Plyler v. Doe, 457 U.S. 202 (1982) (in invalidating a Texas law under the Equal Protection Clause that required children of illegal aliens to pay for their public education whereas children of citizens and documented aliens received a free public education, the Court held that, unlike their parents, the children of undocumented aliens were blameless they were not responsible for creating their status, and the state "could not abandon the innocent"). The Constitution does, however, limit the mobility of some Americans. "No person, except a natural born citizen . . . shall be eligible to the office of president." U.S. Const. art. II, § 1, cl. 5.

17. *Plessy*, 163 U.S. 537, 559 (Harlan, J., dissenting).

18. One of the best discussions of the film is Richard Schickel, *D. W. Griffith: An American Life* (New York: Simon & Schuster, 1984).

19. See, e.g., Christopher D. Totten, "Constitutional Precommitments to Gender Affirmative Action in the European Union, Germany, Canada and the United States: A Comparative Approach," *Berkeley Journal of International Law* 21 (2003): 27n1, 28n8.

20. Grutter v. Bollinger, 539 U.S. 306, 315 (2003) (quoting a school official).

21. Ibid., 330 (sources cited therein).

22. Parents Involved in Community Schools v. Seattle School District No. 1, 551 U.S. 701, 788 (2007) (Kennedy, J., concurring in part).

23. Grutter v. Bollinger, 539 U.S. at 330–331.

24. Meredith Hobbs, "Wal-Mart Demands Diversity in Law Firms," *National Law Journal*, Legal Business, July 11, 2005, http://www.nationallawjournal.com/id=90000543 2489?back=law&slreturn=20160625&20154847 (accessed July 12, 2005).

25. Taylor Cox, *Cultural Diversity in Organizations: Theory, Research & Practice* (San Francisco: Berrett-Koehler Publishers, 1993), 6; "Cultural diversity," Oxford Dictionaries, http://www.oxforddictionaries.com/us/definition/american_english/cultural-diversity

(accessed July 12, 2005). See Richard T. Schaefer, *Racial and Ethnic Diversity in the USA* (Boston: Pearson, 2013).

26. See Roy L. Brooks, *Racial Justice in the Age of Obama* (Princeton, NJ: Princeton University Press, 2009), chap. 2. Traditionalists do not deny the existence of racial oppression or the anthropological claim that racial categories are "constructed"—produced and reproduced ideologically or culturally—to control access to scarce opportunities and resources. But rather than countering such oppression with essentialism, traditionalists would simply file a demur. That is, they would say "So what?"; for they see racial oppression, to quote traditionalist Shelby Steele, as "an oppression of absurd contingencies, not an oppression of absolute determinisms." By "an oppression of absurd contingencies," Steele means an existence in which "it [is] always like living under some inhuman, capricious, intrusive, and fascistic bureaucracy." The constraints imposed on racially oppressed groups, especially African Americans, in this world of "absurd contingencies . . . are in fact racist imperatives," and add an "often unspoken level of meaning in American life to which blacks will have to be accountable." Blacks can experience worldly success and personal happiness only if they do not submit to these "absurd contingencies," give up their aspirations, or become driven by "Bigger Thomas–style determinism," all of which can lead to self-destruction. Traditionalists strongly admonish blacks to never believe that they are unable to compete with whites "because of chronic and apparently immutable handicaps." Shelby Steele, *The Content of Our Character: A New Vision of Race in America* (New York: St. Martin's Press, 1990), 31–32; Adarand v. Peña, 515 U.S. 200, 241 (1995) (Thomas, J., concurring). See Brooks, *Racial Justice in the Age of Obama,* chap. 2. On the construction of racial categories, see, e.g., Lee D. Baker, *From Savage to Negro: Anthropology and the Construction of "Race," 1896–1954* (Berkeley: University of California Press, 1998).

27. John H. McWhorter, *Losing the Race: Self-Sabotage in Black America* (New York: Free Press, 2000), 258.

28. See also Larry Alexander and Maimon Schwarzschild, "Race Matters," *Constitutional Commentary* 29 (2013): 31.

29. See Grutter v. Bollinger, 539 U.S. 306, 355, n3 (2003) (Thomas, J., dissenting).

30. Michelle Adams, "Radical Integration," *California Law Review* 94 (2006): 264, 302 (referencing Dictionary.com's definition of "assimilation").

31. See Michael Barone, *The New Americans: How the Melting Pot Can Work Again* (Washington, DC: Regnery Publishing, 2001). See, e.g., Peter D. Salins, *Assimilation American Style* (New York: Basic Books, 1997), 9–10; Stephan Thernstrom, Ann Orlov, and Oscar Handlin, eds., *Harvard Encyclopedia of American Ethnic Groups* (Cambridge, MA: Belknap Press of Harvard University, 1980), 150. One highly publicized example of the type of social discord traditionalists wish to avoid is the 2004 murder of the prominent Dutch filmmaker Theo van Gogh in Amsterdam by a Dutch-born Islamist, Mohammed Bouyeri, who was enraged by a film van Gogh had made, *Submission.* This film criticized the subjugation of women under Islam. For further discussion, see Brooks, *Racial Justice in the Age of Obama,* 14.

32. Stephan Thernstrom and Abigail Thernstrom, *America in Black and White: One Nation, Indivisible* (New York: Simon & Schuster, 1997), 540.

33. See Brooks, *Racial Justice in the Age of Obama*, chap. 2.

34. Michael S. Schmidt, "F.B.I. Director Speaks Out on Race and Police Bias," *New York Times*, February 12, 2015, http://www.nytimes.com/2015/02/13/us/politics/fbi-director-comey-speaks-frankly-about-police-view-of-blacks.html (accessed June 12, 2015); Barone, *The New Americans*, 3, 21–22.

35. Shelby Steele, *The Content of Our Character: A New Vision of Race in America* (New York: St. Martin's Press, 1990), 58–59, 75, 107–108, 173–174.

36. See Thomas Sowell, *Race, Culture, and Equality* (Stanford, CA: Hoover Institution on War, Revolution, and Peace, 1998), 5, 12–14.

37. This conclusion is based on "a side-by-side comparison of 2000 census data by sociologist John R. Logan at the Mumford Center, State University of New York at Albany." For example, "43.8 percent of African immigrants had achieved a college degree, compared to 42.5 [percent] of Asian-Americans, 28.9 percent for immigrants from Europe, Russia and Canada, and 23.1 percent of the U.S. population as a whole." Clarence Page, "Black Immigrants: An Invisible 'Model Minority,'" *Tribune Media Services*, March 19, 2007, B6, http://www.realclearpolitics.com/articles/2007/03/black_immigrants_an_invisible.html (accessed June 12, 2015).

38. Ibid., Page quoting a Jamaican friend.

39. D'Souza stated, "[T]he slaves are dead and their descendants are better off as a consequence of their ancestors being hauled from Africa to America." But D'Souza did indicate that "Indians have gotten a bad deal." Eric Lach, "D'Souza: African-Americans Better Off Because Ancestors Were 'Hauled from Africa to America,'" Talking Points Memo, June 30, 2014, http://talkingpointsmemo.com/livewire/dinesh-dsouza-african-americans (accessed June 12, 2015). See Dinesh D'Souza, *America: Imagine a World Without Her* (Washington, DC: Regnery, 2014); Dinesh D'Souza, *What's So Great About America* (Washington, DC: Regnery, 2002).

40. Mike Budd and Clay Steinman, "White Racism and *The Cosby Show*," *Jump Cut: A Review of Contemporary Media*, no. 37, July 1992, www.ejumpcut.org/archive/onlinessays/JC37folder/Cosby.html (accessed June 12, 2015). See Renee Graham, "'Cosby Show' Comedy Had a Serious Impact," *Boston Globe*, August 2, 2005 (Arts section).

41. Dr. Poussaint's remarks were given in an interview reported in Denise Hartsough, "The Cosby Show in Historical Context: Explaining Its Appeal to Middle-Class Black Women" (paper presented at Ohio University Film Conference, 1989).

42. Michael Dyson, "Bill Cosby and the Politics of Race," *Zeta*, September 1989, 29.

43. See C. J. Blair, "Writing About 'The Cosby Show,'" *English Journal*, October 1988, 61.

44. John D. H. Downing, "'The Cosby Show' and American Racial Discourse," in *Discourse and Discrimination*, ed. Geneva Smitherman-Donaldson and Teun van Dijk (Detroit: Wayne State University Press, 1988), 67.

45. Sut Jhally and Justin M. Lewis, *Enlightened Racism: The Cosby Show, Audiences, and the Myth of the American Dream* (Boulder, CO: Westview Press, 1992), 2.

46. Henry Louis Gates Jr., "TV's Black World Turns—But Stays Unreal," *New York Times*, November 12, 1989, Arts section, New York ed. See also Leslie B. Inniss and Joe R.

Feagin, "The Cosby Show: The View from the Black Middle Class," *Journal of Black Studies* 25.6 (July 1995): 692–711 (explaining that 100 in-depth interviews from a larger study of 210 middle-class Black Americans in sixteen cities across the United States conveyed that many members of the Black middle class perceived *The Cosby Show* as unrealistic).

47. Dyson, "Bill Cosby and the Politics of Race," 30.

48. Ibid.

49. See Andrew Wallenstein, "Dave Chappelle Inks $50 Million Deal," *Today,* August 3, 2004, http://www.today.com/id/5591225/ns/today-today_entertainment/t/dave-chappelle-inks-million-deal/#.VxKzy9IrKUk (accessed April 16, 2016). In a *60 Minutes* interview with Bob Simon, Chappelle explained his reasons for leaving and wondered whether TV executives would have asked that black characters be added to *Seinfeld* or *Friends.* "60 Minutes: Chappelle," CBS, June 14, 2006, http://www.cbsnews.com/videos/60-minutes-chappelle (accessed April 16, 2016). For background on Dave Chappelle, see, e.g., Devin Gordon, "Fears of a Clown," *Newsweek,* May 15, 2005, 60, available at http://www.newsweek.com/fears-clown-118667 (accessed August 3, 2015); Alex Young, "Dave Chappelle Reveals the Real Reason Why He Left Chappelle's Show," Consequence of Sound, June 10, 2014, http://consequenceofsound.net/2014/06/dave-chappelle-reveals-the-real-reason-why-he-left-chappelles-show/ (accessed April 16, 2016).

50. Thernstrom and Thernstrom, *America in Black and White,* 540. See Jeff Hobbs, *The Short and Tragic Life of Robert Peace: A Brilliant Young Man Who Left Newark for the Ivy League* (New York: Scribner, 2014).

51. Santiago Rodriguez, former director of diversity at Microsoft, would not call this "true diversity." For him, as quoted in a blog posited by Frank Mendelson, "True diversity is exemplified by companies that hire people who are different—knowing and valuing that they will change the way you do business." Frank J. Mendelson, "Workplace Diversity: Beyond Gender and Race," PRI, Business Communications blog, December 12, 2012, http://blog.priworks.com/archives/3527 (accessed April 16, 2016). Dr. Rodriguez's remarks are frequently quoted in publications about diversity, but the original source of the remarks I have yet to find.

52. See Harry G. Hutchison, "Moving Forward? Diversity as a Paradox? A Critical Race View," *Catholic University Law Review* 57 (2008): 1059, 1071; Michelle Adams, "Radical Integration," *California Law Review* 94 (2006): 261, 264. For a discussion regarding discriminatory treatment of racial names, see, e.g., David R. Francis, "Employers' Replies to Racial Names," National Bureau of Economic Research, August 9, 2016, http://www.nber.org/digest/sep03/w9873.html (accessed August 9, 2016); Steven D. Levitt and Stephen J. Dubner, *Freakonomics: A Rogue Economist Explores the Hidden Side of Everything* (New York: William Morrow, 2005), 179–204.

53. Star Parker, "A Defining Moment in Black History," *San Diego Union-Tribune,* June 25, 2005, B10.

54. Page, "Black Immigrants," B6. Michelle Obama's remark was made in a speech given at the Democratic National Convention (DNC) on July 25, 2016, and the DNC made even more history by selecting Hilary Clinton as the first woman to lead a major party's presidential ticket. Michelle Obama had made the same remark a month earlier

in a commencement speech delivered at City College in New York. The remark given at the DNC drew widespread praise as well as some racist commentary. See Zeba Blay, "BLACK VOICES: Why Michelle Obama's 'I Live In A House Built By Slaves' Quote Is Vital, It's Important to Acknowledge America's Dark History," Huffington Post, July 26, 2016, http://www.huffingtonpost.com/entry/why-michelle-obamas-i-live-in-a-house-built-by-slaves-quote-is-vital_us_57976fbce4bc2d5d5ed2dbeb (accessed July 30, 2016). Commenting on the First Lady's speech, Bill O'Reilly of Fox News said, "Slaves did participate in the construction of the White House. . . . In addition, free blacks, whites, and immigrants also worked on the massive building. There were no illegal immigrants at that time. If you could make it here, you could stay here. . . . Slaves that worked there were well-fed and had decent lodgings provided by the government, which stopped hiring slave labor in 1802." The latter statement caused a stir, as it seemed to glide over slavery's incurable flaw, its indelible immorality: the denial of human liberty and human dignity. O'Reilly's commentary was made on the July 26 edition of Fox News's *The O'Reilly Factor.* See "O'Reilly: Slaves Who Built White House Were 'Well-Fed and Had Decent Lodgings Provided by the Government,'" Media Matters, July 26, 2016, http://www.mediamatters.org/video/2016/07/26/oreilly-slaves-who-built-white-house-were-well-fed-and-had-decent-lodgings-provided-government/211921 (accessed July 31, 2016). One should keep in mind the special relationship slave descendants have to slavery and also Jim Crow when reading reports that show that "black immigrants from Africa average the highest educational attainment of any population group in the country, including whites and Asians." Page, "Black Immigrants," B6. Page also cites another interesting study: "Immigrants, who make up 13 percentage of the nation's college-age black population, account for more than a quarter of black students at Ivy League and other elite universities." Ibid. The study looked at twenty-eight selective institutions of higher education. Ibid. Most of the published writings on the socioeconomic success of black immigrants appear to be a bit dated, perhaps indicating that nothing significant has changed to write about. One of the best analyses is Kathryn M. Neckerman, Prudence Carter, and Jennifer Lee, "Segmented Assimilation and Minority Cultures of Mobility," *Ethnic and Racial Studies* 22 (1999): 945–965.

55. Orlando Patterson, "Race and Diversity in the Age of Obama," *New York Times Book Review,* August 16, 2009, 23.

56. Ibid. See also Jennifer Lee and Frank Bean, *The Diversity Paradox: Immigration and the Color Line in Twenty-First Century America,* ppb. ed. (New York: Russell Sage Foundation, 2012); Richard Alba and Victor Nee, *Remaking the American Mainstream: Assimilation and Contemporary Immigration* (Cambridge, MA: Harvard University Press, 2003).

57. Arthur M. Schlesinger Jr., "American Multiculturalism," in *Booknotes on American Character: People, Politics, and Conflict in American History,* ed. Brian Lamb (New York: Public Affairs, 2004), 186. See Arthur M. Schlesinger Jr., *The Disuniting of America,* rev. ed. (New York: W. W. Norton, 1998).

58. Michael Banton, "Assimilation," in *Encyclopedia of Race and Ethnic Studies,* ed. Ellis Cashmore (London: Routledge, 2004), 45.

59. I have explained the issue regarding extremist Muslims in the Netherlands on another occasion as follows: "For more than forty years, large numbers of Islamists from mainly Morocco and Turkey have immigrated to the Netherlands, perhaps the most liberal of Western European democracies. Rather than encouraging its Islamist population to assimilate, the Dutch government tolerated and even supported the Islamist lifestyle. Islamist children were never required to learn the Dutch language, culturally distinct Islamist schools were funded with public money, and illiberal practices within the Islamist community, such as the subordination of women, were permitted even though they were very much at odds with the Dutch mainstream culture. The Dutch attitude of extreme tolerance changed after the murder, in 2004, of the prominent film-maker Theo van Gogh in Amsterdam by a Dutch-born Islamist named Mohammed Bouyeri. A young Islamist extremist, Bouyeri was enraged by a film van Gogh had made with the Somali-born feminist politician, Ayaan Hirsi Ali. The film, titled 'Submission,' portrayed the subjugation of women under Islam. Ali herself had received numerous threats on her life due to her public criticisms of the treatment of women under Islam. In the aftermath of van Gogh's murder, the Dutch have become less tolerant of cultural differences. Before foreigners are allowed to immigrate to the Netherlands, they are now required to view a film produced by the Dutch government that depicts various aspects of the Dutch culture. The film emphasizes the openness of Dutch society and, as if to drive home the point, shows nude swimmers frolicking on public beaches. The message is clear: if you can't tolerate this, then you can't live here. What the government now seeks is less difference and more assimilation; in other words, a society of shared values, a culture that is more homogenous." Brooks, *Racial Justice in the Age of Obama,* 14.

60. See Karen A. Jehn, Gregory B. Northcraft, and Margaret A. Neale, "Why Differences Make a Difference: A Field Study of Diversity, Conflict, and Performance in Workgroups," *Administrative Science Quarterly* 4.4 (December 1999): 758.

61. See Levitt and Dubner, *Freakonomics,* 89–114.

62. Yet if the skill sets of blacks and whites are asymmetrical, value diversity is also likely to be high. That is why corporate America has taken a keen interest in public education in recent years.

63. Derrick A. Bell, "Who's Afraid of Critical Race Theory?" *University of Illinois Law Review* 1995 (1995): 893, 901.

64. Gregory Rodriguez, "A New Way of Joining the Mainstream," *Wall Street Journal,* July 31, 2003, D8.

65. Ibid. See Taunya Lovell Banks, "Two Life Stories," *Berkeley Women's Law Journal* 6 (1990): 46, 49 ("[A black female professor's] presence in the classroom and the academic community creates a potentially richer learning experience because [she] bring[s] a whole segment of life experiences related to law that is missing from the legal landscape"). See Richard Delgado, "Crossroads and Blind Alleys: A Critical Examination of Recent Writings About Race," *Texas Law Review* 82 (2003): 121.

66. See Ruth La Ferla, "The Changing Face of America: With Help from Holly-wood and Madison Avenue, Generation Y Is Challenging the Way America Thinks about Race and Ethnicity," *New York Times Upfront,* February 2, 2004, available at http://www.

thefreelibrary.com/The+changing+face+of+America%3A+with+help+from+Hollywood+and+Madison. . .-a0113051764 (accessed August 4, 2015).

67. James Poniewozik, "Tuned In: How BET's *The Game* Is Adjusting TV's Racial Balance," *Time,* February 28, 2011, available at http://www.time.com/time/magazine/article/0,9171,2050023,00.html (accessed May 14, 2015).

68. See, e.g., Alba and Nee, *Remaking the American Mainstream.*

69. David E. Hayes-Bautista, *La Nueva California* (Berkeley: University of California Press, 2004), 209–214.

70. Schlesinger, "American Multiculturalism," 186. See Schlesinger, *The Disuniting of America,* 38–40.

71. Jeffrey A. Clymer, "Modeling, Diagramming, and Early Twentieth-Century Histories of Invention and Entrepreneurship: Henry Ford, Sherwood Anderson, Samuel Insull," *Journal of American Studies* 36.3 (2002): 491, 498–499. Ford's "melting pot" policy of cultural assimilation was much deeper and faster than Matthew Jacobson's biculturalist position in due course. While Jacobson argued Americans maintained their ethnic identity (to a degree), Ford supported the wholesale replacement of an ethnic identity with one based on American citizenship.

72. Julie A. Su and Eric K. Yamamoto, "Critical Coalitions: Theory and Praxis," in *Crossroads, Directions, and a New Critical Race Theory,* ed. Francisco Valdes, Jerome McCristal Culp, and Angela P. Harris (Philadelphia: Temple University Press, 2002), 382–384.

73. See Chris Moran, "Suit to Fight for Bilingual Testing," *San Diego Union-Tribune,* June 1, 2005, 1.

74. Brooks, *Rethinking the American Race Problem,* 149.

75. See Matthew Frye Jacobson, *Roots Too: White Ethnic Revival in Post–Civil Rights America* (Cambridge, MA: Harvard University Press, 2006), 42.

76. Ibid., 15.

77. Ibid., 12–13, 116. Kennedy wrote *A Nation of Immigrants* (New York: Harper-Collins, 1964) on the contributions of immigrants in America.

78. Jacobson, *Roots Too,* 12–13, 116.

79. See George Yancey, *Who Is White? Latinos, Asians, and the New Black/Nonblack Divide* (Boulder, CO: Lynne Rienner Publishers, 2003), 125–144. For a critique of this book, see Richard Delgado, "Locating Latinos in the Field of Civil Rights: Assessing the Neoliberal Case for Racial Exclusion," *Texas Law Review* 83 (4004): 489.

80. Rodriguez, "A New Way of Joining the Mainstream," D8.

81. Alba and Nee, *Remaking the American Mainstream,* 37–39; Rodriguez, "A New Way of Joining the Mainstream," D8.

82. Brooks, *Rethinking the American Race Problem,* 148–149. This position was taken during my reformist years.

83. Glenn C. Loury, *The Anatomy of Racial Inequality* (Cambridge, MA: Harvard University Press, 2002), 120–121. Loury was explaining why he would be content to work within what the black philosopher Charles Wright Mills called "white philosophy." For a discussion of Mills's views, see Charles W. Mills, *The Racial Contract* (Ithaca, NY:

Cornell University Press, 1997); Charles W. Mills, *Blackness Visible: Essays on Philosophy and Race* (Ithaca, NY: Cornell University Press, 1998).

84. Loury, *The Anatomy of Racial Inequality,* 121.

85. See Joe R. Feagin, *Racist America: Roots, Current Realities, and Future Reparations* (New York: Routledge, 2000), 258–260; West, *Race Matters,* 4. West criticizes Afrocentrism for its "misguided fear" of "cultural hybridization."

86. Grant Hill, "Grant Hill's Response to Jalen Rose," *New York Times,* March 16, 2011, available at http://thequad.blogs.nytimes.com/2011/03/16/grant-hills-response-to-jalen-rose (accessed March 21, 2016).

87. Barone, *The New Americans,* 114.

88. In her majority opinion in Grutter v. Bollinger, 539 U.S. 306, 343 (2003), Justice O'Connor wrote, "It has been 25 years since Justice Powell first approved the use of race to further an interest in student body diversity in the context of public higher education. Since that time, the number of minority applicants with high grades and test scores has indeed increased. We expect that 25 years from now, the use of racial preferences will no longer be necessary to further the interest approved today." In the global context, biculturalism translates into what has been called "cosmopolitanism." Cosmopolitanists seek to establish "multiple affiliations," including subnational and transnational, especially the latter. Mainstream cultural institutions adopt positive cultural traits from other countries—everything from dining to discourse. One mainstream magazine, for example, "offered 30 lessons we can learn from other countries": Susan Headden, "How They Do It Better," CBS, March 20, 2007, http://www.cbsnews.com/news/how-they-do-it-better/ (accessed March 20, 2016). Hence, the dominant culture is not defined by ethnic or racial distinctions, most especially "Anglo-Protestant tribalism." The culture is "post-ethnic." It is characterized by "ethnic eclecticism," shared values and rules. Kwame A. Appiah, *Cosmopolitanism: Ethics in a World of Strangers* (New York: W. W. Norton, 2006), 102; David A. Hollinger, *Postethnic America: Beyond Multiculturalism* (New York: Basic Books, 2000), 199, 202. See Babak Moussavi, "Book Review: Cosmopolitanism: Ethics in a World of Strangers, by Kwame Anthony Appiah," Socialjusticefirst, March 5, 2012, http://socialjusticefirst.com/2012/03/05/book-review-cosmopolitanism-ethics-in-a-world-of-strangers-by-kwame-anthony-appiah (accessed March 20, 2016). Cosmopolitanism is not completely devoid of cultural identity. The mainstream is big and polyglot, but "[i]n this era of globalization—in Asante as in New Jersey—people make pockets of homogeneity." Appiah, *Cosmopolitanism,* 103. Cultural distinctions are maintained in local communities, which provide "individuals with a life-sustaining sense of belonging." These communities need not, however, "be permanent, [and] need not be exclusive of other affiliations." Hollinger, *Postethnic America,* 220. Communities of color, then, create "descent-defined solidarities, not as natural consequences of human difference but in their capacity as chosen instruments for political action and social support." Ibid. Some scholars, however, believe that culturally defined local communities are likely to be temporary. Their survival will likely be threatened through quotidian interactions with elements of the dominant culture. People living in local communities, as Kwame Appiah suggests, have iPods, watch Oprah, listen to hip-hop, and drink

Starbucks coffee. They are tied to a global homogeneity as well as to a local homogeneity. Furthermore, as a minority's immersion in global homogeneity increases, his or her ties to the local community become attenuated. David Hollinger elaborates by way of an example: "[I]t is not that blackness is erased, but the extent and character of its ordinance over an individual's politics, values, art, or lifestyle is not taken for granted." Ibid, 222. But see Appiah, *Cosmopolitanism*, 102–103 (suggesting a more permanent status for local communities). These phenomena—global homogeneity and acculturation—militate against long-term cultural identity.

89. See Brooks, *Racial Justice in the Age of Obama*, chap. 4. For a discussion of blackface and other racist features (e.g., Aunt Jemima) in popular culture, see, e.g., John Strausbaugh, *Black Like You: Blackface, Whiteface, Insult & Imitation in American Popular Culture* (New York: Jeremy P. Tarcher/Penguin, 2006); Randall Kennedy, *Nigger: The Strange Career of a Troublesome Word* (New York: Vintage Books, 2003).

90. Harold Cruse, *The Crisis of the Negro Intellectual* (New York: Morrow, 1967), 3.

91. See Roy L. Brooks, *Integration or Separation? A Strategy for Racial Equality* (Cambridge, MA: Harvard University Press, 1996), 203, 244–246.

92. "Ralph Ellison," in *The Norton Anthology: African American Literature*, ed. Henry Louis Gates Jr. and Nellie Y. McKay (New York: W. W. Norton, 1996), 1515.

93. Shelby Steele, "The Content of His Character," *New Republic*, March 1, 1999, 31.

94. For a discussion of Ms. Dolezal's story, see, e.g., Daniel Victor, "NAACP Leader in Wash. State Posed as Black, Parents Say," *San Diego Union-Tribune*, June 13, 2015, A16.

95. Hollinger, *Postethnic America*, 220.

96. Appiah, *Cosmopolitanism*, 104.

97. Martha C. Nussbaum, *Cultivating Humanity: A Classical Defense of Reform in Liberal Education* (Cambridge, MA: Harvard University Press, 1997) (discussing Allan Bloom's seminal attack on cultural relativism, *The Closing of the American Mind*), 33.

98. Amber Phillips, "Poll Finds Public Opinion on Confederate Flag Mixed," *San Diego Union-Tribune*, July 3, 2015, A9.

99. Postmodernism makes the valid claim that knowledge is limited by our "situatedness." A person living in New York City has knowledge about the human condition that a person living in rural Mississippi may not have. While I acknowledge the contingency of truth, I also believe in the existence of empirical, or common, truth. Universality is discovered through a continuous process of self-reflection and questioning. Differently situated, one person may have access to truths that another person may not. Incorporating other viewpoints in our thinking will overcome our limited perspectives and thereby yield new truths. Thus, I see truth as conditional, as a transitory state in which we accept one proposition over another based upon information available at the moment. This process of considering and weighing the opinions of others will eventually lead to what I have called "hypertruths." "These are truths that are shown to be increasingly fixed or final, truths by which we may judge the world around us. The inherent wrongness of murder and racial bias, and the love one has for one's children are examples of hypertruths." Roy L. Brooks, *Structures of Judicial Decision Making from*

Legal Formalism to Critical Theory, 2nd ed. (Durham, NC: Carolina Academic Press, 2005), 254.

100. This is part of the "social upheaval" that Judge Robert Carter, one of the NAACP lawyers who argued the case before the Supreme Court, saw in *Brown.* See Robert L. Carter, "The Warren Court and Desegregation," *Michigan Law Review* 67 (1968): 237, 246.

101. The prevailing values are truly hypertruths. See my discussion regarding postmodernism in note 99.

102. Personnel Administrator v. Feeney, 442 U.S. 256, 278 (1979).

103. See Kathrin Day Lassila, "Race, Speech, and Value," *Yale Alumni Magazine,* January/February 2016, 41, 42, available at https://yalealumnimagazine.com/articles/4233-race-speech-and-values (accessed April 16, 2016).

104. Roy L. Brooks, *Atonement and Forgiveness: A New Model for Black Reparations* (Berkeley: University of California Press, 2004), xv (quoting Justice Felix Frankfurter).

105. Lassila, "Race, Speech, and Value," 47; e-mail message from President Salovey to Yale Community, subject: "Toward a Better Yale," sent November 17, 2015.

106. Sean McElwee, "The Hidden Racism of Young White Americans," PBS, *NewsHour,* March 24, 2015, http://www.pbs.org/newshour/updates/americas-racism-problem-far-complicated-think (accessed March 21, 2016).

107. Martin Luther King Jr., "Letter from a Birmingham City Jail," in *The African American Book of Values,* 753–767.

108. While I would agree with President Salovey's view that "We are a university, and through teaching and learning about the most troubling aspects of our past, our community will be better prepared to rise to the challenges of the present and the future," I would strongly disagree with his decision not to rename Calhoun College. E-mail message from President Salovey to Yale Community, subject: "Decisions on Residential College Names and 'Master' Title," sent April 27, 2016. Salovey acknowledges that John C. Calhoun was "an egregious defender of slavery." Yet, Salovey argues that "Erasing Calhoun's name from a much-beloved residential college risks masking this past, downplaying the lasting effects of slavery, and substituting a false and misleading narrative, albeit one that might allow us to feel complacent or, even, self-congratulatory. Retaining the name forces us to learn anew and confront one of the most disturbing aspects of Yale's and our nation's past." Ibid. Can't this important lesson be taught without retaining the name of a racist on such an important college building? Retaining the name of Calhoun College is still an honorific designation. It is still an everyday slap in the face to the black community at Yale and the black community of New Haven. It is an unnecessary act of racial subordination—certainly not the least subordinating way to conduct the important discussion that Salovey wants Yale students to undertake. Students can discuss the Holocaust without having a Yale college named after Hitler.

If it stands, Salovey's decision will be yet another piece of evidence of a racial glass ceiling. As of this writing, it appears that Salovey is prepared to revisit his decision, stating in a new message: "However, in recent months, many faculty, students, alumni and staff have raised significant and moving concerns about that decision, and it is now clear to me that the community-wide conversation about these issues could have drawn more effectively on campus expertise." Ed Stannard, "Renaming Calhoun College Still Possible as Yale Forms Committee After Outcry," *New Haven Register*, August 1, 2016, http://www.nhregister.com/general-news/20160801/renaming-calhoun-college-still-possible-as-yale-forms-committee-after-outcry (accessed August 10, 2016).

Bibliography

Adair, Alvis V. *Desegregation: The Illusion of Black Progress.* Lanham, MD: University Press of America, 1984.

Adams, Michelle. "Radical Integration." *California Law Review* 94 (2006): 261.

"African American Perspectives." The Progress of a People. Library of Congress. October 19, 1998. http://memory.loc.gov/ammem/aap/aapexhp.html.

Aka, Philip C. "The Supreme Court and Affirmative Action in Public Education, with Special Reference to the Michigan Cases." *BYU Education and Law Journal* (2006): 1.

Alba, Richard, and Victor Nee. *Remaking the American Mainstream: Assimilation and Contemporary Immigration.* Cambridge, MA: Harvard University Press, 2003.

Alexander, Larry, and Maimon Schwarzchild. "Race Matters." *Constitutional Commentaries* 29 (2013): 31.

Alexander, Michelle. *The New Jim Crow: Mass Incarceration in the Age of Colorblindness.* Rev. ed. New York: New Press, 2011.

Allitt, Patrick. *Religion in America Since 1945: A History.* New York: Columbia University Press, 2003.

Alvi, Shahid, Hannah Scott, and Wendy Stanyon. "We're Locking the Door: Family Histories in a Sample of Homeless Youth." *Qualitative Report* 15.5 (2010): 1210.

Anderson, Jerry L. "Law School Enters the Matrix: Teaching Critical Legal Studies." *Journal of Legal Education* 54 (June 2004): 201.

Anderson, Monica. "6 Key Findings About Black Immigration to the U.S." Pew Research Center. Fact Tank. April 9, 2015. http://www.pewresearch.org/fact-tank/2015 /04/09/6-key-findings-about-black-immigration.

———. "Vast Majority of Blacks View the Criminal Justice System as Unfair." Pew Research Center. Fact Tank. August 12, 2014. http://www.pewresearch.org/fact-tank/2014 /08/12/vast-majority-of-blacks-view-the-criminal-justice-system-as-unfair.

Angelou, Maya. "Voices of Respect." In *The African American Book of Values,* edited by
    Steven Barboza, 822–823. New York: Doubleday, 1998.
Appiah, Kwame A. *Cosmopolitanism: Ethics in a World of Strangers.* New York:
    W. W. Norton, 2006.
Applebone, Peter. "Equal Entry Standards May Hurt Black Students in Mississippi." *San
    Diego Union-Tribune,* April 24, 1996.
Ards, Angela. "In the Twinkling of an Eye." *Black Issues Book Review,* July/August
    2005.
Ariens, Michael. "What Hath Faith Wrought?" Review of *Faith and Law: How Religious
    Traditions from Calvinism to Islam View American Law,* by Robert F. Cochran.
    Journal of Law and Religion 24.1 (2008/2009): 195.
Baker, Houston A. *Betrayal: How Black Intellectuals Have Abandoned the Ideals of the
    Civil Rights Era.* New York: Columbia University Press, 2008.
Baker, Lee D. *From Savage to Negro: Anthropology and the Construction of "Race," 1896–
    1954.* Berkeley: University of California Press, 1998.
Balkin, Jack M., ed. *What Brown v. Board of Education Should Have Said: The Nation's
    Top Legal Experts Rewrite America's Landmark Civil Rights Decision.* New York:
    New York University Press, 2002.
Banks, Taunya Lovell. "Two Life Stories." *Berkeley Women's Law Journal* 6 (1990): 46.
Banton, Michael. "Assimilation." In *Encyclopedia of Race and Ethnic Studies,* edited by
    Ellis Cashmore. London: Routledge, 2004.
Barak, Aharon. "A Judge on Judging: The Role of the Supreme Court in a Democracy."
    Harvard Law Review 116 (2002): 16.
Barone, Michael. *The New Americans: How the Melting Pot Can Work Again.* Washing-
    ton, DC: Regnery Publishing, 2001.
Becker, Jeffrey A. *Ambition in America: Political Power and the Collapse of Citizenship.*
    Lexington: University Press of Kentucky, 2014.
Behrens, Angela, Jeff Manza, and Christopher Uggen. "Ballot Manipulation and the
    'Menace of Negro Domination': Racial Threat and Felon Disenfranchisement in
    the United States, 1850–2002." *American Journal of Sociology* 109 (2003): 559.
Bell, Derrick. *And We Are Not Saved: The Elusive Quest for Racial Justice.* New York: Basic
    Books, 1987.
———. "Brown v. Board of Education: Forty-Five Years After the Fact." *Ohio Northern
    University Law Review* 26 (2000): 171.
———. "Brown v. Board of Education and the Interest-Convergence Dilemma." *Harvard
    Law Review* 93 (1980): 518.
———. "Diversity's Distractions." *Columbia Law Review* 103 (2003): 1622.
———. *Faces at the Bottom of the Well: The Permanence of Racism.* New York: Basic Books,
    1992.
———. *Race, Racism, and American Law.* 2nd ed. Boston: Little, Brown, 1980.
———. "Who's Afraid of Critical Race Theory?" *University of Illinois Law Review* (1995):
    893.
Benedict, Ruth. *Patterns of Culture.* Boston: Houghton Mifflin, 1989.

Berger, Ken. "Sale of Clippers to Steve Ballmer Closes; Donald Sterling Out." CBS Sports. August 12, 2014. http://www.cbssports.com/nba/writer/ken-berger/24657297/sale-of-clippers-to-steve-ballmer-closes-donald-sterling-out.

Berman, Ari. *Give Us the Ballot: The Modern Struggle for Voting Rights in America.* New York: Farrar, Straus and Giroux, 2015.

"Black Beauty Not Valued on International Scale." Black Girl Wondering and Praying. March 2, 2012. https://blacknotwhitedippedinchocolate.wordpress.com/2012/03/02/black-beauty-not-valued-on-international-scale/.

"Black Girl Magic Flashback: Watch the Lupita Nyong'o Speech Heard Around the World." *Essence.* February 27, 2014. http://www.essence.com/2014/02/27/lupita-nyongo-delivers-moving-black-women-hollywood-acceptance-speech.

Blackmon, Douglas. *Slavery by Another Name: The Re-Enslavement of Black Americans from the Civil War to World War II.* New York: Anchor Books, 2008.

Blackwell, James E. *The Black Community: Diversity and Unity.* 2nd ed. New York: Harper & Row, 1985.

Blair, C. J. "Writing About 'The Cosby Show.'" *English Journal* 77 (October 1988): 61.

Blay, Zeba. "Why Michelle Obama's 'I Live In A House Built By Slaves' Quote Is Vital: It's important to acknowledge America's dark history." BLACK VOICES. Huffington Post. July 26, 2016. http://www.huffingtonpost.com/entry/why-michelle-obamas-i-live-in-a-house-built-by-slaves-quote-is-vital_us_57976fbce4b02d5d5ed2dbeb.

Bledstein, Burton J. *The Culture of Professionalism: The Middle Class and the Development of Higher Education in America.* New York: W. W. Norton, 1978.

Blumrosen, Alfred W., and Ruth G. Blumrosen. *Slave Nation: How Slavery United the Colonies & Sparked the American Revolution.* Naperville, IL: Sourcebooks, 2005.

Bonilla-Silva, Eduardo. *Racism without Racist: Color-blind Racism and the Persistence of Racial Inequality in the United States.* 3rd ed. Lanham, MD: Rowman & Littlefield, 2009.

Boyle, Kevin. "White Terrorists." *New York Times,* May 18, 2008.

Brock-Murray, Raymond. "Comparing Racial Identity, Acculturative Stress, and Feelings of Alienation in African-American College Attendees and Non-Attendees." *Seton Hall University Dissertations and Theses (ETDs),* Paper 334, 2010. http://scholarship.shu.edu/cgi/viewcontent.cgi?article=1334&context=dissertations.

Brooks, Roy L. *Atonement and Forgiveness: A New Model for Black Reparations.* Berkeley: University of California Press, 2004.

——. "The Crisis of the Black Politician in the Age of Obama." *Howard Law Journal* 52 (2010): 699.

——. "Cultural Diversity: It's All About the Mainstream." *Monist* 95.1 (2012): 17.

——. *Integration or Separation? A Strategy for Racial Equality.* Cambridge, MA: Harvard University Press, 1996.

——. *Racial Justice in the Age of Obama.* Princeton, NJ: Princeton University Press, 2009.

——. *Rethinking the American Race Problem.* Berkeley: University of California Press, 1990.

——. *Structures of Judicial Decision Making from Legal Formalism to Critical Theory*. 2nd ed. Durham, NC: Carolina Academic Press, 2005.

——. "Use of the Civil Rights Acts of 1866 and 1871 to Redress Employment Discrimination." *Cornell Law Review* 62 (1977): 258.

Brooks, Roy L., Gilbert Paul Carrasco, and Michael Selmi. *The Law of Discrimination: Cases and Perspectives*. New Providence, NJ: LexisNexis, 2011.

Brown, Dorothy A. *Critical Race Theory: Cases, Materials, and Problems*. 2nd ed. St. Paul, MN: Thomson/West, 2007.

Brown, Kevin. "Has the Supreme Court Allowed the Cure for De Jure Segregation to Replicate the Disease?" *Cornell Law Review* 78 (1992): 1.

——. "Review: Robert L. Carter, *A Matter of Law: A Memoir of Struggle in the Cause of Equal Rights*." *Vermont Law Review* 31 (2007): 925.

Broyard, Bliss. "Half and Half." *New York Times Book Review*, February 11, 2007.

——. *One Drop: My Father's Hidden Life—A Story of Race and Family Secrets*. Boston: Little, Brown, 2008.

Budd, Mike, and Clay Steinman. "White Racism and *The Cosby Show*." *Jump Cut: A Review of Contemporary Media*, July 1992. www.ejumpcut.org/archive/onlinessays/JC37folder/Cosby.html.

Carbado, Devan W., and Mitu Gulati. *Acting White? Rethinking Race in "Post-Racial" America*. New York: Oxford University Press, 2013.

Carroll, Bret E., ed. *American Masculinities: A Historical Encyclopedia*. Thousand Oaks, CA: Sage Publications, 2003.

Carter, David G. "Second-Generation School Integration Problems for Blacks." *Journal of Black Studies* 13 (1982): 175.

Carter, Robert. *A Matter of Law: A Memoir of Struggle in the Cause of Equal Rights*. New York: New Press, 2005.

——. "The Warren Court and Desegregation." *Michigan Law Review* 67 (1968): 237.

Carville, James, and Stan Greenberg. *It's the Middle Class, Stupid!* New York: Blue Rider Press, 2012.

Chafe, William H., Raymond Gavins, and Robert Korstad, eds. *Remembering Jim Crow: African Americans Tell About Life in the Segregated South*. New York: New Press, 2001.

Chappelle, Dave. "60 Minutes: Chappelle." CBS, June 14, 2006. http://www.cbsnews.com/videos/60-minutes-chappelle.

Chaves, Mark. *American Religion: Contemporary Trends*. Princeton, NJ: Princeton University Press, 2011.

Clark, William A. V. *Immigrants and the American Dream: Remaking the Middle Class*. New York: The Guilford Press, 2003.

Clymer, Jeffrey A. "Modeling, Diagramming, and Early Twentieth-Century Histories of Invention and Entrepreneurship: Henry Ford, Sherwood Anderson, Samuel Insull." *Journal of American Studies* 36.3 (2002): 491.

Coates, Ta-Nehisi. *Between the World and Me*. New York: Spiegel & Grau, 2015.

Cohn, D'Vera, Gretchen Livingston, and Wendy Wang. "After Decades of Decline, a Rise in Stay-at-Home Mothers." Pew Research Center. Social Trends. April 8, 2014.

http://www.pewsocialtrends.org/2014/04/08/after-decades-of-decline-a-rise-in-stay-at-home-mothers/.

Collins, Andrew P. "Code 3: Investigation Calls Out LA Fire Department for Rampant Nepotism." http://code3.jalopnik.com/investigation-calls-out-la-fire-department-for-rampant-1651020183/+jasontorch.

Comey, James B. "Hard Truths: Law Enforcement and Race." FBI. February 12, 2015. http://www.fbi.gov/news/speeches/hard-truths-law-enforcement-and-race.

Coner-Edwards, Alice F., and Jeanne Spurlock, eds. Black Families in Crisis: The Middle Class. New York: Brunner/Mazel, 1988.

Cox, Taylor. Cultural Diversity in Organizations: Theory, Research & Practice. San Francisco: Berrett-Koehler Publishers, 1993.

Cruse, Harold. The Crisis of the Negro Intellectual. New York: Morrow, 1967.

———. Plural but Equal: Blacks and Minorities in America's Plural Society. New York: William Morrow, 1987.

"Cultural diversity." Oxford Dictionaries. http://www.oxforddictionaries.com/us/definition/american_english/cultural-diversity (accessed July 12, 2005).

Currie, Elliott. The Road to Whatever: Middle-Class Culture and the Crisis of Adolescence. New York: Metropolitan Books, 2008.

Daniels, Maurice C., and Cameron Van Patterson. "(Re)considering Race in the Desegregation of Higher Education." Georgia Law Review 46 (Spring 2012): 521.

Davenport, Lisa E. Jazz Diplomacy: Promoting American in the Cold War Era. Jackson: University Press of Mississippi, 2009.

Davis, David Brion. In the Image of God: Religion, Moral Values, and Our Heritage of Slavery. New Haven, CT: Yale University Press, 2001.

"The Decline of Marriage and Rise of New Families." Pew Research Center. November 18, 2010. www.pewsocialtrends.org/files/2010/11/pew-social-trends-2010-families.pdf.

Delgado, Richard. "Crossroads and Blind Alleys: A Critical Examination of Recent Writings About Race." Texas Law Review 82 (2003): 121.

———. "Explaining the Rise and Fall of African American Fortunes: Interest Convergence and Civil Rights Gains." Harvard Civil Rights–Civil Liberties Law Review 37 (2002): 369.

———. "Locating Latinos in the Field of Civil Rights: Assessing the Neoliberal Case for Racial Exclusion." Texas Law Review 83 (2004): 489.

———. "Recasting the American Race Problem." California Law Review 79 (1991): 1389.

Delgado, Richard, and Jean Stefancic. Critical Race Theory: An Introduction. New York: New York University Press, 2001 (1st ed.); 2012 (2nd ed.).

"Developments in the Law: The Evolution of the State Action Doctrine and the Current Debate." Harvard Law Review 123 (2010): 1255.

DeVitis, Joseph L., and John Martin Rich. The Success Ethic, Education, and the American Dream. New York: State University of New York Press, 1996.

"Donald Sterling Banned for Life from NBA and Fined 2.5 Million for Racist Rant." YouTube. April 29, 2014. https://www.youtube.com/watch?v=gnr7wnRoh6U.

Downing, John D. H. " 'The Cosby Show' and American Racial Discourse." In *Discourse and Discrimination*, edited by Geneva Smithermann-Donaldson and Teun van Dijk. Detroit: Wayne State University Press, 1988.

Dray, Philip. *At the Hands of Persons Unknown: The Lynching of Black America.* New York: Modern Library, 2002.

Dreisinger, Baz. "Blackish in America." *New York Times Book Review,* June 7, 2015.

D'Souza, Dinesh. *America: Imagine a World Without Her.* Washington, DC: Regnery, 2014.

———. *What's So Great About America.* Washington, DC: Regnery, 2002.

Dudziak, Mary L. *Cold War Civil Rights: Race and the Image of American Democracy.* Princeton, NJ: Princeton University Press, 2002.

———. "Desegregation as a Cold War Imperative." *Stanford Law Review* 41 (1988): 61.

Dworking, Ronald. *A Bill of Rights for Britain.* London: Chatto and Windus, 1991.

Dyson, Michael. "Bill Cosby and the Politics of Race." *Zeta,* September 1989.

———. *The Black Presidency: Barack Obama and the Politics of Race in America.* Boston: Houghton Mifflin Harcourt, 2016.

Edwards, Harry T. "The Journey from *Brown v. Board of Education* to *Grutter v. Bollinger*: From Racial Assimilation to Diversity." *Michigan Law Review* 102 (2004): 944.

Ehrenreich, Barbara. *Fear of Falling: The Inner Life of the Middle Class.* New York: Pantheon Books, 1989.

Elliott, Philip. "The Brief: Why Would Democrats Vote for Trump? It's All About Trade." *Time,* March 21, 2016.

Elliot, Stuart. "Vitriol Online for Cheerios Ad with Interracial Family." *New York Times,* May 31, 2013.

Epstein, Joseph. *Snobbery: The American Version.* New York: Houghton Mifflin, 2002.

Estrada, Sheryl. "Serena Williams, New York Times and Body Image." *DiversityInc,* July 15, 2015. http://www.diversityinc.com/news/serena-williams-new-york-times-and-body-image/.

Feagin, Joe R. *Racist America: Roots, Current Realities, and Future Reparations.* New York: Routledge, 2000.

Fehrenbacher, Don E. *The Dred Scott Case: Its Significance in American Law and Politics.* New York: Oxford University Press, 1978.

Fein, Melvyn L. *Human Hierarchies: A General Theory.* Piscataway, NJ: Transaction Publishers, 2012.

Fletcher, Michael A., and Michael D. Shear. "Obama Voices Regret to Policeman." *Washington Post,* July 25, 2009.

Fowler, Robert Booth. "The Roman Catholic Church in 'Protestant' America Today." *Forum* 11.4 (2014): 721.

François, Aderson Bellegarde. "The Brand of Inferiority: The Civil Rights Act of 1875, White Supremacy, and Affirmative Action." *Howard Law Journal* 57 (2014): 573.

Frickey, Philip P. "Revisiting the Revival of Theory in Statutory Interpretation: A Lecture in Honor of Irving Younger." *Minnesota Law Review* 84 (1999): 199.

Friedman, Caitlin, and Kimberly Yorio. *Happy at Work, Happy at Home: The Girl's Guide to Being a Working Mom*. New York: Broadway Books, 2009.

Gabrielson, Ryan, Ryann Grochowski Jones, and Eric Sagara. "Deadly Force, in Black and White: A ProPublica Analysis of Killings by Police Shows Outsize Risk for Young Black Males." ProPublica. October 10, 2014. https://www.propublica.org/article/deadly-force-in-black-and-white.

Garfield, Leslie Yalof. "Adding Colors to the Chameleon: Why the Supreme Court Should Have Adopted a New Compelling Governmental Interest Test for Race-Preference Student Assignment Plans." *Kansas Law Review* 56 (2008): 277.

———. "Back to *Bakke*: Defining the Strict Scrutiny Test for Affirmative Action Policies Aimed at Achieving Diversity in the Classroom." *Nebraska Law Review* 83 (2005): 631.

Gates, Henry Louis, Jr. "TV's Black World Turns—But Stays Unreal." *New York Times*, November 12, 1989.

Gates, Henry Louis, Jr., and Nellie Y. McKay, eds. "Ralph Ellison." In *The Norton Anthology: African American Literature*. New York: W. W. Norton, 1996.

"The Generation Gap and the 2012 Election." Pew Research Center. November 3, 2011. www.people-press.org/files/legacy-pdf/11-3-11%20Generations%20Release.pdf.

Gilbert, Dennis. *The American Class Structure in an Age of Growing Inequality. 6th ed.* Belmont: Thomson Wadsworth, 2003.

Gladwell, Malcolm. *Outliers: The Story of Success*. New York: Little, Brown, 2008.

Goldstone, Lawrence. *Inherently Unequal: The Betrayal of Equal Rights by the Supreme Court, 1865–1903*. New York: Walker, 2011.

Gomez, Laura E. "Understanding Law and Race as Mutually Constitutive." *Journal of Scholarly Perspectives* 8.1 (2012): 47, 50.

Gordon, Devin. "Fears of a Clown." *Newsweek*, May 15, 2005, available at http://www.newsweek.com/fears-clown-118667.

Graham, Renee. " 'Cosby Show' Comedy Had a Serious Impact." *Boston Globe*, August 2, 2005.

Greene, Jamal. "The Anticanon." *Harvard Law Review* 125 (2011): 379.

Guelzo, Allen C. *Lincoln's Emancipation Proclamation: The End of Slavery in America*. New York: Simon & Schuster, 2004.

Harnden, Toby. "Barack Obama's Support Falls Among White Votes." *Telegraph*, August 2, 2009.

Hart, H. L. A. "American Jurisprudence Through English Eyes: The Nightmare and the Noble Dream." *Georgia Law Review* 11 (1977): 969.

———. *The Concept of Law*. New York: Oxford University Press, 1961; 1965 (corrected pp. of 1st ed.).

———. "Discretion." *Harvard Law Review* 127 (2013): 652.

Hartmann, Thom. *Screwed: The Undeclared War Against the Middle Class—and What We Can Do About It*. San Francisco: Berrett-Koehler Publishers, 2006.

Hartsough, Denise. "The Cosby Show in Historical Context: Explaining Its Appeal to Middle-Class Black Women." Paper presented at Ohio University Film Conference, 1989.

Hayes-Bautista, David E. *La Nueva California.* Berkeley: University of California Press, 2004.

Headden, Susan. "How They Do It Better." CBS. March 20, 2007. http://www.cbsnews.com/news/how-they-do-it-better/.

Hebert, James. "1 After 1: In Pop Culture, Who or What Is No. 1 Changes in a Flash." *San Diego Union-Tribune,* October 9, 2006.

Hevesi, Dennis. "Louis H. Pollak, Civil Rights Advocate and Federal Judge, Dies at 89." *New York Times,* May 12, 2012.

Higginbotham, A. Leon, Jr. *In the Matter of Color: Race and the American Legal Process: The Colonial Period.* New York: Oxford University Press, 1978.

Hill, Brenna Lermon. "A Call to Congress: Amend Education Legislation and Ensure That President Obama's 'Race to the Top' Leaves No Child Behind." *Houston Law Review* 51 (2014): 1177.

Hill, Grant. "Grant Hill's Response to Jalen Rose." *New York Times,* March 16, 2011, available at http://thequad.blogs.nytimes.com/2011/03/16/grant-hills-response-to-jalen-rose.

Hirsch, Nicole Arlette, and Anthony Abraham Jack. "What We Face: Framing Problems in the Black Community." *Du Bois Review: Social Science Research on Race* 9.1 (2012): 133.

Hobbs, Jeff. *The Short and Tragic Life of Robert Peace: A Brilliant Young Man Who Left Newark for the Ivy League.* New York: Scribner, 2014.

Hobbs, Meredith. "Wal-Mart Demands Diversity in Law Firms." *National Law Journal.* Legal Business. July 11, 2005, available at http://www.nationallawjournal.com/id=900005432489?back=law&slreturn=20160625154847.

Hochschild, Jennifer L. *Facing Up to the American Dream: Race, Class, and the Soul of the Nation.* Princeton, NJ: Princeton University Press, 1995.

Hollinger, David A. *Postethnic America: Beyond Multiculturalism.* New York: Basic Books, 2000.

Holmes, Oliver Wendell. *The Common Law.* Edited by Mark DeWolfe Howe. Cambridge, MA: Harvard University Press, 1963.

Howard, John R. *The Shifting Wind: The Supreme Court and Civil Rights from Reconstruction to Brown.* New York: State University of New York Press, 1999.

Hughes, Langston. "The Negro Mother." In *The African American Book of Values,* edited by Steven Barboza, 552–553. New York: Doubleday, 1998.

Huhn, Wilson R. "The Legacy of Slaughterhouse, Bradwell, and Cruikshank in Constitutional Interpretation." *Akron Law Review* 42 (2009): 1051.

Hutchison, Harry G. "Moving Forward? Diversity as a Paradox? A Critical Race View." *Catholic University Law Review* 57 (2008): 1059.

Ifill, Sherrilyn A. "Creating a Truth and Reconciliation Commission for Lynching." *Law and Inequality* 21 (2003): 263.

Inniss, Leslie B., and Joe Feagin. "The Cosby Show: The View from the Black Middle Class." *Journal of Black Studies* 25.6 (July 1995): 692.

"Inside the Middle Class: Bad Times Hit the Good Life." Pew Research Center. April 9, 2008. http://www.pewsocialtrends.org/2008/04/09/inside-the-middle-class-bad-times-hit-the-good-life.

Jacobson, Matthew Frye. *Roots Too: White Ethnic Revival in Post–Civil Rights America.* Cambridge, MA: Harvard University Press, 2006.

Jehn, Karen A., Gregory B. Northcraft, and Margaret A. Neale. "Why Differences Make a Difference: A Field Study of Diversity, Conflict, and Performance in Workgroups." *Administrative Science Quarterly* 4.4 (December 1999).

Jensen, Robert. "White Privilege Shapes the U.S.: Affirmative Action for Whites Is a Fact of Life." *Baltimore Sun,* July 19, 1998.

Jhabvala, Nicki. "Mark Cuban Talks Donald Sterling, Admits His Own Prejudices." *Denver Post,* May 22, 2014, available at http://blogs.denverpost.com/nuggets/2014/05/22/mark-cuban-talks-donald-sterling-admits-prejudices/10717.

Jhally, Sut, and Justin M. Lewis. *Enlightened Racism: The Cosby Show, Audiences, and the Myth of the American Dream.* Boulder, CO: Westview Press, 1992.

Joffe, Josef. "The Perils of Soft Power: Why America's Cultural Influence Makes Enemies Too." *New York Times Magazine,* May 14, 2006.

Kahl, Joseph A. *The American Class Structure.* New York: Rinehart, 1957.

Kalman, Laura. *Legal Realism at Yale, 1927–1960.* Chapel Hill: University of North Carolina Press, 1986; Clark, NJ: Lawbook Exchange, 2010 (repr. ed.).

Kanfer, Stefan. *Tough Without a Gun: The Life and Extraordinary Afterlife of Humphrey Bogart.* New York: Vintage Books, 2011.

Keepnews, Peter. "Culture's Ambassador." *New York Times Book Review,* June 6, 2010.

Kelly, Amita. "WATCH: Black GOP Senator Says He's Been Stopped by Police 7 Times in a Year." NPR. Politics. July 14, 2016. http://www.npr.org/2016/07/14/485995136/watch-black-gop-senator-says-hes-been-stopped-7-times-by-police-in-a-year.

Kendall, Diana. *Framing Class: Media Representations of Wealth and Poverty in America,* 2nd ed. Lanham, MD: Rowman and Littlefield Publishers, 2011.

Kennedy, Randall. *Nigger: The Strange Career of a Troublesome Word.* New York: Vintage Books, 2003.

Kerbo, Harold R. *Social Stratification and Inequality: Class Conflict in Historical, Comparative, and Global Perspective.* 4th ed. Boston: McGraw-Hill, 2000.

Kiel, Daniel. "An Ounce of Prevention Is Worth a Pound of Cure: Reframing the Debate About Law School Affirmative Action." *Denver University Law Review* 88 (2011): 791.

Killenbeck, Ann Millott. "Bakke, with Teeth? The Implication of *Grutter v. Bollinger* in and Outcomes-Based World." *Journal of College and University Law* 36 (2009): 1.

Kluger, Richard. *Simple Justice: The History of Brown v. Board of Education and Black America's Struggle for Equality.* New York: Knopf, 2004.

Korzec, Rebecca. "Working on the Mommy-Track: Motherhood and Women Lawyers." *Hastings Women's Law Journal* 8 (Winter 1997): 117.

Kreider, Rose M., and Diana B. Elliott. "Historical Changes in Stay-at-Home Mothers: 1969 to 2009." U.S. Census Bureau. Fertility and Family Statistics Branch. Paper Presented at American Sociological Association 2010 annual meeting. https://www.census.gov/hhes/families/files/ASA2010_Kreider_Elliott.pdf.

Kuper, Adam. *Culture: The Anthropologists' Account.* Cambridge, MA: Harvard University Press, 1999.

Lacey, Nicola. "The Path Not Taken: H. L. A. Hart's Harvard Essay on Discretion." *Harvard Law Review* 127 (2013): 636.

Lach, Eric. "D'Souza: African-Americans Better Off Because Ancestors Were 'Hauled from Africa to America.'" Talking Points Memo. TPM LiveWire, June 30, 2014, available at http://talkingpointsmemo.com/livewire/dinesh-dsouza-african-americans.

Lacy, Karyn R. *Blue-Chip Black: Race, Class, and Status in the New Black Middle Class.* Berkeley: University of California Press, 2007.

La Ferla, Ruth. "The changing face of America: with help from Hollywood and Madison Avenue, Generation Y is challenging the way America thinks about race and ethnicity." *New York Times Upfront,* February 2, 2004, available at http://www.thefreelibrary.com/The+changing+face+of+America%3A+with+help+from+Hollywood+and+Madison. . .-a0113051764.

Lamont, Michele. *The Dignity of Working Men: Morality and the Boundaries of Race, Class, and Immigration.* New York: Russell Sage Foundation, 2009.

Landry, Bart. *The New Black Middle Class.* Berkeley: University of California Press, 1987.

Landry, Bart, and Kris Marsh. "The Evolution of the New Black Middle Class." *Annual Review of Sociology* 37 (2011): 373.

Lane, Charles. *The Day Freedom Died: The Colfax Massacre, the Supreme Court, and the Betrayal of Reconstruction.* New York: Henry Holt, 2008.

Lareau, Annette. *Unequal Childhoods: Class, Race and Family Life.* 2nd ed. Berkeley: University of California Press, 2011.

Lareau, Annette, and Dalton Conley, eds. *Social Class: How Does It Work?* New York: Russell Sage Foundation, 2008.

Lasch, Christopher. *The True and Only Heaven: Progress and Its Critics.* New York: W. W. Norton, 1991.

Lassila, Kathrin Day. "Race, Speech, and Value." *Yale Alumni Magazine,* January/February 2016, available at https://yalealumnimagazine.com/articles/4233-race-speech-and-values (accessed April 16, 2016).

Lawrence, Charles, and Mari J. Matsuda. *We Won't Go Back: Making the Case for Affirmative Action.* New York: Houghton Mifflin, 1997.

Lee, Jaeah. "BJS Arrest-Related Deaths 2003–2009." https://docs.google.com/spreadsheets/d/1Tx7gUUqFgd2wLYVd161uuR6bnnfEz4Ouo7PYqa6aHKE/edit#gid=0.

Lee, Jennifer, and Frank Bean. *The Diversity Paradox: Immigration and the Color Line in Twenty-First Century America.* New York: Russell Sage Foundation, 2012.

Levitt, Steven D., and Stephen J. Dubner. *Freakonomics: A Rogue Economist Explores the Hidden Side of Everything.* New York: William Morrow, 2005.

Linder, Douglas. *Lynching in America: Statistics, Information, Images.* University of Missouri–Kansas City. http://law2.umkc.edu/faculty/projects/ftrials/shipp/lynchingyear.html.

Loury, Glenn C. *The Anatomy of Racial Inequality.* Cambridge, MA: Harvard University Press, 2004.

Lucas, Kristen. "The Working Class Promise: A Communicative Account of Mobility-Based Ambivalences" (2011). Papers in Communication Studies. Paper 12. Communication Studies Department, University of Nebraska-Lincoln. http://digitalcommons.unl.edu/commstudiespapers/12.

Lucas, Samuel R., and Marcel Paret. "Law, Race, and Education in the United States." *Annual Review of Law and Social Science* 1 (2005): 203.

Luhby, Tami. "Typical American Family Earned $53,657 Last Year." CNN Money. American Opportunity. September 16, 2014. http://money.cnn.com/2015/09/16/news/economy/census-poverty-income.

MacMahon, Tim. "Cuban Not in Favor of Booting Sterling." ESPN. April 29, 2014. http://espn.go.com/nba/story/_/id/10854381/mark-cuban-dallas-mavericks-rails-donald-sterling-not-favor-kicking-owner.

Mangum, Charles S., Jr. *The Legal Status of the Negro.* Chapel Hill: University of North Carolina Press, 1940.

Marshall, Thurgood. "Reflections on the Bicentennial of the United States Constitution." *Harvard Law Review* 101 (1987): 1.

Martin, Lori Latrice. "Strategic Assimilation or Creation of Symbolic Blackness: Middle-Class Blacks in Suburban Contexts." *Journal of African American* 14.2 (2010): 234.

Mason, Linda. *The Working Mother's Guide to Life: Strategies, Secrets, and Solutions.* New York: Three Rivers Press, 2002.

Mason, Patrick L., ed. *Encyclopedia of Race and Racism.* Vol. 3. 2nd ed. Detroit: Macmillan Reference USA, 2013.

Matthews, David. *Ace of Spades: A Memoir.* New York: Henry Holt, 2007.

McCormack, Karen. "Credit and Credibility: Homeownership and Identity Management in the Midst of the Foreclosure Crisis." *Sociological Quarterly* 55.2 (2014): 261.

McElwee, Sean. "The Hidden Racism of Young White Americans." PBS. *NewsHour.* March 24, 2015. http://www.pbs.org/newshour/updates/americas-racism-problem-far-complicated-think.

McPherson, James M. *For Cause and Comrades: Why Men Fought in the Civil War.* New York: Oxford University Press, 1997.

McWhorter, John. *Authentically Black: Essays for the Black Silent Majority.* New York: Gotham Books, 2003.

———. *Losing the Race: Self-Sabotage in Black America.* New York: Free Press, 2000.

Memmott, Mark. "15 Years Later, Tawana Brawley Has Paid 1 Percent of Penalty." NPR. August 5, 2013. http://www.npr.org/sections/thetwo-way/2013/08/05/209194252/15-years-later-tawana-brawley-has-paid-1-percent-of-penalty.

Mendelson, Frank. "Workplace Diversity: Beyond Gender and Race." PRI. Business Communications blog, December 12, 2012. http://blog.priworks.com/archives/3527.

Mendes, Elizabeth, Lydia Saad, and Kyley McGeeney. "Stay-at-Home Moms Report More Depression, Sadness, Anger." Gallup. Well-Being. May 18, 2012. http://www.gallup.com/poll/154685/Stay-Home-Moms-Report-Depression-Sadness-Anger.aspx.

Meroe, Aundra Saa. "Democracy, Meritocracy, and the Uses of Education." *Journal of Negro Education* 83.4 (2014): 485.

Merry, Michael S. *Equality, Citizenship, and Segregation*. New York: Palgrave Macmillan, 2013.

Mills, Charles W. *Blackness Visible: Essays on Philosophy and Race*. Ithaca, NY: Cornell University Press, 1998.

———. *The Racial Contract*. Ithaca, NY: Cornell University Press, 1997.

Minow, Martha. *In Brown's Wake: Legacies of America's Educational Landmark*. New York: Oxford University Press, 2010.

Moran, Chris. "Suit to Fight for Bilingual Testing." *San Diego Union-Tribune*, June 1, 2005.

Morial, Marc H. "Solving Old Racial Murders." *San Diego Union-Tribune*, March 23, 2007.

Motley, Constance Baker. *Equal Justice Under the Law: An Autobiography*. New York: Farrar, Straus and Giroux, 1998.

Moussavi, Babak. "Book Review: Cosmopolitanism: Ethics in a World of Strangers, by Kwame Anthony Appiah," Socialjusticefirst. March 5, 2012. http://socialjusticefirst.com/2012/03/05/book-review-cosmopolitanism-ethics-in-a-world-of-strangers-by-kwame-anthony-appiah.

Murray, Charles. *Coming Apart: The State of White America 1960–2010*. New York: Crown Forum, 2012.

Myrdal, Gunnar. *An American Dilemma: The Negro Problem and Modern Democracy*. New York: Harper & Row, 1994.

Nakashima, Ryan. "UCLA: Movies Make More $$$ When Half the Cast Is White." *San Diego Union-Tribune*, February 25, 2016, available at http://www.sandiegouniontribune.com/news/2016/feb/25/ucla-diversely-cast-films-do-better-at-the-box/.

Neckerman, Kathryn M., Prudence Carter, and Jennifer Lee. "Segmented Assimilation and Minority Cultures of Mobility." *Ethnic and Racial Studies* 22 (1999): 945.

Nussbaum, Martha C. *Cultivating Humanity: A Classical Defense of Reform in Liberal Education*. Cambridge, MA: Harvard University Press, 1997.

"Optimism About Black Progress Declines: Blacks See Growing Values Gap Between Poor and Middle Class." Pew Research Center. November 13, 2007. www.pewsocialtrends.org/files/2010/10/Race-2007.pdf.

"O'Reilly: Slaves Who Built White House Were 'Well-Fed and Had Decent Lodgings Provided by the Government.'" Media Matters. July 26, 2016. http://www.mediamatters.org/video/2016/07/26/oreilly-slaves-who-built-white-house-were-well-fed-and-had-decent-lodgings-provided-government/211921.

Orentlicher, David. "Diversity: A Fundamental American Principle." *Missouri Law Review* 70 (2005): 777.

Orfield, Gary, and Chungmei Lee. "The Civil Rights Project, Historic Reversals, Accelerating Resegregation, and the Need for New Integration Strategies." UCLA. August 2007. http://civilrightsproject.ucla.edu/research/k-12-education/integration-and-diversity/historic-reversals-accelerating-resegregation-and-the-need-for-new-integration-strategies-1/orfield-historic-reversals-accelerating.pdf.

Oxford Dictionaries. "Definition of *cultural diversity* in English." http://www.oxforddictionaries.com/us/definition/american_english/cultural-diversity.

Page, Clarence. "Black Immigrants: An Invisible 'Model Minority.'" Real Clear Politics. March 19, 2007. http://www.realclearpolitics.com/articles/2007/03/black_immigrants_an_invisible.html.

Parks, Rosa, and Jim Haskins. *Rosa Parks: My Story.* New York: Dial Books, 1992.

"Partisan Polarization Surges in Bush, Obama Years: Trends in American Values: 1987–2012." At section 8: "Values About Immigration and Race." Pew Research Center. U.S. Politics & Policy. June 4, 2012. http://www.people-press.org/2012/06/04/partisan-polarization-surges-in-bush-obama-years/.

Patillo, Mary. *Black Picket Fences: Privilege and Peril Among the Black Middle Class.* 2nd ed. Chicago: University of Chicago Press, 1999, 2013.

Patten, Eileen, and Kim Parker. "A Gender Reversal on Career Aspirations: Young Women Now Top Young Men in Valuing High-Paying Career." Pew Research Center. Social Trends. April 19, 2012. http://www.pewsocialtrends.org/files/2012/04/Women-in-the-Workplace.pdf.

Patterson, Orlando. "Race and Diversity in the Age of Obama." *New York Times Book Review,* August 16, 2009.

Paulsen, Michael Stokes. "The Worst Constitutional Decisions of All Time." *Notre Dame Law Review* 78 (2003): 995.

Phillips, Amber. "Poll Finds Public Opinion on Confederate Flag Mixed." *San Diego Union-Tribune,* July 3, 2015.

Pica, Leslie Houts, and Joe R. Feagin. *Two-Faced Racism: Whites in the Backstage and Frontstage.* New York: Routledge, 2007.

"Pluralism—Cultural Pluralism." Science Encyclopedia. JRank Science & Philosophy. Net Industries. 2016. http://science.jrank.org/pages/10750/Pluralism-Cultural-Pluralism.html.

Poiewozik, James. "Tuned In: How BET's *The Game* Is Adjusting TV's Racial Balance." *Time,* February 28, 2011.

Posner, Richard A. *Divergent Paths: The Academy and the Judiciary.* Cambridge, MA: Harvard University Press, 2016.

Rampell, Catherine. "Defining Middle Class." *New York Times.* Economix. September 14, 2012. http://economix.blogs.nytimes.com/2012/09/14/defining-middle-class.

Rampersad, Arnold. *Ralph Ellison: A Biography.* New York: Alfred A. Knopf, 2007.

Rankine, Claudia. *Citizen: An American Lyric.* Minneapolis: Graywolf Press, 2014.

Reich, Charles A. *The Greening of America.* New York: Random House, 1970.

Ribbhagen, Christina. "What Makes a Technocrat? Explaining Variation Thinking Among Elite Bureaucrats." *Public Policy and Administration* 26.1 (2011): 23.

Robinson, Eugene. *Disintegration: The Splintering of Black America.* New York: Doubleday, 2010.

Rodriguez, Gregory. "A New Way of Joining the Mainstream." *Wall Street Journal,* July 31, 2003.

Rogers, Harrell R., Jr., and Charles S. Bullock III. *Law and Social Change: Civil Rights Laws and Their Consequences.* New York: McGraw-Hill, 1972.

Rollock, Nicola, David Gilborn, Carol Vincent, and Steven Ball. "The Public Identities of the Black Middle Classes: Managing Race in Public Spaces." *Sociology* 45.6 (2011): 1078.

Rosak, Theodore. *The Making of a Counter Culture: Reflections on the Technocratic Society and Its Youthful Opposition.* Berkeley: University of California Press, 1995.

Rosen, Jeffrey. "Rights Unraveled: A Narrative History of the Continuing Efforts to Weaken the Voting Rights Act of 1965." *New York Times Book Review,* August 30, 2015.

Roth, Zachary. "93-Year-Old Black Man Disenfranchised by Alabama Voter ID Law." MSNBC. June 3, 2014. http://www.msnbc.com/msnbc/voter-id-law-disenfranchises-93-year-old-black-man.

———. "Voting Rights in Danger One Year After Shelby County Supreme Court Ruling." MSNBC. June 25, 2014. http://www.msnbc.com/msnbc/voting-rights-danger-one-year-after-shelby-county-supreme-court-ruling.

Saatcioglu, Bige, and Julie L. Ozanne. "Moral Habitus and Status Negotiation in a Marginalized Working-Class Neighborhood." *Journal of Consumer Research* 40 (2013): 692.

Sahgal, Neha, and Greg Smith. "A Religious Portrait of African-Americans." Pew Research Center. January 30, 2009. http://www.pewforum.org/2009/01/30/a-religious-portrait-of-african-americans.

Salins, Peter D. *Assimilation American Style.* New York: Basic Books, 1997.

Sandberg, Sheryl. *Lean In: Women, Work, and the Will to Lead.* New York: Random House, 2013.

"San Diego Datebook." *San Diego Union-Tribune,* May 23, 2015.

Schaefer, Richard T. *Racial and Ethnic Diversity in the USA.* Upper Saddle River, NJ: Pearson, 2013.

Schickel, Richard. *D. W. Griffith: An American Life.* New York: Simon and Schuster, 1984.

Schilken, Chuck. "Mark Cuban on Donald Sterling: 'People Are Allowed to be Morons.'" *Los Angeles Times,* April 29, 2014, available at http://www.latimes.com/sports/sportsnow/la-sp-sn-mark-cuban-donald-sterling-20140429-story.html.

Schlesinger, Arthur M., Jr. "American Multiculturalism." In *Booknotes on American Character: People, Politics, and Conflict in American History,* edited by Brian Lamb. New York: Public Affairs, 2004.

———. *The Disuniting of America.* Rev. ed. New York: W. W. Norton, 1998.

Schmidt, Michael S. "F.B.I. Director Speaks Out on Race and Police Bias." *New York Times,* February 12, 2015, available at http://www.nytimes.com/2015/02/13/us/politics/fbi-director-comey-speaks-frankly-about-police-view-of-blacks.html.

Schultz, David, and Sarah Clark. "Wealth v. Democracy: The Unfulfilled Promise of the Twenty-Fourth Amendment." *Quinnipiac Law Review* 29 (2011): 375.

Scott, Janny, and David Leonhardt. "Class Matters: Shadowy Lines That Still Divide." *New York Times,* May 15, 2005.

Sebok, Anthony. *Legal Positivism in American Jurisprudence.* New York: Cambridge University Press, 1998.

Sharkey, Patrick. "Spatial Segmentation and the Black Middle Class." *American Journal of Sociology* 119 (2014): 903.

Shaw, Geoffrey C. "H. L. A. Hart's Lost Essay: Discretion and the Legal Process School." *Harvard Law Review* 127 (2013): 666.

Shelby, Tommie. Interview by Tavis Smiley. February 17, 2016. PBS. Tavis Smiley Archives. www.pbs.org/kcet/tavissmiley/archive/200602/20060217_transcript.html (hard copy of interview on file with author).

——. *We Who Are Dark: The Philosophical Foundations of Black Solidarity.* Cambridge, MA: Harvard University Press, 2005.

"Shelly Sterling Can Proceed with Sale." ESPN. July 29, 2014. http://espn.go.com/los-angeles/nba/story/_/id/11277942/judge-rules-donald-sterling-attempt-block-sale-los-angeles-clippers.

"Simple Justice: About the Book." http://www.richardkluger.com/AboutSimpleJustice.htm.

Slaughter, Anne-Marie. "Why Women Still Can't Have it All." *Atlantic,* July/August 2012.

Smiley, Tavis. Interview of Tommie Shelby. February 17, 2016. PBS. Tavis Smiley Archives. www.pbs.org/kcet/tavissmiley/archive/200602/20060217_transcript.html (hard copy of interview on file with author.

Smith, Robert C., and Richard Seltzer. *Race, Class and Culture: A Study in Afro-American Mass Opinion.* Albany: State University of New York Press, 1992.

Sokol, Jason. *All Eyes Are Upon Us: Race and Politics from Boston to Brooklyn.* New York: Basic Books, 2014.

Sotomayor, Sonia. *My Beloved World.* New York: Alfred A. Knopf, 2013.

Sowell, Thomas. "Race, Culture, and Equality." Stanford: Hoover Institution, July 17, 1998.

Spears, Brooks H. "'If the Plaintiffs Are Right, Grutter Is Wrong': Why Fisher v. University of Texas Presents an Opportunity for the Supreme Court to Overturn a Flawed Decision." *University of Richmond Law Review* 46 (2012): 1113.

Staples, Brent. "F.B.I. Director James Comey on How Everyone's a Little Bit Racist." *New York Times.* Taking Note. February 12, 2015. http://takingnote.blogs.nytimes.com/2015/02/12/f-b-i-director-james-comey-on-how-everyones-a-little-bit-racist/?action=click&contentCollection=Politics&module=RelatedCoverage&region—arginalia&pgtype=article.

Steel, Lewis. "A Critic's View of the Warren Court—Nine Men in Black Who Think White." *New York Times,* October 13, 1968.

Steele, Shelby. *The Content of Our Character: A New Vision of Race in America.* New York: St. Martin's Press, 1990.

Strausbaugh, John. *Black Like You: Blackface, Whiteface, Insult & Imitation in American Popular Culture.* New York: Jeremy P. Tarcher/Penguin, 2006.

Strmic-Pawl, Hephzibah V., and Phyllis K. Leffler. "Black Families and Fostering of Leadership." *Ethnicities* 11.2 (June 2011): 139–162. http://etn.sagepub.com/content/11/2/139.full.pdf.

Su, Julie A., and Eric K. Yamamoto. "Critical Coalitions: Theory and Praxis." In *Crossroads, Directions, and a New Critical Race Theory,* edited by Francisco Valdes, Jerome McCristal Culp, and Angela P. Harris. Philadelphia: Temple University Press, 2002.

Sullivan, Kathleen M., and Gerald Gunther. *Constitutional Law.* 15th ed. New York: Foundation Press, 2004.

Sullivan, Teresa A., Elizabeth Warren, and Jay Lawrence Westbrook. *The Fragile Middle Class: Americans in Debt.* New Haven, CT: Yale University Press, 2000.

Terrell, Francis, and Sandra L. Terrell. "Effects of Race of Examiner and Cultural Mistrust on the WAIS Performance of Black Students." *Journal of Consulting and Clinical Psychology* 49.5 (1981): 750.

Terrell, Mark T. "Bucking Grutter: Why Critical Mass Should Be Thrown Off the Affirmative-Action Horse." *Texas Journal on Civil Liberties and Civil Rights* 16 (2011): 233.

Thernstrom, Stephan, Ann Orlov, and Oscar Handlin, eds. *Harvard Encyclopedia of American Ethnic Groups.* Cambridge, MA: Belknap Press of Harvard University, 1980.

Thernstrom, Stephan, and Abigail Thernstrom. *America in Black and White: One Nation, Indivisible.* New York: Simon & Schuster, 1997.

Thompson, Joshua P., and Damien M. Schiff. "Divisive Diversity at the University of Texas: An Opportunity for the Supreme Court to Overturn Its Flawed Decision in Grutter." *Texas Review of Law and Politics* 15 (2011): 437.

Thompson, Krissah, and Cheryl W. Thompson. "Officer Tells His Side of the Story in Arrest of Harvard Scholar." *Washington Post,* July 24, 2009.

Toliver, Susan D. "Critical Perspectives on Black Family Theory: A Revised ABC-X Model for Understanding Black Family Stress and Black Family Strengths." *European Scientific Journal* 1 (2015): 380.

Torlina, Jeff. *Working Class: Challenging Myths About Blue-Collar Labor.* Boulder, CO: Lynne Rienner Publishers, 2011.

Totten, Christopher D. "Constitutional Precommitments to Gender Affirmative Action in the European Union, Germany, Canada, and the United States: A Comparative Approach." *Berkeley Journal of International Law* 21 (2003): 27.

Touré. "How to Talk to Young Black Boys About Trayvon Martin." *Time,* April 2, 2012.

——. "Visible Young Man." *New York Times Book Review,* May 3, 2009.

Touré and Michael Eric Dyson. *Who's Afraid of Post-Blackness? What It Means to Be Black Now.* New York: Free Press, 2011.

Turner, Ani. "The Business Case for Racial Equity." W. K. Kellogg Foundation. October 24, 2013. http://www.wkkf.org/resource-directory/resource/2013/10/the-business-case-for-racial-equity.

——. "The Business Case for Racial Equity in Michigan." W. K. Kellogg Foundation. June 11, 2015. https://www.wkkf.org/news-and-media/article/2015/05/the-business-case-for-racial-equity-in-michigan-report-released.

U.S. Department of Justice, Civil Rights Division. *Investigation of the Ferguson Police Department.* http://www.justice.gov/sites/default/files/opa/pressreleases/attachments/2015/03/04/ferguson_police_department_report.pdf.

U.S. House of Representatives. "The Legislative Process." http://www.house.gov/content/learn/legislative_process/.

Victor, Daniel. "NAACP Leader in Washington State Posed as Black, Parents Say." *San Diego Union-Tribune,* June 13, 2015.

Wallenstein, Andrew. "Dave Chappelle Inks $50 Million Deal." *Today.* August 3, 2004. http://www.today.com/id/5591225/ns/today-today_entertainment/t/dave-chappelle-inks-million-deal/#.VxKzy9IrKUk.

Wang, Wendy. "Interracial Marriage: Who Is 'Marrying Out'?" Pew Research Center. Fact Tank. June 12, 2015. http://www.pewresearch.org/fact-tank/2015/06/12/interracial-marriage-who-is-marrying-out.

Wang, Xi. "The Making of Federal Enforcement Laws, 1870–1872." *Chicago-Kent Law Review* 70 (1995): 1013.

Ware, Leland, and Theodore J. Davis. "Ordinary People in an Extraordinary Time: The Black Middle-Class in the Age of Obama." *Howard Law Journal* 55 (2012): 533.

Weis, Lois, ed. *Class, Race & Gender in American Education.* Albany: State University of New York Press, 1988.

Weis, Lois, and Michelle Fine. "Narrating the 1980s and 1990s: Voices of Poor and Working-Class White and African American Men." *Anthropology and Education Quarterly* 27.4 (December 1996): 493.

West, Cornel. *Race Matters.* Boston: Beacon Press, 2001.

West, Cornel, and Christa Buschendorf. *Black Prophetic Fire.* Boston: Beacon Press, 2014.

West, Kanyé. "Gorgeous." *My Beautiful Dark Twisted Fantasy.* Def Jam Records, 2010.

White, Daniel. "Nearly 20% of Trump Fans Think Freeing the Slaves Was a Bad Idea." *Time,* February 24, 2016, available at http://time.com/4236640/donald-trump-racist-supporters.

Wickman, Forrest. "Working Man's Blues: Why Do We Call Manual Laborers *Blue Collar*?" *Slate,* May 1, 2012. www.slate.com/articles/business/explainer/2012/05/blue_collar_white_collar_why_do_we_use_these_terms_.html.

Wikens, John. "Prolific Writer Bears Witness to Suffering." *San Diego Union-Tribune,* February 22, 2015.

Wilcox, W. Bradford, Andrew J. Cherlin, Jeremy E. Uecker, and Matthew Messel. "No Money, No Hunny, No Church: The Deinstitutionalization of Religious Life Among the White Working Class." *Research in Sociology of Work* 23 (2012): 227.

Will, George F. "Why Civil Rights No Longer Are Rights." *San Diego Union-Tribune,* March 10, 2005.

Williams, Joan C. "The Class Culture Gap." In *Facing Social Class: How Societal Rank Influences Interaction,* edited by Susan Fiske and Hazel Rose Markus. New York: Russell Sage Foundation, 2012.

Willie, Charles Vert, and Richard J. Reddick. *A New Look at Black Families.* Walnut Creek, CA: Rowman and Littlefield Publishers, 2003.

Willis, Sherman P. "Bridging the Gap: A Look at the Higher Education Cases Between *Plessy* and *Brown.*" *Thurgood Marshall Law Review* 30 (2004): 1.

Winkler, Adam. "Fatal in Theory and Strict in Fact: An Empirical Analysis of Strict Scrutiny in the Federal Courts." *Vanderbilt Law Review* 59 (2006): 793.

Wise, Steven M. *Though the Heavens May Fall: The Landmark Trial That Led to the End of Human Slavery.* Boston: Da Capo Press, 2005.

Wise, Tim. *Dear White America: Letter to a New Minority.* San Francisco: City Lights
    Books, 2012.
Womack, Ytasha L. *Post Black: How a New Generation Is Redefining African American
    Identity.* Chicago: Lawrence Hill Books, 2010.
Yancey, George. *Who Is White? Latinos, Asians, and the New Black/Nonblack Divide.*
    Boulder, CO: Lynne Rienner Publishers, 2003.
Young, Alex. "Dave Chappelle Reveals the Real Reason Why He Left Chappelle's Show."
    Consequence of Sound. June 10, 2014. http://consequenceofsound.net/2014/06/
    dave-chappelle-reveals-the-real-reason-why-he-left-chappelles-show/.
Zelden, Charles L. *The Battle for the Black Ballot.* Lawrence: University Press of Kansas,
    2004.
Zellner, William W. *Countercultures: A Sociological Analysis.* New York: St. Martin's Press,
    1995.
Zweig, Michael, ed. *What's Class Got to Do With It? American Society in the Twenty-First
    Century.* Ithaca, NY: Cornell University Press, 2004.

Index

racial abyss, 6

racial classification: Broyard on, 73; Gladwell on, 72; Gomez on, 183n1; Lucas and Paret on, 71–72; strict scrutiny test, 37

racial democracy, 104, 144

racial equality: benefits of advancing, 153n9; compared to other minorities, 6–7, 153n5, 153n7, 177n70; Reconstruction Amendments and postamendment statutes, 14, 16, 158–60n2, 161n10, 161n11; separate treatment for blacks, 40, 85, 193n8; status of blacks, 6–7, 153n5–7; theories of, 13

racial glass ceiling, 2, 7, 9, 144

racial identity: Broyard on, 73; as cultural expression, 71, 72–73; Gladwell on, 72; limited separatists on, 129–31; Lucas and Paret on, 71–72, 84; "passing" for white, 72–73; Supreme Court on, 143

racial identity norm, 38

racial inequality: in contemporary American society, 3, 6–7, 153n5–7; disparate treatment, 52, 53, 153n3; financially successful blacks and, 3, 6, 8; process of, 5. See also racial subordination

racial integration norms: about, 33–35, 167n2; critical race theorists on, 46; formal equal opportunity defined by, 34; limited separatists on, 64; reformists on, 13, 41–42, 48, 63, 143, 170n18; Ricci v. DeStefano (2009), 53, 54; Robinson v. Shell Oil Co. (1997), 51; Supreme Court and, 12–13, 41–42; traditionalists on, 39

Racial Justice in the Age of Obama (Brooks), 157n1, 177n70

racial neutrality, 34

"racial occupancy controls" quotas, 168n5

racial omission norms: about, 33–38; critical race theorists on, 46;

Historically Black Colleges and Universities (HBCUs), 44; limited separatists on, 43–44; Plessy v. Ferguson (1896) and, 44; reformists on, 41, 42, 62–63, 143, 167n2; Ricci v. DeStefano (2009), 53, 54; Robinson v. Shell Oil Co. (1997), 51; Supreme Court and, 12–13; traditionalists on, 39, 48, 62, 143

racial oppression, traditionalists on, 196n26

racial-preference law, in post–civil rights era, 58–69

racial preferences: as a remedy, 36; federal statutes proscribing, 35–37, 167nn3–5; as form of reverse racial discrimination, 62, 63

racial reductionism, 6

racial self-sufficiency, 54, 56, 64

racial solidarity, 13, 95, 99, 128

racial subordination: about, 2, 5, 7, 68, 142–43; critical race theorists on, 4; defined, ix, 4, 5; impact on blacks, 5, 7; legal liability from, 152n3; racism vs., 4–5; reformism and, 127; Supreme Court and, ix–x, 3, 12–32, 33–69; use of term, 4; Yale University administrative action, 137–39. See also cultural subordination; juridical subordination

"racial uplift," 85

racial violence, 18, 161n13

"racing," 81, 82

racism: about, 117, 157n19; campus racist acts at colleges and universities, 137–38; Coates on, 5; defined, 4; economic impact of, 153n9; "elegant racism," 5; "frontstage"/"backstage," 41, 157n19; middle-class blacks and, 83; in National Basketball Association (NBA), 1–2, 4, 151n1; nature of, 4; racial subordination vs., 4–5; university administrators' inaction on, 137–38; in white working-class culture, 92